D0908923

POSITIVE
ACADEMIC
LEADERSHIP

Other Books by Jeffrey L. Buller

Academic Leadership Day by Day: Small Steps That Lead to Great Success

The Essential Department Chair: A Comprehensive Desk Reference, Second Edition

The Essential Academic Dean: A Practical Guide to College Leadership

The Essential College Professor: A Practical Guide to an Academic Career

Best Practices in Faculty Evaluation: A Practical Guide for Academic Leaders

Classically Romantic: Classical Form and Meaning in Wagner's Ring

POSITIVE
ACADEMIC
LEADERSHIP

How to Stop Putting Out Fires and Start Making a Difference

Jeffrey L. Buller

JB JOSSEY-BASS™

A Wiley Brand

Library of Congress Cataloging-in-Publication Data

Buller, Jeffrey L.
Positive academic leadership : how to stop putting out fires and begin making a difference / Jeffrey L. Buller.
pages cm. – (The Jossey-Bass higher and adult education series)
Includes bibliographical references and index.
ISBN 978-1-118-53192-1 (cloth); ISBN 978-1-118-55221-6 (ebk);
ISBN 978-1-118-55222-3 (ebk); ISBN 978-1-118-55737-2 (ebk)
1. Universities and colleges–Administration. I. Title.
LB2341.B746 2013
378.1'11–dc23   2012048730

CONTENTS

About the Author ix

Introduction xi

PART ONE
Exploring Positive Academic Leadership

1 What Positive Leadership Means 3

2 Alternative Approaches to Academic Leadership 25

3 Applying the Positive Leadership Model to Higher Education 43

PART TWO
Positive Approaches for Yourself

4 Positive Language 67

5 Positive Perspectives 83

6 Positive Strategies 101

PART THREE
Positive Approaches for Faculty, Staff, and Students

7 The Academic Leader as Coach 123

8 The Academic Leader as Counselor 143

9 The Academic Leader as Conductor 161

PART FOUR
Positive Approaches for Higher Education as a Whole

10 Positive Administration Throughout the Institution   183

11 The Crisis Industry and How Positive Leaders
    Should Respond to It   205

12 Playing to Our Strengths   227

Index   249

The Jossey-Bass Higher and Adult Education Series

To James Barta, Warren Jones, Harry Carter, Cynthia Tyson, Brenda Bryant, Edward Scott, Christine Licata, Bob Smith, Walt Gmelch, Bob Cipriano, John Pritchett, Anne Boykin, and Eliah Watlington—the most positive academic leaders I've ever met. It's been my honor to work with you. I'm sure you'll all recognize yourselves in the anecdotes told here. (Hint: They're the stories where the administrator comes off looking pretty good. The other stories—well, those are about somebody else. You'll probably know who they are too.)

ABOUT THE AUTHOR

Jeffrey L. Buller has served in administrative positions ranging from department chair to vice president for academic affairs at a diverse group of institutions: Loras College, Georgia Southern University, Mary Baldwin College, and Florida Atlantic University. He is the author of *Best Practices in Faculty Evaluation: A Practical Guide for Academic Leaders; The Essential Department Chair: A Comprehensive Desk Reference; Academic Leadership Day by Day: Small Steps That Lead to Great Success; The Essential College Professor: A Practical Guide to an Academic Career;* and *The Essential Academic Dean: A Practical Guide to College Leadership.* Buller has also written numerous articles on Greek and Latin literature, nineteenth- and twentieth-century opera, and college administration. From 2003 to 2005, he served as the principal English-language lecturer at the International Wagner Festival in Bayreuth, Germany. More recently, he has been active as a consultant to Sistema Universitario Ana G. Méndez in Puerto Rico and to the Ministry of Higher Education in Saudi Arabia, where he is assisting with the creation of a kingdom-wide academic leadership center. Along with Robert E. Cipriano, Buller is a senior partner in ATLAS: Academic Training, Leadership, & Assessment Services, through which he has presented numerous workshops on positive academic leadership.

INTRODUCTION

What is it that makes some academic administrators successful while others struggle? Certainly there's no one answer to this question. The leader who may be perfect for one situation may not be at all right in another context. Different administrators have different skill sets, levels of experience, and amounts of formal administrative training. But through observation of hundreds of different academic leaders at hundreds of institutions, I've increasingly come to observe one repeated phenomenon: successful academic leaders generally practice what I call *positive academic leadership;* struggling or failing academic leaders generally take a more negative approach. Negative leaders become fixated on problems; positive leaders are aware of possibilities and can build something useful out of even the worst type of problem.

In the pages that follow, I explain in detail what distinguishes positive academic leadership as an administrative approach. But one central point can't be repeated too frequently: positive academic leadership isn't a matter of coming to work each day with feigned optimism, pretending to see the sunny side of disasters, or acting as though bad things don't happen in academic life. It's also not about filling your walls with those annoying motivational posters. (Okay, full disclosure here: I do suggest one poster at the very end of the book. But it's intended to be a reminder to us as positive leaders, not a stratagem to manipulate unmotivated employees.) Even curmudgeons and grumps can become positive academic leaders, and their levels of achievement will grow as a result. I've seen it happen too many times for it to be a fluke. Change your language, change your perspective, change your strategies—and you'll begin seeing more achievements than frustrations. No matter how you define productivity in your programs, it will increase—not immediately and not overnight, but eventually and noticeably. And in the meantime you'll feel better about what you do. Your morale will improve; the morale of your faculty and staff will improve. Then someday you may find yourself coming to work each day with more optimism, not feigned this time but as genuine as it comes.

Still—don't go putting up any annoying posters.

One of the goals of this book is to make positive academic leadership easy for administrators to implement. As you'll see by the sheer number of references (works from which quotes or ideas have been taken and cited in the chapter) and resources (additional useful materials that haven't been directly cited) that appear at the end of each chapter, there's a huge body of scholarly research on the subject of positive leadership. Experts in neuroscience, psychology, management, organizational behavior, and a host of other fields are all validating the effectiveness of the very strategies I outline in this book. But many of these studies are written in the type of dense academic jargon that makes it extremely difficult for anyone outside that specialty to figure out how to apply these ideas in day-to-day situations. Here's an actual example:

> We expand the conceptualization of positive leadership and hypothesize that leaders' ability to influence followers across varied complex situations will be enhanced through the development of a rich and multifaceted self-construct. Utilizing self-complexity theory and other aspects of research on self-representation, we show how the *structure* and *structural dynamics* of leaders' self-constructs are linked to their varied role demands by calling forth cognitions, affects, goals, and values, expectancies, and self-regulatory plans that enhance performance. Through this process, a leader is able to bring the "right stuff" (the appropriate ensemble of attributes) to bear on and succeed in the multiple challenges of leadership. We suggest future research to develop dimensional typologies related to leadership-relevant aspects of the self and also to link individual positive self-complexity to more aggregate positive organizational processes. (Hannah, Woolfolk, and Lord, 2009, p. 269)

That particular article happens to contain a great deal of valuable information, but busy academic leaders won't have the time to make their way through such dense academic verbiage in order to learn how to improve their administrative technique. They want ideas they can use *now*, and *Positive Academic Leadership* seeks to meet that desire for immediate information. With that objective in mind, I've tried to make the range of current research as accessible as possible, sometimes blending the findings of scholars with examples drawn from popular entertainment or the types of management books you see people reading on long flights. I'm firmly convinced that people with Ph.D.s don't own the patent on wisdom and insight, so it's possible to draw valid parallels, applications, and illustrations from an exceptionally wide range of sources.

Furthermore, my goal in this book is never simply to give you information about positive academic leadership but rather to demonstrate how you can practice this leadership. In the end, your own experience in trying out these ideas will matter more than the reams of studies that led to their development.

Positive academic leadership isn't just something I train others to do. It's also how I try to approach my own responsibilities at my college and in my university. For this reason, there are a lot more personal anecdotes in this book than in any other I've written. That's intentional: positive academic leadership is an approach best taught by example, and all of us are familiar with situations (both good and bad) that we've experienced ourselves. But I'll admit it: I'm not successful at positive academic leadership every single day, and you won't be either. If you try it, however, and stick with it, you'll eventually notice improvements—a little bit at first, then more, then a flood. You may even become an advocate of this administrative approach and want to spread it throughout your institution and through academia as a whole, as I recommend in the last two chapters. That's a good thing.

We face a wide range of challenges in higher education. There's never enough money to meet our needs. Competition among institutions is increasing. Enrollment limits on courses are higher than ever before. And the amount of respect the public at large gives to four-year undergraduate education in general, and college professors in particular, seems to decline each year. (Community colleges and graduate programs still often receive widespread admiration, but not what is too often referred to as "that overpriced, ineffective, meaningless bachelor's degree.") We can see all these developments as catastrophes and go into crisis mode as we try to solve them, but then we'll just be running from fire to fire, putting out one blaze only to see another erupt from a different quarter. Problems at universities are like candies in a PEZ dispenser: as soon as you remove one, another pops right up. But we do have alternatives. We can say, "It's not a crisis. It's just the environment in which I work. Now how do I go about making things better?" And then we can create something wonderful out of the materials we have at hand. That's the essence of positive academic leadership, and that's what you'll learn about in this book.

I'm grateful to Magna Publications for allowing me to adapt and reuse some material that originally appeared in *Academic Leader*. (Reprint permission was granted by Magna Publications and *Academic Leader*.) In addition, I thank Tamara Howard for her contributions in researching this material; Megan Geiger, Sandy Ogden, and Cecilia Chin-Pallés for editorial assistance; and Lawrence Abele, Heather Coltman, and everyone involved in the annual K-State Academic Chairpersons Conference (particularly Kathryn Harth and Sharon Brookshire) for their generosity in letting me pilot this material in its rough, initial form. I'm greatly indebted to all those scholars whose work contributed to the concept of positive academic leadership. You'll notice their names cited repeatedly throughout this book: Martin Seligman, Mihály Csíkszentmihályi, Kim Cameron, Ian MacDonald, Catherine Burke, Karl Stewart, Kaye Herth, Kina Mallard, and Mark Sargent. Finally I'm indebted to all the positive academic leaders I've met in so many colleges and universities around the world. They're the people who taught me what truly transformative academic leadership can be.

Jupiter, Florida   Jeffrey L. Buller
September 1, 2012

Reference

Hannah, S. T., Woolfolk, R. L., & Lord, R. G. (2009). Leader self-structure: A framework for positive leadership. *Journal of Organizational Behavior, 30*(2), 269–290.

POSITIVE
ACADEMIC
LEADERSHIP

PART ONE

EXPLORING POSITIVE ACADEMIC LEADERSHIP

CHAPTER 1

WHAT POSITIVE LEADERSHIP MEANS

Very few administrators begin their positions as confirmed cynics or pessimists, although some of them end up that way. It's just human nature. When most people are offered their first leadership position, they're enthusiastic about the opportunity, excited by the possibilities, and eager to make a real difference in the world. They want to help shape a program, guide students and faculty members toward achieving their goals, and leave their college or university better than they found it. So why is it that this initial optimism all too often gets stifled by the reality of the job, and day after day gets spent on countless vexing problems, those petty little details we know collectively as "administrivia"? Here's how Frederick L. Ahearn, a former dean at the Catholic University of America, describes his work in his essay "A Day in the Life of a Dean":

> Another day begins, and my agenda, as usual, is full. Sometimes I wonder if my life has become one long meeting. Fitting things into my schedule is becoming a juggling act—so much to do in so little time . . . An angry student complains that she is not able to register for an elective course that her faculty adviser has recommended she take: "With the high tuition that students must pay today, the school should have extra sections of the important courses that students need for their professional training." . . . As I walk back to my office, I think about how much more difficult it is to be a dean when you have to cut a budget that is already inadequate, and when the AVP [academic vice president] has little regard for the school. I have always tried to emphasize how the school contributes to the university and its mission, but I feel that the AVP does not understand the school or its mission . . . The five members of the school's Committee on Appointment and Promotion (CAP), all senior faculty, enter as I finish

3

my phone call. As dean, I am an ex officio member of this committee, and I chair the meetings. However, I do not vote with the CAP; I express my vote separately on each matter that comes before the committee . . . I finally end the meeting knowing that this split will continue to interfere with other business in the school. How will I be able to manage these differences? How can I breach the differences and negotiate a compromise? I will have to end up siding with one group over the other. I am disgusted! . . . Driving home this night, I feel tired. I am not happy with my meetings with the academic vice president and the senior faculty on the Committee on Appointment and Promotion. (Ahearn, 1997, pp. 9, 10, 13, 17, 18, 20)

Who in the world would ever want a job like *that*? One problem to be solved after another. Angry or apathetic stakeholders. A feeling of exhaustion, disgust, and disappointment at the end of the day. There are probably lots of department chairs, deans, vice presidents, provosts, presidents, and chancellors who can sympathize with the situation Ahearn describes. We come to our positions with the impression that we'll be dealing with major issues and key decisions, but we often find our days weighed down by one crisis after another. Once we've spent a year or two on the job, we discover that we've become so focused on solving problems that we hardly have any time left to achieve all the goals we had when we started.

Part of the problem stems from the way in which administrative positions have been designed at most colleges and universities. If you do an Internet search on such phrases as "job description department chair" or "responsibilities university dean," you'll find numerous listings where administrative duties are fragmented, ill defined, and occasionally even contradictory. For example, visionary assignments like "provides leadership in all areas of the discipline" or "recruits, retains, and develops a faculty recognized for excellence in both instruction and research" often stand side by side with paper pushing: "ensures that all book orders are submitted in a timely manner," "verifies the accuracy of catalogue information," "requisitions supplies as needed," and so on. It's no wonder that some academic leaders find their energy sapped by minutiae. Is there any way to improve this situation?

New Models for Leadership

The USA Network series *Royal Pains* brought fresh attention to the practice known as "concierge medicine": a type of care in which a patient pays a special fee to a physician for an expanded array of services. The additional service provided varies from doctor to doctor, but it often includes house calls, longer appointments, 24/7 telephone access, no copays on routine medical procedures, and similar privileges. "In addition, wellness care and preventative care are often provided. A comprehensive approach to healthcare allows time to address the unique needs of the individual" (Knope, 2008, p. 9). What concierge medicine illustrates is a different way of thinking about the relationship between doctor and patient. Rather than assuming that offices and hospitals have to be run the way they are because "that's just how we've always done things," it demonstrates an innovative approach that provides improved service, reorganizes the relationship between the doctor and patient, and is extremely cost effective. What if we were to rethink how colleges and universities are administered in an equally radical way?

It may initially shock academic leaders to think so, but in many ways, what highly innovative college administrators are trying to do is bring a kind of concierge service to their programs. Like concierge doctors, university administrators tend to be on call outside normal business hours, strive to match their efforts to the specific needs of their constituents, and often go wherever their stakeholders happen to be instead of always expecting their stakeholders to come to them. Even more important, both administrators and physicians prefer to prevent problems before they arise. Yet despite this preference, they end up spending 90 percent of their time or more treating existing conditions or problems rather than planning for the future. To change metaphors for a moment, although both groups try extremely hard to make a real and positive difference, they still end up putting out a lot of fires.

For this reason, an approach known as the P4 Medicine Institute (2010) has attempted to give the contributions of concierge doctors even greater impact. The program receives its name from its four primary goals of developing a holistic approach to health care that is

Predictive, using genomics and molecular biomarkers to assess the unique risk factors of each patient

Preventative, developing therapies to forestall illnesses before they occur rather than just treat them once they have already developed

Personalized, creating therapeutic and wellness plans tailored to the patient's specific history, needs, and prognosis

Participatory, transforming patients from passive consumers of health care into active contributors to their own well-being.

"This approach," notes the institute (P4 Medicine Institute, 2010), "will result in healthcare that predicts and prevents illness, focuses on health and wellness, and considers the consumer as the central figure in care." Concierge medicine and the P4 initiative represent significant changes from what we might call the surgeon model of health care in which patients often felt treated as problems to be solved or as collections of parts to be fixed and replaced rather than as organic, three-dimensional people with distinctive personalities, needs, social situations, and dreams.

In both cases, what these doctors are doing is to combine their traditional healing role with a new role centered on training and coaching. We'll examine coaching in greater detail in chapter 7, but for now, suffice it to say that coaches and personal trainers aren't in the business of fixing something that's broken but rather in improving something that's already working well. Benign neglect and the old adage that "if it ain't broke, don't fix it" can't really be applied to coaching and training. The fundamental principle of a trainer is that improvement is always possible, and so a program is custom-designed for the individual athlete that will best achieve his or her desired goals. Trainers and coaches start at whatever level a person happens to have reached and seek to build on existing strengths. While physicians have traditionally had patients, the new concept of the physician as trainer or coach means that they now have clients. The goal isn't simply to solve problems but to increase success. As the author and entrepreneur Timothy Ferriss (2009) notes:

> It is far more lucrative and fun to leverage your strengths instead of attempting to fix all the chinks in your armor. The choice is between multiplication of results using strengths or incremental improvement fixing weaknesses that will, at best, become mediocre. Focus on better use of your best weapons instead of constant repair. (p. 34)

In the expression made famous by Jim Collins (2001), doctors as trainers help their clients advance from "good to great"; their focus remains on possibilities for the future, not on the problems of the past. So if we extrapolate from the major differences between what we might call the surgeon model of medicine and the newer model that incorporates concierge medicine, the goals of the P4 Institute, and the personal trainer approach to health and wellness, we notice three important factors:

1. The latter three approaches represent a movement away from merely asking, "What is wrong?" to also asking, "What is possible?"

2. They represent a personalized and customized approach that takes into account the unique history, needs, situation, and potentialities of each individual.

3. They represent a future-oriented strategy that assumes importance equal to, if not greater than, the strategy of repairing the damage resulting from past mistakes and problems.

Those same three factors can also be found in one other major approach that has revolutionized concepts of health, wellness, and personal success: positive psychology.

The Models of Traditional Psychology and Positive Psychology

Martin Seligman and Mihály Csíkszentmihályi (2000), two of the founding members of the positive psychology movement, suggest that what's now regarded as the traditional approach to psychology—essentially the behaviorist school that dominated American universities for half a century after World War II—produced many great advances:

> In the 50 years since psychology and psychiatry became healing disciplines, they have developed a highly transferable science of mental illness. They developed a usable taxonomy, as well as reliable and valid ways of measuring such fuzzy concepts as schizophrenia, anger, and depression. They developed sophisticated methods—both experimental and longitudinal—for understanding the causal pathways that lead to such undesirable outcomes. Most important, they developed pharmacological and psychological interventions that have allowed many untreatable mental disorders to become highly treatable and, in a couple of cases, even curable. (p. 13)

The ability to treat, even cure, these troubling and life-altering diseases must be regarded as a major accomplishment of psychology by any standard. In addition, the behaviorist method contributed a great deal to make psychology a genuine science and to amass a body of data that vastly improved our understanding of mental illness. At the same time, however, there were consequences of the scientific, clinical, behaviorist approach to psychology—what we'll now refer to as the traditional approach—that were both unintentional and undesirable:

> [Psychologists] came to see themselves as part of a mere subfield of the health professions, and psychology became a victimology.

> Psychologists saw human beings as passive foci: Stimuli came on and elicited responses (what an extraordinarily passive word!). External reinforcements weakened or strengthened responses. Drive, tissue needs, instincts, and conflicts from childhood pushed each of us around. (Seligman and Csíkszentmihályi, 2000, p. 6)

In other words, when you view the field of mental health primarily as the study of mental illness and consider the most significant subjects for research to be diseases and behavioral problems, you can produce significant benefits in alleviating suffering. But you also ultimately come to view human beings from a very limited perspective. You start to see people as collections of symptoms rather than as complete persons, and the goal of the psychologist is reduced to eliminating misery rather than increasing happiness.

That realization led Seligman and Csíkszentmihályi, along with such other pioneers as Ed Diener, Nancy Etcoff, and Daniel Gilbert, to adopt an expression originally coined by Abraham Maslow (1954) to designate a significant new emphasis within their discipline:

> If we are interested in the psychology of the human species we should limit ourselves to the use of the self-actualizing, the psychologically healthy, the mature, the fulfilled, for they are more truly representative of the human species than the usual average or normal group. The *psychology generated by the study of healthy people could fairly be called positive* by contrast with the negative psychology we now have, which has been generated by the study of sick or average people. (p. 361, emphasis added)

This new approach, positive psychology, has a great deal in common with the other health care models we've been discussing. For one thing, its focus is less on curing illness than it is on increasing well-being (e.g., Carr, 2004; Snyder and Lopez, 2007). Whereas the traditional psychological approach sought to reduce misery and unhappiness in those who had problems, the model of positive psychology aims to increase happiness and well-being in people who are generally content. As Seligman and Csíkszentmihályi (2000) have concluded, "Psychology is not just the study of pathology, weakness, and damage; it is also the study of strength and virtue. Treatment is not just fixing what is broken; it is nurturing what is best" (p. 7).

For this reason, we might outline the differences between traditional and positive psychology in the following way:

TRADITIONAL APPROACH	POSITIVE APPROACH
Focuses on disease	Focuses on health
Repairs what is wrong	Improves what is right
Addresses weaknesses, often ignoring strengths	Addresses strengths and recognizes weaknesses
Eliminates sadness	Increases happiness
Seeks to transform mental states from bad to good	Seeks to transform mental states from good to excellent
Reactive	Proactive
Treats people as patients who suffer from things that happen to them	Treats people as clients who make rational choices and are active participants in their own well-being

Since the inception of positive psychology, a number of critics have charged that it's based on assumptions about human nature and happiness that are solely Eurocentric in focus, fails to provide a sufficient challenge to the methods and approaches it criticizes, and doesn't give adequate attention to the interplay between the individual and his or her social environment (see Becker and Marecek, 2008; Richardson and Guignon, 2008; Christopher and Hickinbottom, 2008). Yet despite these objections, positive psychology remains a significant and influential corrective to the view that strategies that cure diseases are somehow more legitimate than those that boost existing fitness. It replaces the outdated perspective that the counselor or therapist has little to offer people who aren't suffering from an abnormal condition.

The Positive Approach to Leadership

In a similar way, it seems likely that many people in leadership roles feel frustrated by their positions today because they've been trained in management strategies that emphasize fixing what's broken, not nurturing what's best. Despite their good intentions, bosses of all kinds are faced each day with a growing list of problems to solve: interpersonal disputes, complaints from dissatisfied customers, delayed shipments, network breakdowns, insufficient resources, inconsistency in the quality of production, unexpected areas of competition, rivalry with other managers, and a host of other issues. Even the influx of information that arrives on a daily basis can often seem like an insurmountable problem. There are e-mails to be answered, items to check off on the to-do list, and new tasks imposed by the manager's own supervisor, all of which can make leaders today feel as though they're running an endless race. They clear this hurdle, then that hurdle, then still another, with no end in sight. Perhaps the problem isn't the nature of the work itself but rather the strategy we bring to our responsibilities. We see our roles as surgeons repairing damage and excising unhealthy tissue rather than as genuine leaders who build on strengths, create a shared sense of constructive energy, and develop what's positive in our organizations. But if we were to change our overall approach to how we supervise others and adopt some of the lessons learned from concierge medicine, the P4 Institute, personal training, and positive psychology, an entirely new type of leadership would result. What would this new form of leadership look like?

In his book *Positive Leadership: Strategies for Effective Performance* (2008), Kim Cameron, the William Russell Professor of Management and Organizations at the University of Michigan, summarizes several decades of research on positive leadership and finds that it depends on four key strategies:

1. *Positive climate,* demonstrated through compassion, forgiveness, and gratitude
2. *Positive relationships,* demonstrated through the reinforcement of strength and the creation of "energy networks" (the types of interactions we have that make us feel more motivated and optimistic)
3. *Positive communication,* demonstrated through supportive collaborations and emphasizing what others see as their strengths and major contributions
4. *Positive meaning,* demonstrated through building a sense of community, recognizing what people see as their calling, and grounding actions in a set of core values

This perspective, which Cameron presents in both *Positive Leadership* and *Positive Organizational Scholarship: Foundations of a New Discipline* (2003, coauthored with Jane Dutton and Robert Quinn), will guide our discussion in the chapters that follow. I'll rely on Cameron's works to provide a foundation for what *positive leadership* means and how it benefits the organizations that adopt it.

At the same time, I also provide a set of criteria by which we can recognize positive leadership in ourselves and others. So building outward from Cameron's four strategies, here are ten principles that we might describe as the indicators of genuinely positive leadership:

1. *Positive leaders place greater emphasis on developing what's already working than on correcting what's flawed.* No one would deny that in order for organizations to change, they have to be aware of anything

that's not working properly and address those problems through new techniques, ideas, or strategies. But if leaders come to see their roles solely as spotting the flaws in what people do, an atmosphere of distrust and anxiety often arises. Employees become reluctant to share bad news with their supervisors because they fear being blamed for the problem. Creativity becomes stifled, since no one wants to be held responsible for a new idea that doesn't work. As Kenneth Blanchard and Spencer Johnson (1982) noted long ago, "the most important thing in training somebody to be a winner is to catch them doing something right" (p. 81). For this reason, positive leaders identify what's already working, support and reward those who are responsible, and don't become preoccupied with blaming those who have made mistakes.

2. *Positive leaders encourage everyone in a supervisory position to devote time to their best performers rather than having their energy drained by troublemakers, chronically dissatisfied employees, or squeaky wheels.* Everyone is familiar with the type of employee who acts almost like a black hole for all the optimism and satisfaction in the organization. Frequently these are the same people who can consume a disproportionate amount of the leader's time presenting their complaints, tattling on coworkers, and expressing their discontent with everything from the salaries they're paid to the choice of coffee in the break room. The Italian economist Vilfredo Pareto (1848–1923) once articulated what has come to be known as the Pareto principle or 80/20 rule: in any system of unequal distribution, 20 percent of the people tend to control 80 percent of the resources. In its original formulation, the Pareto principle was concerned with land ownership in Italy, where the wealthiest 20 percent of the population came to own 80 percent of the land. (The Occupy Wall Street movement replaced this formula with an even more pessimistic view: the 1 percent versus the 99 percent.) But managers often apply the same rule to problematic employees: they find that 20 percent of the people they supervise take up 80 percent of their time. The negativity of this troublesome fifth can be contagious, and morale often plummets as a result. The positive leader tries to avoid this situation by systematically spending as much time as possible with his or her best colleagues. The leader learns from these superior performers, encourages them, and guides them to becoming even better.

3. *Positive leaders personalize the type of guidance they give to each employee rather than assuming that a single leadership style works equally well for all people.* We already know that each person we work with is unique. Our colleagues all have their own goals,

hopes, fears, plans, dreams, and histories. What motivates one person quite successfully sometimes proves to be a disincentive for someone else. Recognizing this diversity, positive leaders tailor their leadership approach to the individual or group they're working with. While a traditional leader may describe his or her management style as consistently participatory, visionary, or transformational, the positive leader sees all of these approaches as simply different tools in a toolbox, each useful in its own way. As Tony Alessandra and Michael O'Connor (1996) have observed, the golden rule—Do onto others as you'd have them do unto you—goes only so far. The other person may not want to be treated as you'd like to be. For this reason, Alessandra and O'Connor have proposed what they call the platinum rule: "Do unto others as they'd like done unto them" (p. 3). This type of personalized motivation and reward need not always involve salary increases or significant expenditures. Bob Nelson's books, *1001 Ways to Reward Employees* (2005) and *1001 Ways to Energize Employees* (1997), are great resources for ideas about how to motivate employees in a way that's meaningful to them and costs little or nothing at all. Positive leaders can thus select from a wide variety of morale-building approaches in order to adopt those that are most appropriate to the person and situation.

4. *Positive leaders adopt a systems approach, emphasizing the efficient operation of the group as well as the unique contributions of each member.* As we'll see in greater detail in chapter 9, systems—such as ecosystems, computer systems, and organ systems of the body—generally share two features. First, they're composed of distinct individual members. In other words, a monitor has a different function from a CPU, just as the heart has a different function from the arteries. Second, these individual elements work together in an interrelated and interconnected manner, or at least they simultaneously affect and are affected by other elements in the system. The pieces of an ecosystem may not be described as working together in the same way that the brain interacts with the nerves, but they ultimately depend on one another and develop a type of balance. Positive leaders recognize both that employees are individuals with individual needs, talents, and operating styles and that the unit gains strengths from this type of diversity operating together. A synergy is produced by the system that wouldn't occur if all the employees were identical. Positive leadership thus tries to make the best use of different individuals' strongest assets, creating work groups and task forces, taking full advantage of opportunities as they arise, and using the gifts of one person to compensate for the challenges of another.

5. *Positive leaders are future oriented and proactive, constantly exploring what's possible instead of being bound by past decisions and disappointments.* Since it doesn't merely focus on problems and mistakes, positive leadership is free to emphasize what might be rather than what has been. For the unit as a whole, the positive leader considers ways to take full advantage of opportunities as they occur and how to remain agile and versatile enough to adapt to even unexpected occurrences. Positive leadership includes the recognition that although you can't plan for everything, you can prepare for anything. In this way, the leader gets locked into neither the habit of always responding to the latest setback nor the rigidity of highly detailed strategic plans that, contrary to the intentions behind them, limit rather than increase the options available. Positive leaders also understand that just as their entire units must prepare for the future, so must each member of the team prepare for his or her own future. They encourage the professional and personal growth of their colleagues and always provide them with opportunities for training, not only in how to do their current jobs more effectively but also in how they can succeed in assuming greater responsibility—or even in obtaining their next jobs. Positive leaders don't measure success by how irreplaceable they are to the organization. They measure success by how well their unit can function without them.

6. *Positive leaders emphasize rewards and recognitions over punishments and penalties.* One of the pioneering contributions to the understanding of how people learn was made by Edward Thorndike (1874–1949), who observed that punishments and penalties only teach people what not to do, while positive reinforcements such as rewards and recognitions encourage people to engage in more of what they should do (Thorndike, 1932; see also Jones and Page, 1993; Martin and Pear, 1999; Flora, 2004; and Bernstein, 2010). Positive leaders understand the full implication of Thorndike's observation. It's not that positive leaders never see the need for penalties. Certain behaviors—sexual harassment, misappropriation of funds, insubordination, and the like—can't be ignored and call for sanctions. In these cases, penalties are appropriate because the supervisor wants the employee to refrain from engaging in a specific undesirable behavior. But positive leaders know that these occurrences are relatively rare, while situations that call for rewards or recognitions occur daily, even hourly. By acknowledging desirable behavior in a positive and constructive manner, the leader increases the likelihood that this type of behavior will be repeated by both the employee who's being acknowledged and anyone else who happens to witness the

supervisor's response. As the minister and author Victor Parachin (2006) puts it,

> *Express appreciation; accept responsibility.* Catherine the Great said, "I praise loudly, I blame softly." Sadly, some leaders are quick to accept credit and even quicker to assign blame. The best leaders reverse that pattern. They give credit to subordinates for work well done and they do that both privately and publicly. (pp. 17–18)

7. *Positive leaders are at least as people oriented as they are goal oriented.* After studying numerous cases of businesses and other organizations that flourished during times of change while others failed, Ian Macdonald, Catherine Burke, and Karl Stewart (2006) concluded that the very first principle for success is:

> *People are not machines.* This "common sense" statement is nevertheless central to understanding change processes. Change processes are often described as "organisational change", "culture change", "re-engineering". We look for "efficiency improvement", "performance enhancement" and "productivity gains" . . . If we really can be disciplined about not treating people as machines or objects then we can try to understand how people view the world. We need to understand not only what "the organisation" needs, but what people need and what they value. Only then can we be really effective in introducing change and begin building a positive organization. (pp. 11, 14).

Even our professional language sometimes dehumanizes our colleagues and employees when we begin to look at an organization as not a network of people but as engines of productivity that we can reengineer if things aren't going well. Of course, no organization can be successful if it doesn't adhere to its mission and achieve its ultimate goals. But too many organizations (and too many leaders) view success only in terms of the goals achieved and the increases in productivity that can be documented. They confuse being data driven with becoming data obsessed and fail to realize that information consists of more than just numbers alone.

In much the same way as positive psychology regards happiness as a worthy object of study and pursuit, so does positive leadership regard the morale, job satisfaction, and personal growth of employees as a worthwhile aspiration. From a practical perspective, a high level of employee contentment frequently translates into better productivity, lower turnover, and improved customer relations (Taylor, 2011; Karl, Harland, Peluchette, and Rodie, 2010; Liao, Hu, and Chung, 2009). From the perspective of sound leadership, it's desirable to promote collegiality and mutual sup-port within the team for its own sake. Groups that are optimistic and have good working relationships are more willing to share information and step in when help is needed. Groups that are immersed in fear or distrust—whether of one another or of their supervisor—are more likely to become fragmented and limit their communication. In other words, all members of the work group function better when it's clear that their supervisor values them as three-dimensional human beings with diverse goals, problems, and personal situations rather than as human machines that create whatever product they've been assigned to manufacture.

8. *Positive leaders prefer team-based and collaborative approaches to rigid hierarchies and chains of command.* In a top-down management system, decisions can often be made and implemented very quickly since only a few people are in a position of authority. But that greater speed—and some might say greater efficiency—comes at a very high cost. Employees further down the institutional ladder may have insights that could avoid costly problems or provide greater effectiveness in the long run. Moreover, people tend to develop very little buy-in when decisions are made without their consultation and advice. For this reason, positive leadership avoids rigid hierarchies as much as possible and includes a broader range of the organization when decisions are made. Adopting a modified version of the quality circles pioneered by William Edwards Deming (1900–1993) and Kaoru Ishikawa (1915–1989), positive leadership regards all members of a unit as full partners in the activities vital to the mission of the organization. Even when responsibility for a decision must rest with an individual, positive leadership fosters an atmosphere of consultation and the free exchange of ideas in order that the final decision will be made on the basis of a well-informed consensus.

9. *Positive leaders treat each member of a group as a rational, capable member of the team, not as someone who needs to be led or manipulated.* Many management books treat employees as though they were problems to be solved or mindless robots needing to be directed when performing their tasks. In fact, the very word *management* conveys the idea that everyone in an organization, except those in supervisory positions, are challenges to "manage." Since positive leadership prefers people-oriented approaches and alternatives to inflexible chains of command, it also tends to treat employees with greater respect, valuing their ability to make reasonable decisions. For instance, rather than demonstrating to someone every step of a process and expecting that person to follow the procedure in precisely the way it was demonstrated, positive leaders will (except in cases where safety is at stake) illustrate the end result that's

desired and trust the employee to find a rational, creative, and efficient way to accomplish that goal.

10. *Positive leaders rely on a subtle, at times nearly invisible type of guidance rather than the "my way or the highway" style of management that authoritarian leaders adopt.* Perhaps the biggest difference between positive leadership and more traditional forms of organizational management is that its leaders don't always appear to be leading—at least not in an obvious manner. In other words, rather than telling people to do this or that, positive leaders spend much of their time creating environments that increase the likelihood of a successful result. They often work behind the scenes, not creating secret cliques and cabals but helping others form the connections they need in order to exercise their own originality. They eliminate the obstacles that can prevent employees from putting forth their best efforts. The effectiveness of positive leaders can't be judged by the number of memos they produce, meetings they call, or reprimands they issue but by the overall success of their organizations. They lead without making the people they work with continually feel that they are constantly being led, even though everyone senses the energy and progress that results from the collective efforts.

In this way, positive leadership provides a viable alternative to organizational models based on hierarchy, fear of penalties for honest mistakes, and other factors that inhibit creativity and destroy initiative. As Cameron (2008) observes:

> Positive leadership . . . refers to an *affirmative bias*—or a focus on strengths and capabilities and on affirming human potential. Its orientation is toward enabling thriving and flourishing rather than toward addressing obstacles and impediments . . . Positive leadership does not ignore negative events but builds on them to develop positive outcomes . . . In sum, *positive leadership* refers to an emphasis on what elevates individuals and organizations (in addition to what challenges them), what goes right in organizations (in addition to what goes wrong), . . . what is experienced as good (in addition to what is objectionable), [and] what is extraordinary (in addition to what is merely effective). (pp. 2–3)

What Positive Leadership Is Not

When they hear the term *positive leadership,* many people immediately think of those cheerful motivational posters that are all too often found on the walls of conference rooms, supervisors who are so far removed from reality that they remain unnaturally optimistic even in the face of disastrous news, or efforts adopted by upper management to make employees exhibit false fronts of exuberance no matter what their own feelings, challenges, and preferences may be. This sort of manipulative optimism has little lasting effect in most work environments and is often counterproductive (Grandey, Fisk, and Steiner, 2005; Butler, Egloff, Wilhelm, Smith, Erickson, and Gross, 2003; Snee, 2006). For this reason, let's eliminate immediately the following false impressions of what positive leadership might be:

1. *Positive leadership doesn't consist of motivational speaking or filling the workplace with inspirational messages.* Every good supervisor has to be a bit of a cheerleader from time to time, encouraging people to try harder when their energy is flagging or restoring confidence when it is lost. But many workers find an endless barrage of motivational messages to be ineffectual, even irritating. Positive leadership is about shaping work environments and the supervisor's perspective, not trying to fit all workers into the same cheery mold.

2. *Positive leadership isn't a matter of simply going along to get along and suppression of one's own feelings.* Some people associate positive leadership with forcing everyone to be nice to everyone else. While positive leadership, like all other effective approaches to success in organizational situations, certainly insists on collegial and professional interaction in the workplace, it doesn't require people to act like happy automatons at work or pretend that there's never such a thing as a bad day. Positive leadership is based on the principle that employees don't always have to like one another, but they do have to work effectively together. In order to achieve this result, positive leadership seeks strategies intended to make that collegiality and professionalism easier to achieve.

3. *Positive leadership doesn't require supervisors to provide life coaching to employees.* Life coaching, the practice of counseling others to identify and achieve their personal goals, can be highly beneficial for many people, even for many supervisors. But it's morally (and often legally) wrong to practice counseling without a license, and the supervisor who becomes too involved in the personal lives and goals of employees has entered a dangerous area. Positive leadership respects the rights of colleagues to set and pursue their own objectives in their private lives, while seeking more effective ways of attaining professional objectives at work.

4. *Positive leadership doesn't provide an excuse for supervisors to impose their religious or political views on others.* Some supervisors derive their motivation and positive outlook from their belief in a certain set of religious or political principles. While that source of support may

be extremely valuable for that person, positive leadership doesn't open the door to imposing those convictions on others or creating environments in which advocates of certain creeds or beliefs feel disenfranchised. The strategies that are discussed in this book are not limited to a single religious tradition or political philosophy, and, in fact, they should help to create environments in which everyone feels more valued and respected for the contribution that he or she is making to the overall enterprise.

5. *Positive leadership isn't blind optimism, the power of positive thinking, or simply hoping that things will eventually get better.* Ignoring a problem isn't the same as solving it. But to take the other side of the issue for a moment, becoming fixated on problems—and seeking to root out every possible imperfection before moving forward—can create an environment where everyone feels that supervisors distrust their workers and where morale (and productivity) quickly suffer. Martin Seligman (2006) discusses what he calls *learned optimism* as a strategy that even naturally pessimistic people can adopt in order to create positive outcomes in largely negative situations. Learned optimism is the rational conviction that regardless of how troubling the situation is right now, it's possible to learn from it, recover from it, derive benefit from it, and then move on from it. As Seligman notes,

> The defining characteristic of pessimists is that they tend to believe bad events will last a long time, will undermine everything they do, and are their own fault. The optimists, who are confronted with the same hard knocks of this world, think about misfortune in the opposite way. They tend to believe defeat is just a temporary setback, that its causes are confined to this one case. The optimists believe defeat is not their fault: Circumstances, bad luck, or other people brought it about. Such people are unfazed by defeat. Confronted by a bad situation, they perceive it as a challenge and try harder. (pp. 4–5)

In other words, it's possible to learn how to become optimistic even if you don't have a naturally sunny disposition. People who treat success as though it were the expected outcome of their efforts, while regarding failure as something that occurs occasionally because of circumstances beyond their control, tend to develop a more positive outlook on life over time. Viewed from this perspective, optimism isn't blind faith; it's an intentional cognitive strategy that anyone can adopt. Even cynics, curmudgeons, and worrywarts—perhaps *especially* these people—can adopt an attitude that tells others, "It's not me; it's the world," when things are going wrong and think, "I helped contribute to this huge success" when things are going well. In a similar way, in order for leadership to be positive, leaders don't have to ignore problems and act as though they see nothing but joy and happiness all around them. They merely have to seek positive outcomes in every situation, even when they are dealing with a frustration or failure.

These clarifications will be useful as we shift our discussion from positive leadership in general to positive academic leadership. The purpose of this book is, after all, to help administrators understand how they can change their default mode from solving problems to creating something phenomenal. But in order to provide a different type of leadership, administrators need to be trained in new ways and interpret their roles differently. They have to start leading with what Kim Cameron calls a *positive bias* (What's right? And how can I make it even better?) and stop leading with a *negative bias* (What's wrong? And how can I fix it?). They need to learn how to identify strengths, not just solve problems.

Negative Leadership

When Maslow (1954) coined the term *positive psychology,* he also mentioned "the negative psychology we now have" (p. 361). In a similar way, if leadership with a positive bias involves identifying assets, then a fixation on problems and liabilities might be termed negative leadership. What's distressing, however, is that negative leadership is what most people think of when they think of leadership at all. That view of what a leader does is implicit in the high-pressure "give no quarter and take no prisoners" approach to management outlined in books like Donald Trump's *Time to Get Tough: Making America #1 Again* (2011) and, with B. Zanker, *Think Big and Kick Ass in Business and Life* (2007). But there is an alternative. Consider the way in which psychologist Daniel Goleman (2006) distinguishes good bosses from bad bosses, based on dozens of discussions he's had with employees from the entire spectrum of the labor market:

GOOD BOSS	BAD BOSS
Great listener	Blank wall
Encourager	Doubter
Communicator	Secretive
Courageous	Intimidating
Sense of humor	Bad temper
Shows empathy	Self-centered
Decisive	Indecisive
Takes responsibility	Blames
Humble	Arrogant
Shares authority	Mistrusts

Goleman writes, "The best bosses are people who are trustworthy, empathetic and connected, who make us feel calm, appreciated, and inspired. The worst—distant, difficult, and arrogant—make us feel uneasy at best and resentful at worst" (p. 277; for a similar conclusion, see Longenecker, 2011). Replace the phrase "bad boss" with "negative leader," and you'll come up with almost the same list and draw the same conclusion. We've all known supervisors who thought that they needed to threaten others, either openly or by implication, in order to receive "respect" and mistook arrogance for confidence. Negative leaders are the bosses who routinely suspect others of having ulterior motives because they always have their own and who distrust any idea they didn't think of themselves. To judge from movies and the stories we've heard from our parents, negative leaders were once rampant in military, corporate, and academic life. But there's another way to lead—one that brings about greater benefits in the long run. That's what the rest of this book is about.

Conclusion

We seem to have come a long way from Frederick Ahearn's descriptions of the frustrations facing college administrators. We've taken a detour through alternative models of health care like concierge medicine and the P4 Institute and ended by encountering the principles of positive psychology and positive leadership. You may be asking at this point, "What does the last topic have to do with the first? How might positive leadership provide an alternative to the sort of challenges that Ahearn was describing?" In order to answer these questions, we turn next to various alternative types of academic leadership and see what different administrators have discovered when they made a conscious effort to lead their programs in new, more constructive ways.

References

Ahearn, F. L. (1997). A day in the life of a dean. *New Directions for Higher Education, 98*, 9–20.

Alessandra, A. J., & O'Connor, M. J. (1996). *The platinum rule: Discover the four basic business personalities—and how they can lead you to success*. New York, NY: Warner.

Becker, D., & Marecek, J. (2008). Positive psychology: History in the remaking? *Theory and Psychology, 18*, 591–604.

Bernstein, D. (2010). *Essentials of psychology*. Florence, KY: Wadsworth/Cengage.

Blanchard, K. H., & Johnson, S. (1982). *The one minute manager*. New York, NY: Morrow.

Butler, E. A., Egloff, B., Wilhelm, F. H., Smith, N. C., Erickson, E. A., & Gross, J. J. (2003). The social consequences of expressive suppression. *Emotion, 3*(1), 48–67.

Cameron, K. S. (2008). *Positive leadership: Strategies for extraordinary performance*. San Francisco, CA: Berrett-Koehler.

Cameron, K. S., Dutton, J. E., & Quinn, R. E. (2003). *Positive organizational scholarship: Foundations of a new discipline*. San Francisco, CA: Berrett-Koehler.

Carr, A. (2004). *Positive psychology: The science of happiness and human strengths*. New York, NY: Brunner-Routledge.

Christopher, J., & Hickinbottom, S. (2008). Positive psychology, ethnocentrism, and the disguised ideology of individualism. *Theory and Psychology, 18*, 563–589.

Collins, J. C. (2001). *Good to great: Why some companies make the leap— and others don't*. New York, NY: HarperBusiness.

Ferriss, T. (2009). *The four-hour workweek: Escape 9–5, live anywhere, and join the new rich*. New York, NY: Crown.

Flora, S. R. (2004). *The power of reinforcement*. Albany: State University of New York Press.

Goleman, D. (2006). *Social intelligence: The new science of human relationships*. New York, NY: Bantam Books.

Grandey, A. A., Fisk, G. M., & Steiner, D. D. (2005). Must "service with a smile" be stressful? The moderating role of personal control for American and French employees. *Journal of Applied Psychology, 90*, 893–904.

Jones, L., & Page, D. (1993). Punishment: Its use and abuse. *Education and Training, 25*, 35–37.

Karl, K., Harland, L., Peluchette, J., & Rodie, A. (2010). Perceptions of service quality: What's fun got to do with it? *Health Marketing Quarterly, 27*, 155–172.

Knope, S. D. (2008). *Concierge medicine: A new system to get the best healthcare*. Westport, CT: Praeger.

Liao, S.-H., Hu, D.-C., & Chung, H.-Y. (2009). The relationship between leader-member relations, job satisfaction and organizational commitment in international tourist hotels in Taiwan. *International Journal of Human Resource Management, 20.8*, 1810–1826.

Longenecker, C. O. (2011). Characteristics of really bad bosses: An applied research study ferreted out the top "dirty dozen" characteristics of bad bosses. *Industrial Management, 53*(5), 10–15.

Macdonald, I., Burke, C. G., & Stewart, K. (2006). *Systems leadership: Creating positive organizations*. Aldershot, England: Gower.

Martin, G., & Pear, J. (1999). *Behavior modification: What it is and how to do it*. Upper Saddle River, NJ: Prentice Hall.

Maslow, A. H. (1954). Toward a positive psychology. In A. H. Maslow, R. Frager, & J. Fadiman, *Motivation and personality* (pp. 353–363). New York, NY: Harper.

Nelson, B. (1997). *1001 ways to energize employees*. New York, NY: Workman.

Nelson, B. (2005). *1001 ways to reward employees*. New York, NY: Workman.

P4 Medicine Institute. (2010). *Mission*. Retrieved April 1, 2011, from http://p4mi.org/mission.

P4 Medicine Institute. (2012). *P4 medicine*. Retrieved April 1, 2011, from p4mi.org/p4-medicine.

Parachin, V. (2006, September). Laws for positive leadership: How to be a leader others want to follow. *Toastmaster*, 16–18. Retrieved April 29, 2011, from www.toastmasters.org/laws.aspx.

Richardson, F., & Guignon, C. (2008). Positive psychology and philosophy of social science. *Theory and Psychology, 18*, 605–627.

Seligman, M.E.P. (2006). *Learned optimism: How to change your mind and your life*. New York, NY: Vintage Books.

Seligman, M.E.P., & Csíkszentmihályi, M. (2000). Positive psychology: An introduction. *American Psychologist, 55*, 5–14.

Snee, T. (2006). Break room posters: Motivational or mockable? UI business professor says big picture more important. *FYI: Faculty and Staff News, University of Iowa*. Retrieved April 16, 2011, from http://www.uiowa.edu/~fyi/issues/issues2009_v46/07062009/posters.html.

Snyder, C. R., & Lopez, S. J. (2007). *Positive psychology: The scientific and practical explorations of human strengths*. Thousand Oaks, CA: Sage.

Taylor, W. (2011). Booster breaks: An easy-to-implement workplace policy designed to improve employee health, increase productivity, and lower health care costs. *Journal of Workplace Behavioral Health, 26*, 70–84.

Thorndike, E. L. (1932). *The fundamentals of learning*. New York, NY: Teachers College Press of Columbia University.

Trump, D. (2011). *Time to get tough: Making America #1 again*. Washington, DC: Regnery.

Trump, D., & Zanker, B. (2007). *Think big and kick ass in business and life*. New York, NY: Collins.

Resources

Buller, J. L. (2012). The deceptive allure of negative academic leadership. *Department Chair*, 22(4), 19–21.

Lewis, S. (2011). *Positive psychology at work: How positive leadership and appreciative inquiry create inspiring organizations.* Hoboken, NJ: Wiley.

Macdonald, I., Burke, C. G., & Stewart, K. (2006). *Systems leadership: Creating positive organizations.* Burlington, VT: Ashgate.

Nelson, B., & Spitzer, D.R. (2003). *The 1001 rewards and recognition fieldbook: The complete guide.* New York, NY: Workman.

Whitney, D. K., Trosten-Bloom, A., & Rader, K. (2010). *Appreciative leadership: Focus on what works to drive winning performance and build a thriving organization.* New York, NY: McGraw-Hill.

CHAPTER 2

ALTERNATIVE APPROACHES TO ACADEMIC LEADERSHIP

If you attend nearly any conference on higher education administration, you'll find a program filled with sessions about outcomes assessment, program review, strategic planning, and promoting greater efficiency in times of decreasing resources. (Of course, colleges and universities are always in times of decreasing resources.) What you usually won't find are panels that explore how leadership in higher education isn't at all the same thing as leading a battalion or a Fortune 500 company. It isn't even the same thing as leading an elementary or high school. Working with professors requires completely different strategies from those that are effective in a command-based environment where the supervisor is a boss, not a colleague. Fortunately, there have always been a few visionary administrators who've been willing to consider alternative approaches to leadership in higher education, and it's to their examples that we turn in this chapter.

Kaye Herth's Hope-Based Leadership

Kaye Herth, the former dean of the College of Allied Health and Nursing at Minnesota State University, Mankato, made a career of studying the effect that the presence or absence of hope has on people. Beginning with research into how the homeless and critically ill view the future, she then applied her discoveries to leadership roles among nurses and college administrators. Herth's conclusions—coupled with those of Charles Snyder, Shane Lopez, Martha Helland, and Bruce Winston—are that the preservation and development of hope have a demonstrable correlation with effective leadership. After all, few people in an organization will want to work hard, endure the discomforts of change, or learn new skills if they don't believe that a better future is possible. Moreover, the degree to which a person preserves hope is related to his or her ability to be creative, achieve significant goals, and carry out plans in an effective manner (Herth, 2007a; Helland and Winston, 2005; Hunt, 1997). Since the term *hope* often means different things to different people, Herth and her fellow researchers defined it in their studies as "a positive motivational state that is based on an interactively derived sense of successful (a) agency (goal-directed energy), and (b) pathways (planning to meet goals)" (Snyder, Irving, and Anderson, 1991, p. 287; see also Beck, Weissman, Lester, and Trexler, 1974; and Snyder et al., 1991). Or to phrase it more simply, hope is the positive feeling that results from a person's belief that he or she controls a situation and can thus be successful in achieving important goals. Hopelessness or despair is the opposite: the sense that one isn't in control and that extremely important goals are thus likely to be unattainable.

In her research, Herth (2007b) found that hope-centered leadership is usually based on three major components:

1. Building the leader's own sense of hope
2. Minimizing the factors that limit hope or promote despair
3. Creating a vision of hope in others

The implication of this conclusion is that in order for institutions and the units within them to improve, people have to be supported in their belief that improvement is both possible and within their power to achieve. We can easily see this idea at work at a college or university. Unless members of the faculty and staff are convinced that circumstances will be better in the future, they won't try to make things better, and the result will be a self-fulfilling prophecy: improvements won't be made because no one has enough confidence to make them. In order to avoid this problem, a major task of academic leaders has to be conveying a sense of hope and opportunity. In Herth's (2007b) words, "It is absolutely critical that hope be present within the leader and be modeled by the leader" (p. 4).

Even so, the most important question about hope-based leadership still remains: How do academic leaders convey this air of confidence, particularly if they're not optimistic people themselves or are confronted with truly difficult circumstances? Without a meaningful answer to this question, we're reduced to doing exactly what we've said we won't do in our desire to build a positive environment: simply fake it, surrender to blind optimism, and lie to others about the severity of our challenges. But that's not what Herth wants us to do. She provides several key strategies leaders can use to create an environment of genuine hope-based leadership:

o *We should lead by building relationships among our colleagues, not merely setting strategic goals and improving the bottom line.* The hope-centered leader should view his or her role as "empowering others through coaching, teaching, mentoring, . . . and celebrating one another's victories" (Herth, 2007b, p. 4). In other words, that stereotypical image of the powerful leader as a stern boss who strikes fear into employees and humiliates anyone who fails even slightly—what we might call the bully model of leadership—simply doesn't work in higher education. (It probably doesn't work all that well anywhere else.) To the contrary, negative leaders cause people to give up and stop trying. Hope-filled leaders, in contrast, encourage others by celebrating their successes, supporting them even when they don't happen to reach their goals, and guiding them toward objectives they may have thought beyond their ability to achieve.

o *We should make it a priority to underscore the meaning and importance of the tasks our colleagues perform together.* A frequently repeated anecdote in management books sounds rather ancient but it seems to have arisen only at the start of the twentieth century. Here's what may be the first recorded version, which appears in a 1920 training course for supervisors written by Dudley Kennedy:

> The story is told of a man who stopped one day to watch some men digging on the site of a new structure.
> "What are you doing?" he asked.
> "I'm digging out the dirt," answered one.
> "I'm earning my three squares a day," replied a second man.
> The third man was different. He straightened up at the question and said with a glint of real pride in his eye, "I'm building a cathedral." (p. 26)

The moral of this story is that the person who understands the purpose of a task and how it fits into the future is more likely to view each day's work as contributing to a worthwhile enterprise, not as an exercise in drudgery. Hope-based leadership recognizes the need we all have for knowing that our work is important. Many people develop that understanding on their own, but for those who don't, the hope-based leader can help make the difference between success and failure.

o *We should take time to reflect on our achievements rather than simply rushing into the next project.* Dalton Conley in *Elsewhere, U.S.A.*

(2009) describes the impulse many have to focus solely on what's still ahead and what they need to plan. As a result, they rarely take time to enjoy what's happening at that very moment or what they've achieved in the past. Many faculty members and administrators fall into precisely this trap. They've achieved a certain level of success by being extremely goal oriented, with the result that each new goal becomes an end in itself. They wind up confusing the number of checkmarks on their to-do lists with actually getting something done. Our evaluation systems in higher education contribute to this mind-set. We force people to become so fixated on their next publication, next million-dollar grant, next increase on their course evaluations, or next major award that their attention becomes directed anywhere but where they are right now. We create promotion timetables and merit pay scales that pay scant attention to the rhythms of life and the totality of a person's overall career path. Annual evaluations become like needy relatives who ask, "Sure, but what have you done for academia lately?" Herth's hope-filled leaders break this cycle by making it a priority to celebrate achievements of all kinds: individual and group, small and large. They don't become so obsessed with what they want to accomplish next that they lose sight of what they've already achieved.

o *We should set meaningful goals for the institution as a whole, the unit, and each member of that unit.* Although we've just seen that hope-filled leaders don't become preoccupied with goals, we shouldn't conclude that they don't have any goals at all. They understand that when members of a group share a vision about where the group is going, they're less likely to give up during difficult times and more likely to derive satisfaction from even small victories. In short, they know that articulating a vision is quite a different thing from obsessing about the future. Pursuing a common vision provides members of the faculty and staff with a much-needed sense that the institution is heading in the right direction; people don't end up feeling that their college or department is languishing or, at best, reacting to the latest catastrophe. Effective leaders support their confidence in the future with an appreciation of all the effort that made their confidence possible. In fact, hope-based administrators recognize that you can't have energy for your existing tasks if you don't take pride in your past accomplishments and look forward to a better future.

In the end, what Herth means by *hope* turns out to be similar to what Seligman meant by *learned optimism*. It's a way of approaching our work with a sense of excitement for what may go right rather than a sense of anxiety over what may go wrong. And it's that very focus on strength rather than weakness that makes hope-based leadership such an important component of positive academic leadership.

Administrative Resilience

Yet hope-based leadership isn't identical to the type of leadership we'll be exploring throughout this book. Positive academic leadership is about more than just confidence in your ability to create a better future. In fact, one objection that's often raised about hope-based academic leadership is that any administrative philosophy based largely on optimism—even learned optimism—ignores the dire realities surrounding us in higher education today. Later on, in chapter 11, we'll see that many of these "dire realities" are really just the product of despair and negative academic leadership. But for now let's admit that the pessimists do have a point: there are serious challenges in higher education today, and you don't solve a problem simply by pretending it doesn't exist. So hope-based leadership won't get you very far when you're trying to demonstrate to a governing board, state legislature, or accrediting agency that your college or university is fulfilling its mission in terms of teaching, research, and service. In the words of Rick Page (2002), founder and CEO of the Complex Sale, "overoptimism has overcome critical thinking. Hope is not a strategy" (p. 3). Moreover, we have to remember that parallel conclusion commonly cited in the armed forces: "Hope is not a plan" (see Mowle, 2007; Krugman, 2008). So what's our strategy? What's our plan?

As we'll see in the next chapter, college administrators should always see a bright red flag whenever anyone starts adopting military or corporate language in an academic context. Our ultimate goals in higher education are different from those in other types of organizations, and our plans and strategies need to reflect that difference. As academic leaders, when we talk about hope, we're not talking about the victory of our desires over our reason. We're talking about something that we might call administrative resilience: the awareness that our programs have the ability to bounce back even when they've encountered what may seem like overwhelming challenges. In recent years, *resilience* has become something of a buzzword. It was the title of a 2009 memoir by the late Elizabeth Edwards that dealt with the author's struggles following the loss of her son, the recurrence of her cancer, and the very public troubles that destroyed her marriage. But in academic circles, resilience is the subject of a great deal of research in the field of positive psychology and is concerned with how counselors help people overcome adversity (Liebenberg and Ungar, 2009; Windle, 2011; Krovetz, 2008; Luthar, 2006). In addition, it was incorporated into the U.S. Army's Comprehensive Soldier Fitness program (n.d.). And whole shelves of self-help books have touted resilience as an effective strategy for dealing with stress, change, and personal loss. The following titles provide a small taste of how this idea has permeated popular culture.

o *The Resilience Factor: Seven Keys to Finding Your Inner Strength and Overcoming Life's Hurdles* (Reivich and Shatté, 2003)

o *The Power of Resilience: Achieving Balance, Confidence, and Personal Strength in Your Life* (Brooks and Goldstein, 2004)

o *The Resiliency Advantage: Master Change, Thrive Under Pressure, and Bounce Back from Setbacks* (Siebert, 2005)

o *Designing Resilience: Preparing for Extreme Events* (Comfort, Boin, and Demchak, 2010)

o *It's Not the End of the World: Developing Resilience in Times of Change* (Borysenko, 2009)

Properly understood, resilience can help us deal with loss, change, setbacks, and crushing disappointment, all challenges that are familiar to most academic administrators. So resilience seems to be a really good thing to have. But what *is* administrative resilience, and how can we apply it in our academic leadership?

Andrew Zolli, the executive director of Pop! Tech, a nonprofit organization that deals with issues of technology and the media, defines resilience as "the ability to maintain core function under the widest variety of operating conditions" (Southern Association of Colleges and Schools Commission on Colleges, 2010, slide 6). In other words, resilient people and organizations can keep ultimate goals in perspective when things are going well and recover easily when things are going poorly. Like hope and learned optimism, resilience is based on the conviction that disappointment doesn't have to become a permanent state and that useful lessons can be learned in even the most disastrous circumstances. If the word *hope* strikes some people as veering a bit too close to a Pollyanna-like belief that the future's going to be bright whether we prepare for it or not, the word *resilience* provides a valuable corrective. Resilient people and organizations are optimistic because they're prepared to deal with unforeseen circumstances. They understand that their objectives can always be affected by unpredictable external events such as health issues, economic cycles, and emerging trends. But they're also adaptable enough to respond to these eventualities in a manner that helps them maintain their focus on their most important goals, even if it means pursuing those goals in ways they hadn't originally intended.

In academic leadership, resilience has particular significance because college and university programs are affected by so many factors beyond our control: demographics, political agendas, natural and man-made disasters, unpredictable shifts in enrollment trends, changes in the governing board or upper administration, and so forth. Universities are extremely complex communities, and although administrators do their best to develop their plans based on institutional mission, demographic trends, probable enrollment patterns, and anticipated budgets, they can't predict the impact of every possible external factor. A new invention, a national crisis, or even the role played by a character in a film or television series can cause the popularity of certain programs to skyrocket while enrollments in other areas plummet. An economic crisis could entail additional budget cuts, while an unexpected gift from a donor could cause the institution to realign its priorities. The progress of any program in higher education is thus rarely consistent or predictable. So in order to remain effective in whatever new environment may arise, academic administrators have to be adaptable and innovative—in a word, resilient. They need to inspire others not with the false hope that "everything is going to work out somehow" but with justified confidence that the entire community can weather any storm that may arise if it works together.

Like optimism, resilience is an approach that can be learned. If you don't feel like a naturally resilient person, there are several strategies you can adopt to improve this skill:

o *Accept the fact that change is inevitable.* Even the most seemingly stable academic environment is bound to change. Students come and go, and so do faculty members. Once you stop fighting the existence of change, you can begin to affect how things change. The evangelical author and preacher Charles Swindoll (1980) wrote, "We are all faced with a series of great opportunities brilliantly disguised as impossible situations" (p. 194). Once at a workshop on positive academic leadership I was leading, one of the participants said she found it helpful to rephrase this sentiment as, "Change is merely opportunity disguised as discomfort." Resilient leaders don't mistake discomfort for a terminal illness.

o *Finding the right answers is important, but asking the right questions is even more important.* Answers give us the feeling that we're at the end of a process. Questions keep that process moving. If you decide that the only reasonable answer is, "We just can't afford to do it," then everything comes to a halt. But if you ask instead, "How can we do it even though we can't afford it?" you open the door to creative alternatives you wouldn't have investigated otherwise. In *Smart Questions* (1987), Dorothy Leeds provides practical lessons in how to develop the right sorts of questions for different types of situations. Negative academic leaders give answers; they speak in sentences that end with a period. Resilient academic leaders ask questions; they keep a process moving forward through liberal use of the question mark.

o *Be experimental.* Not every strategy works, but we often don't know what will work until we try. It's always surprising to me when scholars become administrators after success as scientists or artists, but then approach their leadership roles with unwavering determination never to make a mistake. That approach would've been disastrous in their scholarly careers. Fear of doing something wrong can paralyze us. Sure, it's unpleasant to take the blame for an initiative that didn't work. But the truth of the matter is that not every initiative will work. We can develop our resilience by learning that failure doesn't hurt as much as we think. In fact, it might even teach us what we need to know for our next success.

Kina Mallard and Mark Sargent's Joyful Leadership

Hope-based leadership and administrative resilience appear to turn ordinary thinking on its head: we usually think of hope and resilience as products of what we do, not as prerequisites for successful academic leadership. But as we've seen, we have a lot more control over the amount of hope and resilience our institutions have than we may initially believe. That same principle has to be applied to the next alternative administrative strategy we'll explore, Mallard and Sargent's joyful leadership. In fact, in this case, the need to transform our thinking seems even greater. After all, it's one thing to accept the notion that hope and resilience can be intentional. But how can happiness be intentional? How do you make yourself feel joy?

In 2008–2009, Kina Mallard, provost at Carson-Newman College, and Mark Sargent, provost at Gordon College, published a three-part series in *Department Chair* on the way in which positive attitudes increase how effective we are as college administrators (Mallard and Sargent, 2008, 2009a, 2009b). Their overall finding was as follows: "The best chairs we have worked with are joy-filled chairs. They breathe excellence into their faculty and programs, they approach their jobs with a sense of purpose and respect for their faculty, they appreciate the uniqueness of their department members, and they are able to match faculty strengths with departmental needs" (2009b, p. 3).

From this conclusion, we can identify four primary behaviors that Mallard and Sargent observed in what they called "the best chairs." These chairs

1. Have a sense of vision
2. Respect the people they work with
3. Appreciate the uniqueness of each member of their programs
4. Try to match individual strengths to group needs

We'll encounter these same four elements again and again throughout this book. But even at this early point in our discussion, we need to understand precisely what Mallard and Sargent mean when they say that good administrators derive joy from their positions. Here's what they discovered: administrators who are happy by nature aren't necessarily the ones who describe themselves as satisfied in their jobs, are well regarded by their peers, and build strong, successful programs. Rather, leaders who are successful in those three areas (job satisfaction, reputation, and program strength) have learned to view their responsibilities as "good work, meaningful and transformative" (Mallard and Sargent, 2008, p. 9). In other words, like optimism and resilience, finding significance in our work is a skill we can develop. Administrators do so, Mallard and Sargent discovered, by approaching their duties not as an endless series of unconnected problems but as part of an important ongoing process. Successful academic leaders view themselves as continuing the work begun by all the chairs (or deans, vice presidents, presidents, chancellors, or whatever title they happen to hold) who came before them and as building a legacy for all of those who will follow in the future.

The first step in joyful leadership is thus to begin looking at everything you do vertically through time: How do my duties today fit into the sweep of history? The second step is to supplement this view by considering your work horizontally across the academic world as a whole: How do my duties today improve higher education? Certainly our work as academic leaders has become more and more specialized because of the vast increase in information we have available and the responsibilities administrators didn't have a generation or two ago. But we're more likely to see our work as part of a big picture if we stop defining ourselves in terms of our academic or administrative specialties. As we'll see in the next chapter, our worldview becomes smaller—and our achievements less significant—if we define our role narrowly in terms of the closed system of just the department, college, or school in which we work. Viewing ourselves as part of a larger, more important enterprise can make our day-to-day problems seem less aggravating and provide us with the knowledge that what we're doing matters.

Mallard and Sargent also discuss the importance of enforcing administrative policies as collegially as possible. If administrators convey an air of cynicism about such activities as tenure and promotion reviews, treating them as little more than meaningless hurdles or politicized nuisances, then our institutional procedures will eventually become meaningless hurdles and politicized nuisances. They suggest that it matters how we describe something like the tenure process when we're speaking to faculty. We should say things like:

> If you are going to invest your career in an institution, you'll want colleagues who have proven their mettle. In addition, you want to belong to an institution that encourages the freedom and trust that tenure offers. Colleges with a tradition of strong, tenured faculty members generally have a culture of open dialogue and a spirit of mutual respect between educators and administrative leaders. (2009b, p. 2)

In other words, putting together that tenure binder isn't just a matter of jumping through hoops. It's a matter of strengthening our disciplines and supporting academic freedom. By placing issues within their larger context, we help faculty members see themselves as part of their own big picture and create an environment where it's easier for faculty members to overcome the distrust that sometimes emerges between administrators and instructors. By guaranteeing that the work of others isn't ignored, undervalued, or taken for granted, we help build an institution in which our own work is also less likely to be ignored, undervalued, or taken for granted.

Naturally I can't promise you that if you follow Mallard and Sargent's advice, you'll immediately begin to feel joy at work and that your problems will become pleasures overnight. But the idea of joyful chairing underscores the notion that few approaches to leadership (and probably no approach to academic leadership) are likely to be successful if supervisors regard their own duties as a burden, the people with whom they work as lazy, their own bosses as incompetent, and the entire organization as unworthy of their remarkable talents. Contempt and resentment are contagious. But so are hope, resilience, and joy. When we change the way we lead, the effect becomes noticeable throughout the institution as a whole.

Appreciative Inquiry and Positive Change

Just as hope-based leadership and joyful leadership may strike some people as impractical until they realize what *hope* and *joy* really mean in an administrative context, so will there be those who believe suggesting that change can be fun is little more than a utopian dream. But David Cooperrider and Diana Whitney (2005), who helped found the Taos Institute (a loose affiliation of scholars dedicated to the philosophical perspective known as social constructionism), have concluded that what they call *appreciative inquiry* can lead to positive change through a process that people actually enjoy:

> Appreciative Inquiry is the cooperative . . . search for the best in people, their organizations, and the world around them. It involves systematic discovery of what gives life to an organization or a community when it is most effective and most capable in economic, ecological, and human terms . . . Instead of negation, criticism, and spiraling diagnosis, there is discovery, dream, and design . . . Positive change can be defined as follows: Any form of organization[al] change, redesign, or planning that begins with a comprehensive inquiry, analysis, and dialogue of an organization's positive core, that involves multiple stake-holders, and then links this knowledge to the organization's strategic change agenda and priorities. (pp. 8, 12)

In other words, appreciative inquiry means exploring future possibilities, not because what we're doing now is wrong but because we're strong enough to pursue a more compelling vision. In the same way, positive change isn't about abandoning what works; it's about making what works even more effective. Since its inception, appreciative inquiry has been used to guide discussions at many institutional levels, ranging from the mayor of Cleveland's annual summits on sustainability (see http://www.city.cleveland.oh.us/CityofCleveland/Home/Community /ThingsToDo/AISummit) to gatherings of global business leaders at the United Nations (see http://www.unglobalcompact.org/docs/news _events/8.1/summit_rep_fin.pdf). It can also be applied to the day-to-day operations of a department, college, or university.

Traditional administrators ask questions like, "Where are our deficiencies that we need to improve?" and, "Where are our problems that we need to solve?" That mind-set filters down into everything we do. For example, when we are evaluating faculty, it causes us (consciously or not) to ask such questions as, "What is this person doing wrong?" and, "What makes this applicant fall short of our promotion criteria?" We become preoccupied with the negative and with uncovering where the flaws are rather than where each person's strengths reside. Appreciative inquiry reverses this process, asking instead such questions as, "Where do we have assets we can capitalize on?" "Where do we have successes we can celebrate?" and "Where is this person successful so that I can better match talents to responsibilities?" By their very nature, most of our administrative approaches are backward looking: assessment and evaluation examine data from the past. Appreciative inquiry is far more forward looking: it considers what's possible and desirable for the future, treating hope and joy as powerful motivating factors.

According to organizational consultant Richard Seel, appreciative inquiry is based on two complementary models: the 4-D model and the 4-I model (http://www.new-paradigm.co.uk/introduction_to_ai.htm). Each model has four sequential steps.

4-D Model

Discover: The organization engages in discussions to find out where its successes are and which factors are producing them.

Dream: A cross-section of the organization then speculates about future possibilities, challenges itself to think even more creatively and ambitiously, and presents these ideas to the organization as a whole.

Design: The organization next develops practical plans to attain the goals developed during the previous step.

Deliver: Those plans are then implemented through the process of positive change.

4-I Model

Initiate: The concept of appreciative inquiry is explained to everyone in the organization, and various task forces are created.

Inquire: Interviews and discussions are held throughout the organization about possibilities for the future.

Imagine: Important themes that emerged during the previous step are integrated into a comprehensive plan for change.

Innovate: The plan is improved through discussions across the entire organization, implemented through positive change, and assessed to determine its progress toward long-term goals.

In higher education, both of these approaches suggest effective ways of implementing change. Instead of focusing on the structures, policies, and procedures that created problems in the past, the 4-D and 4-I models encourage academic leaders to be more innovative and move in new directions because they lead to exciting opportunities. People become pulled along by the future rather than futilely trying to push away their past failures. In essence, appreciative inquiry and positive change require administrators to see their roles at the institution differently. They require us to stop viewing change as a necessary inconvenience and start seeing it as a way of making our lives better.

Daniel Wheeler's Servant Leadership in Higher Education

One final alternative leadership strategy has a long and respected heritage. The term *servant leadership* was developed by Robert K. Greenleaf, the founder of the Center for Applied Ethics, to describe an improvement over the authoritarian, top-down style of leadership so prevalent in post–World War II corporate life. As Greenleaf envisioned his idea, a servant leader would be a person who assumed a leadership role not out of a desire for wealth or power, but out of a sincere desire to help others. Servant leaders wouldn't be content with merely making the organization better; they would also want to make the lives of all the individuals who composed that organization better. Greenleaf felt that leaders should help people grow as individuals, improving their daily experience both within and outside the workplace and encouraging them to adopt a similar philosophy of helping others: "The best test of the servant leader is: do those served grow as persons; do they, while being served, become healthier, wiser, freer, more autonomous, more likely themselves to become servants?" (Greenleaf, 1970, p. 7).

Larry Spears (2005), who succeeded Greenleaf as head of the Center for Applied Ethics (and renamed the Greenleaf Center for Servant-Leadership), identified ten qualities that he said characterized the servant leader: listening, empathy, healing, awareness, persuasion, conceptualization, foresight, stewardship, commitment to the growth of people, and building community. The meaning of most of these terms is obvious, but a few of them require a bit more explanation. By *healing*, Spears meant that servant leaders help the members of their organizations become "whole people," successful not just as employees but also as human beings. By *conceptualization*, he meant that servant leaders encourage others not to be bogged down by existing challenges but to dream of possibilities for the future. And by *foresight*, he meant that servant leaders understand the long-term consequences of their decisions, aware that short-term benefits can sometimes arise at the cost of long-term progress.

Perhaps the best image of how servant leaders approach their work appeared in an open letter that David Dudley, chair of the Department of Literature and Philosophy at Georgia Southern University, wrote to his faculty about challenges that he saw arising at his school. The letter quickly went viral, largely because it spoke so vividly about the troubled nature of administrator-faculty relationships today, using metaphors like the following:

> My friend Tim used to teach a course in church leadership, designed for people interested in various kinds of ministry, including pastoral ministry. At the end of the course, each graduate received a gift. Not a diploma. Not an engraved plaque. Not a gift certificate. A toilet brush.
>
> A reminder that true leadership is servant leadership. The higher the level of leadership, the greater the responsibility. The greater the call to service. (Dudley, 2012)

In 2012, Daniel Wheeler, professor emeritus of leadership studies at the University of Nebraska-Lincoln, applied that philosophy to what it is we do as department chairs, deans, provosts, and chancellors. Like Spears, Wheeler suggests that leaders should "promote emotional healing in people and in organizations (Wheeler's principle 4). In much the same way that Spears spoke of conceptualization, Wheeler encourages academic leaders to "leave a legacy to society" (principle 8) instead of just putting in the time their contracts require. And in a manner reminiscent of what Spears called foresight, Wheeler recommends that administrators "keep one eye on the present and one on the future" (principle 6) to help reduce the likelihood of unintended consequences (Wheeler, 2012, pp. 28–32). Most important of all is Wheeler's conviction that for academic leaders, service to others must be their highest priority. Administrators must see their roles as meeting the needs of the faculty, staff, and students, not standing at the pinnacle of some imaginary pyramid. In fact, academic servant leaders aren't at the top of anything; rather, they act as the hub of an organizational wheel. Wheeler isn't saying that administrators should feel as though everything revolves around them. Instead they should feel that support and compassion radiate outward from them, proving strength and permitting the whole unit to move forward. That image is one that we'll encounter again in chapter 10 in connection with what we'll call *centrifugal leadership*. Like Kaye

Herth, Wheeler sees the academic servant leader's greatest contribution as hope:

> Servants have the ability to project light rather than darkness; they are dealers in hope. Nothing is more discouraging than to have an administrator who constantly paints a discouraging picture and engenders little or no hope. It kills the spirit of those involved and results in people just going through the motions. Because servants have a passion for their commitments, they are not going to be in situations where they are just going to be passive in their efforts. (p. 41)

Like Kina Mallard and Mark Sargent, Wheeler (2012) believes that by acting in this way, academic servant leaders can derive joy from their job. In fact, he notes that this type of leader often describes work as a calling instead of a job, deriving satisfaction from the opportunity to help others. Servant leaders, Wheeler wrote, respect their colleagues because they "are committed to valuing everyone in their sphere of influence" (p. 90). They put the needs of their programs ahead of their own, recognizing that no organization belongs any one individual.

The Road to Positive Academic Leadership

Throughout these five approaches to academic leadership, certain themes echo:

o Effective academic leadership can be stifled by rigid hierarchies.
o The best administrators are those who have confidence that the future will be better than the past.
o It's possible to gain something important even from a setback.
o Building relationships is just as important as completing tasks.
o Change does not have to be threatening.
o Strengths are ultimately more important than weaknesses.

If we combine all of these elements—keeping in mind what we've learned from the research outlined in chapter 1—we produce the topic of the chapters that follow: positive academic leadership. Yet in order to understand why positive academic leadership can't simply be equated with positive organizational leadership, we first must understand why colleges and universities are different from other types of organizations and require different strategies to lead them. And so it's the unique nature of higher education as an organizational environment that we turn to in the next chapter.

Conclusion

> Forget about those age-old images of the stern, dour-faced manager, cracking the whip and doling out punishments and hard work to embittered employees. In today's world, great leaders are recognized by the positive effects they have on people. They promote teamwork, encourage excellence, foster growth, and offer criticism in a productive way. (Toastmasters International 2011)

Positive academic leadership is grounded in what psychologists and organizational theorists have discovered about what actually works in moving a program forward. Although positive academic leaders are not blind to the many significant challenges that plague higher education, they don't give into despair. They place a premium on hope, resilience, joy, appreciation of others, positive change, and a commitment to service. In this way, they don't mistake organizational charts for the organization itself, and they don't confuse issuing commands with being in charge.

References

Beck, A. T., Weissman, A., Lester, D., & Trexler, L. (1974). The measurement of pessimism: The hopelessness scale. *Journal of Consulting and Clinical Psychology, 42,* 861–865.

Borysenko, J. (2009). *It's not the end of the world: Developing resilience in times of change.* Carlsbad, CA: Hay House.

Brooks, R. B., & Goldstein, S. (2004). *The power of resilience: Achieving balance, confidence, and personal strength in your life.* Chicago, IL: Contemporary Books.

Comfort, L. K., Boin, A., & Demchak, C. C. (2010). *Designing resilience: Preparing for extreme events.* Pittsburgh, PA: University of Pittsburgh Press.

Comprehensive Soldier Fitness. (n.d.). *Resilience materials.* Retrieved April 25, 2011, from csf.army.mil/resilience/index.html.

Conley, D. (2009). *Elsewhere, U.S.A.* New York, NY: Pantheon Books.

Cooperrider, D. L., & Whitney, D. K. (2005). *Appreciative inquiry: A positive revolution in change.* San Francisco, CA: Berrett-Koehler.

Dudley, D. (2012, June 14). *An open letter to the GSU community.* http://class.georgiasouthern.edu/litphi/dd-openletter.pdf.

Edwards, E. (2009). *Resilience: Reflections on the burdens and gifts of facing life's adversities.* New York, NY: Broadway Books.

Greenleaf, R. K. (1970). *The servant as leader.* Cambridge, MA: Center for Applied Studies.

Helland, M., & Winston, B. (2005). Towards a deeper understanding of hope and leadership. *Journal of Leadership and Organizational Studies*, *12*(2), 42–54.

Herth, K. (2007a). Leadership from a hope paradigm. *Leadership*, *14*(1), 10–19.

Herth, K. (2007b). Hope-centered leadership in practice. *Academic Leader*, *23*(8), 4–5.

Hunt, T. L. (1997). *Self-concept, hope and achievement: A look at the relationship between the individual self-concept, level of hope, and academic achievement.* Retrieved from http://www.missouriwestern.edu/psychology /research/psy302/spring97/teresa_hunt.html.

Kennedy, D. R. (1920). *Better foremanship: A practical training course in the requirements, functions and opportunities of up-to-date foremanship.* Chicago, IL: American School of Correspondence.

Krovetz, M. L. (2008). *Fostering resilience: Expecting all students to use their minds and hearts well* (2nd ed.). Thousand Oaks, CA: Corwin Press

Krugman, P. (2008, March 11). Craziness. *New York Times*.krugman.blogs .nytimes.com/2008/03/11/craziness/.

Leeds, D. (1987). *Smart questions: A new strategy for successful managers.* New York, NY: McGraw-Hill

Liebenberg, L., & Ungar, M. (2009). *Researching resilience.* Toronto: University of Toronto Press.

Luthar, S. S. (2006). Resilience in development: A synthesis of research across five decades. In D.Cicchetti & D. J. Cohen (Eds.), *Developmental psychopathology*, Vol. 3: *Risk, disorder, and adaptation* (2nd ed.). Hoboken, NJ: Wiley.

Mallard, K. S., & Sargent, M. L. (2008, Fall). Joyful chairing: Finding joy in your department's heritage. *Department Chair*, *19*(2), 9–10.

Mallard, K. S., & Sargent, M. L. (2009a). Joyful chairing: Finding joy in committee work. *Department Chair*, *19*(3), 11–13.

Mallard, K. S., & Sargent, M. L. (2009b). Joyful chairing: Finding joy in your faculty. *Department Chair*, *19*(4), 1–3.

Mowle, T. S. (2007). *Hope is not a plan: The war in Iraq from inside the Green Zone.* Westport, CT: Praeger Security International.

Page, R. (2002). *Hope is not a strategy: The six keys to winning the complex sale.* New York, NY: McGraw-Hill.

Reivich, K., & Shatté, A. (2003). *The resilience factor: Seven keys to finding your inner strength and overcoming life's hurdles.* New York, NY: Broadway Books.

Siebert, A. (2005). *The resiliency advantage: Master change, thrive under pressure, and bounce back from setbacks.* San Francisco, CA: Berrett-Koehler.

Snyder, C. R., Harris, C., Anderson, J. R., Holleran, S. A., Irving, L. M., Sigmon, S. T., . . . Harney, P. (1991). The will and the ways: Development and validation of an individual-differences measure of hope. *Journal of Personality and Social Psychology, 60,* 570–585.

Snyder, C. R., Irving, L. M., & Anderson, J. R. (1991). Hope and health: Measuring the will and the ways. In C. R. Snyder & D. R. Forsyth (Eds.), *Handbook of social and clinical psychology: The health perspective* (pp. 285–307). New York, NY: Pergamon Press.

Southern Association of Colleges and Schools Commission on Colleges. (2010). *Photo gallery: 2010 SACSCOC annual meeting.* Retrieved April 25, 2011, from http://www.sacscoc.org/annmtg/2010/2010%20 Highlights.pdf.

Spears, L. C. (2005). *The understanding and practice of servant-leadership.* Retrieved March 26, 2012, from http://www.regent.edu/acad/global /publications/sl_proceedings/2005/spears_practice.pdf.

Swindoll, C. R. (1980). *Three steps forward, two steps back: Persevering through pressure.* Nashville, TN: T. Nelson.

Toastmasters International. (2011). *Positive leadership.* Retrieved April 29, 2011, from www.toastmasters.org/MainMenuCategories/FreeResources /QuestionsaboutLeadership/PositiveLeadership.aspx.

Wheeler, D. W. (2012). *Servant leadership for higher education: Principles and practices.* San Francisco, CA: Jossey-Bass.

Windle, G. (2011). What is resilience? A review and concept analysis. *Reviews in Clinical Gerontology, 21,* 152–169.

Resources

Cockrell, J., & McArthur-Blair, J. (2012). *Appreciative inquiry in higher education: A transformative force.* San Francisco, CA: Jossey-Bass.

Eliott, J. (2005). *Interdisciplinary perspectives on hope.* New York, NY: Nova Science Publishers.

Sutcliffe, K. M., & Vogus, T. J. (2003). Organizing for resilience. In K. S. Cameron, J. E. Dutton, & R. E. Quinn (Eds.), *Positive organizational scholarship: Foundations of a new discipline* (pp. 94–110). San Francisco, CA: Berrett-Koehler.

Yeasting, K., & Jung, S. (2010). Hope in motion. *Journal of Creativity in Mental Health, 5,* 305–319.

CHAPTER 3

APPLYING THE POSITIVE LEADERSHIP
MODEL TO HIGHER EDUCATION

As we saw at the end of chapter 2, leadership in higher education provides opportunities and challenges that are quite different from those found in other types of organizations. One important reason for this difference is that shared governance and academic collegiality play a much more important role in higher education than they do, for instance, on the factory floor, in a military unit, or even among the faculty of an elementary or high school. The result is that colleges and universities adhere much more closely to what we might call a client/professional model of interaction than to a customer/business or soldier/command model of interaction (Buller, 2007).

The distinction may best be understood as follows. Imagine that someone goes into a department store, asks a sales clerk for an extra-small, red, lightweight cotton, turtleneck sweater; makes the purchase; and goes home only to find that the package he or she was given actually contains an extra large, navy blue, heavy wool, V-neck sweater. The customer returns to the store to exchange the item, but the clerk insists that all sales are final and that neither refunds nor exchanges are possible. If the clerk refuses to compromise, the customer will then almost certainly demand to see the manager, who's likely to overturn the clerk's decision, apologize for the poor level of service the customer received, and remind the sales staff to be more "customer friendly." If the incident is serious enough, the customer is important enough, or the problem has occurred often enough, the manager may even terminate the clerk on the spot. While the working environment and job responsibilities are dramatically different in a military unit, we can still find certain similarities to this sequence of events. If a major is dissatisfied with a decision made by a captain in his or her chain of command, the major could overturn that decision, reprimand the captain, and (if the poor decision was bad enough or had occurred often enough) initiate appropriate disciplinary measures.

Now imagine a comparable occurrence at a college or university. A student goes to a faculty member, says that she "really needs at least a B in this course in order to graduate next semester." But when the term is over and grades have been posted, the student discovers that she has been given a C minus. The student then meets with the professor to object, but the professor refuses to change the grade and insists that the student got what she earned. Frustrated, the student makes an appointment with the faculty member's chair or dean, says that she "worked really, really hard in the course," paid the tuition that funds the faculty member's salary (as well as that of the administrator), and demands that the grade be changed, an apology issued, and the professor fired. The administrator's response is likely to be quite different from that of either the major or the department store manager. As long as a suitable grading policy appeared on the faculty member's syllabus, that policy was followed in assigning the grade, and the grade the student received didn't involve any favoritism, retribution, or other form of irregularity, the dean or department chair will almost certainly defer to the faculty member's professional judgment and declare the matter closed. The student may argue that she is a customer of the institution, has paid handsomely for a good grade and timely diploma, and is being refused the "product" that she purchased. But the truth of the matter is that despite what we hear so often from state legislatures, university governing boards, and the parents of our students, students don't really interact with us in a customer/business type of relationship. Moreover, despite all the elaborate organizational charts we post on our websites, faculty members don't report to us in a soldier/command model type of relationship. The role the student plays at a college or university is far more similar to that of a client who's interacting with a professional.

Here's the difference. When a client goes to a professional such as a doctor or lawyer, the "product" or "service" that's purchased is a process, not an outcome. The doctor can't guarantee that the patient will be cured, the lawyer can't guarantee that the client will be acquitted, and the professor can't guarantee that the student will get an A, master the material, or graduate on time. There are too many other factors—not least of which is the client's responsibility to take the medication at the proper time, be innocent of the charges filed, and study for the course—that affect the outcome. All the professional can do is promise to apply his or her knowledge in an appropriate manner, make the best possible effort, offer sound advice, and rely on his or her expert training, experience, and judgment. The rest is up to the client—and to chance. So if a patient storms into the office of a hospital director, claims that he or she has been misdiagnosed by a physician on the staff, and "really, really needs" those pain medications the doctor has refused, the administrator isn't going to overturn the doctor's decision. Even if the hospital director appears to be the doctor's supervisor on the organizational chart, the doctor has specialized expertise that the administrator will respect and trust. Ultimately they're colleagues at the same time that they're supervisor and employee. In a similar way, no self-respecting partner in a law firm is going to risk that firm's reputation and future by acting illegally in order to help a client after an associate has refused to do so. In client/professional models of interaction, the supervisor may review the process that led to the decision, but if appropriate procedures were followed, the judgment of the professional will be respected.

This difference between client/professional models of interaction and other institutional models of interaction can sometimes be seen in the shape of the organizational chart. In the military and corporate worlds, reporting relationships assume a familiar triangle or pyramid shape: authority rises as you go up the pyramid; numbers of employees increase at each level as you go down the pyramid (figure 3.1). In addition, there are important structures that exist outside this internal chain of command. For example, in the military, the commander in chief and Department of Defense stand above the formal structure; the enemy and the unit's mission are below it, together providing the reason for the entire structure. In the corporate world, the board of directors and stockholders stand above the formal, internal line of command; the end user and customer are below it, again providing the ultimate reason that the organization exists (figure 3.2).

In client/professional models of interaction, although it's still possible to talk about a hierarchy or chain of command, the entire organizational chart works differently. For one thing, it's a lot flatter and messier that the two examples we've just seen (figure 3.3). While in hospitals, doctors

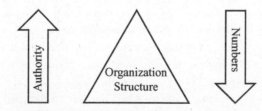

FIGURE 3.1 Pyramid-Shaped Organizational Chart

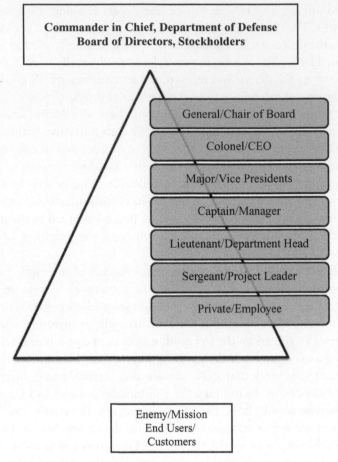

FIGURE 3.2   Military and Corporate Hierarchies

may be said to "report to" chiefs of various areas, who in turn "report to" the hospital director, each level retains much more autonomy than their counterparts elsewhere. Similarly, at colleges and universities, faculty members technically "report to" department chairs, who in turn "report to" a dean, but in fact a great deal of autonomy is possible at each level. Indeed, that autonomy is usually spelled out in detail by the institution's bylaws or in the faculty handbook. It's essential to how the school works.

For this reason, we can speak of pyramid-shaped, chain-of-command organizations as consisting of superiors and subordinates (officers and enlisted, management and labor), while client/professional environments are composed of colleagues. I'm not saying that chairs and deans don't evaluate faculty members and make decisions about them. And there are

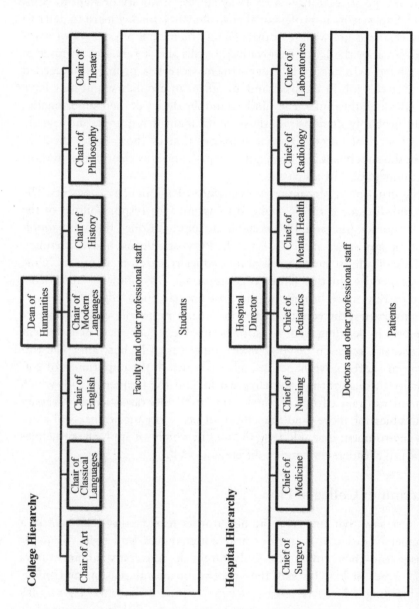

FIGURE 3.3   Examples of a Client/Professional Model

many ways in which associate professors "outrank" assistant professors and instructors. But in the vast majority of cases, these levels result from merit and prestige, not from an assigned responsibility or right to command. Supervisors in professional environments quickly learn to defer to the specialized knowledge of their faculty members, physicians, or associates because the latter have valuable skills the supervisors themselves don't have. A manager in a department store has probably succeeded at the clerk's job in the past, and an officer in a military unit may have risen through the ranks. They understand the duties of their subordinates, could probably demonstrate those skills again if required, and usually have a level of knowledge that surpasses that of those under them. In short, the supervisor is a boss, not an equal, and this clear line of authority is understood by all parties.

The situation is very different in client/professional environments. The hospital director is rarely qualified to assume the responsibilities of the cardiothoracic surgeon, the neonatal nurse practitioner, the ophthalmologist, or any other specialist on staff. Provosts, deans, and department chairs can almost never teach and conduct research in every discipline they supervise. In this flatter organizational environment, supervisors have to rely more heavily on the professional knowledge of the staff. At universities, the result is that administrators usually defer to faculty members in deciding what constitutes suitable standards of achievement for courses, research projects, and promotion to higher rank. The tradition of shared governance in higher education, the importance of collegiality throughout the academic world, and the frequency with which administrators rise from and later return to faculty ranks make university hierarchies far more fluid than those of other organizations. And since this environment is so different, the way in which we apply the principles of positive leadership must be different as well.

Maximum Collegial Flow

We just saw that university administrators lead faculty members in a completely different way from how commanders lead their troops or bosses lead their employees. Only rarely do university administrators issue direct orders. Instead, they depend on moral suasion or consensus building. Moreover, in cases where commands have to be given, it's almost always a sign that something's gone wrong. Either a genuine crisis has occurred or the relationship between the administrator and the faculty member has broken down in some way. It could be simply that the administrator has become angry or exasperated. It could be that he or she hasn't thought carefully about every option. It could be that there's a legitimate crisis where actions have to be taken now. Or it could be that this administrator's style just isn't suited to the environment of higher education today. Either way, when orders are given in a college or department where no true emergency exists, it almost always indicates a failure in leadership—the type of failure that portends greater problems for the future.

Ian Macdonald, Catherine Burke, and Karl Stewart, whose study of change in highly effective organizations became the basis for *Systems Leadership: Creating Positive Organizations* (2006), argue that issuing commands decreases the effectiveness of any organization, not just universities:

> Our view is that, to be effective, leaders must work so that organisations can run without needing to resort to force or manipulation, that is, power. It is a more difficult route to put aside such techniques but we have seen the toll this takes on members of organisations. Whilst the people at the top of the power pecking order may enjoy it, and it may appear more exciting and dramatic, it causes significant harm to people—not least a sense of cynicism and mistrust in a failed authority. Most people find these "power" organisations demoralising and debilitating. "Office politics", unclear accountabilities, shifting blame and making decisions on the basis of who will gain power rather than their effects on the long-term viability of the enterprise are all evident in such organisations. Power struggles may also lead to good people being dismissed because they are part of a group where the leader has lost the political power struggle, and all the supporters must go too. (p. 83)

Yet as true as this observation may be of corporations and nonprofit groups, it's all the more true in academic settings where professionalism, collegiality, and shared governance are major goals. As I've noted elsewhere,

> Power politics is . . . the great bane of academic life today. Many faculty members seem to spend a distressing amount of time forming alliances, grandstanding at public meetings, cutting secret deals, and undermining the initiatives of others, not for any fundamental principles in support of academic integrity or the welfare of students, but because they are convinced that "that's how the world works." Anyone who suggests that perhaps seeing everything in terms of political struggles is either not really how the world . . . works or

how we in academic life *have* to work is likely to be dismissed as naïve, ineffective, or out of touch with the harsh realities of the professoriate today. (2012, p. 85)

So at the risk of being dismissed as naïve, ineffective, or out of touch, if we want to reap the benefits of positive leadership in an academic setting, we need to set ourselves a loftier goal than simply settling for the status quo. We must strive for a result that's possible only in the flatter organizational structure of the client/professional model of interaction, a result that I call *maximum collegial flow.* The last term in this expression, *flow,* relates to a concept proposed and developed by Mihály Csíkszentmihályi, whose name we encountered earlier in our discussion of positive psychology. Flow, according to Csíkszentmihályi (1990), refers to that highly absorbed or focused state that can occur when we're so involved in an activity we lose all track of time, even lose track of ourselves and our worries. He suggests that people tend to be at their happiest when they're regularly operating in a state of flow.

We can easily see the operation of this concept in our own lives. If we think back to a time when we were gardening, running, playing tennis, writing a paper on a topic of great interest to us, listening to or performing music, telling or absorbed in a fascinating story, or following some similar pursuit in which we became totally engaged, we've already encountered a high state of flow. In most cases, we were probably functioning in what the psychologist Lev Vygotsky once called "the zone of proximal development": the point where we were sufficiently challenged that we needed to stretch ourselves a little bit, but not so overwhelmingly challenged that we became frustrated or discouraged (Vygotsky and Kozulin, 1986; Vygotsky, 1978). The point where this experience occurs is a "Goldilocks" moment when the work is neither too easy nor too difficult, but just right. In Zen, flow is sometimes identified with the state of mindfulness that can be attained through archery, flower arranging, calligraphy, the tea ceremony, and similar activities that absorb one's entire focus and immerse one in the moment.

But in order for administrators to promote positive academic leadership, they need to recognize that groups can achieve a state of flow no less than individuals can. The string quartet whose performances meld perfectly, the athletic team that's playing "in the zone," the married couple who have such perfect harmony that they can finish each other sentences, the operating room staff that's so focused on what they're doing that nothing else seems to matter—all of these are examples of collective experiences in which a state of flow has been achieved. It's part of what can elevate a group of individuals into a tightly interconnected team. Shared governance and flat administrative structures encourage maximum collegial flow. Strict hierarchies impede it. It's extremely difficult to achieve effortless group spontaneity when you see yourselves as "just obeying orders" or are constantly aware that the boss is looking disapprovingly over your shoulder. Notice that I say difficult, but not impossible. The incredible teamwork of military and corporate entities like SEAL Team Six, the Tuskegee Airmen, Southwest Airlines at its height, and Apple demonstrate that maximum collegial flow is possible even in environments that might be expected to staunch it. But these are all exceptions that prove the rule. They're remarkable specifically because they're different from the norm. But in athletic, cultural, medical, and intellectual environments, examples of maximum collegial flow seem to be all around us. In fact, you've probably had this experience yourself, even if it was only short-lived. When we're working with others whom we view as highly capable peers, a team mentality rather than a command mentality often emerges. And that's precisely the type of environment that's most conducive to a shared sense of flow.

Of course, there's no guarantee that maximum collegial flow will emerge in academia. Judging from the articles that regularly appear in the *Chronicle of Higher Education* and from books like Darle Twale and Barbara De Luca's *Faculty Incivility* (2008), most people might conclude that bullying and rancor have become the norm among university faculties today. But positive academic leaders realize that a better alternative is possible. They understand, through experience or a natural insight into human nature, that (to paraphrase Lincoln) you can achieve maximum collegial flow with some of the people all of the time or with all of the people some of the time, but not with all of the people all of the time. Even so, wherever this incredible team spirit does occur, it results in better teaching and research, higher morale, and the sort of academic environment where both students and faculty members long to be.

Although flow won't occur in our programs simply because we decide we want it, it's equally true that it's more likely to emerge if we make a conscious decision to pursue it. In other words, if we buy into the corporate and military models that focus exclusively on the product of our programs with little or no attention paid to the means adopted to deliver that product, we're setting ourselves up for failure. Progress may appear to occur in the short term—after all, creating "products" is a form of progress—but that progress won't be sustainable. As we saw at the beginning of this book, positive leaders must be at least as people oriented as they are goal oriented. In higher education, this means that rather than seeing our role as generating outcomes that happen to arise from whatever type of academic environment we may have, we should view our role as building a constructive environment that's conducive to generating one highly desirable outcome after another. It's a matter of turning our entire approach upside down, just as positive psychology turned the traditional approach to psychology on its head by emphasizing strength rather than weakness, health rather than disease, and success rather than failure.

This notion is the polar opposite of the direction in which so much of higher education has been moving for the past twenty to thirty years. Think of how many times you've read that the way to success at colleges today is through careful strategic planning (identifying desirable outcomes and the tactics we'll need to attain them), rigorous assessment (measuring whether we've attained the outcomes we've identified), and pursuing more and more accreditation and accountability (making the case to others that we're really attaining and measuring the outcomes we've identified). Look closely at that vocabulary. It's borrowed from the corporate and military worlds, not the professional/client world where collegiality and shared governance are the goal. *Strategy, tactics, objectives*—these are terms used to describe success on the battlefield, not in the studio or laboratory. *Strategic planning, quality assurance, productivity*—these are appropriate concerns for the factory floor, not the world of research, scholarship, and ideas. (For an interesting discussion of the rise of strategic planning and quality assurance in higher education, as well as their limited utility, see Birnbaum, 2000.) To be fair, there have been important achievements in higher education because of these approaches. But we've made the mistake of assuming that if a little bit of strategic planning and assessment is good, a lot must be better. We've become so preoccupied with institutional effectiveness that we devote increasing portions of our limited budgets to administration rather than education. We concentrate so exclusively on measuring our results that we forget all about collegiality, shared governance, and the fact that people are the center of our entire enterprise.

It's no wonder that so many administrators experience severe stress and faculty morale is low. They've been encouraged to buy into an industrial and military mind-set when what higher education needs is more of an academic and professional mind-set. Positive academic leadership provides an antidote to this problem. It's based on the principle that if you strive to create the right sort of environment, the right sort of results will follow. After all, the basketball team that's "in the zone" isn't thinking about the score or its standing in the league, at least not while it's out on the court. And it's certainly not relying on strategic planning, assessment, or accreditation to execute each play. When members of a team that's achieved maximum collegial flow become completely immersed in the game (the process) itself, the points (the results) follow almost effortlessly. And positive academic leaders approach their jobs in precisely the same way. They build superb departments and colleges that happen to have high retention rates, large pools of applicants, and increasing morale. They don't pursue better retention rates, expanded pools of applicants, improved standardized test scores, and higher ratings on morale surveys that just happen to result from any environment whatsoever. For positive academic leaders, the journey is the destination; arrival is merely a wonderful by-product.

Peak-End Rule

In situations where the journey does indeed become the destination, we sometimes becomes so caught up in the activity itself that we don't even realize how well things are going until we reflect on the experience later. Then we'll make statements like, "Now *that* was a great department!" or "We all just knew instinctively where our program was headed." Those recollections don't result from a strict arithmetic average of our feelings throughout the process. They're more likely to be based on certain key moments, experiences that were particularly positive or particularly negative, and our final experience before the process ended.

Let me illustrate this point with a personal example. One of my great joys in life is international travel, and when you travel a lot, people ask you about your favorite place to visit. It's a difficult question to answer. Almost no one is fascinated by just one place. When musicians are asked to name their favorite composer or avid readers are questioned about the author they like best, they frequently don't know what to reply. "It depends on the mood I'm in that particular day," they want to answer, "or what I've read or listened to most recently." But that response never satisfies anyone, and pressed for a response, people usually come up with a stock answer that may be true but is rarely the entire story. That was my experience when it came to travel. After years of hemming and hawing and giving bland or unsatisfactory answers, I finally decided what to say: I'd tell people that the isle of Capri was my favorite place on earth. Every time I'd been there, I'd had a wonderful time. The weather was always beautiful, the scenery never less than gorgeous, and the food consistently incredible. So Capri was long my stock answer to the inevitable question about the one place in the world I liked the best.

At least that was my answer until March 2007. My earlier trips to Italy had always been in the summer, but this time I went over spring break, and spring break happened to come early that year. The whole visit began poorly and then rapidly went even further downhill. The hydrofoil from Sorrento bounced uncomfortably on choppy seas. When I arrived, a little queasy from the difficult passage, the sky over Anacapri was a dull gray. The winds were fierce and unrelenting. The tourist season hadn't quite begun yet, so every shop and restaurant I wanted to visit was closed. I decided simply to spend my time taking pictures with my new camera. I was particularly excited about it since I'd invested quite a bit in the camera and lens so that I could capture some of the beauty I'd encountered in my earlier travels. But while I was framing a photo of that splendid rock formation known as the Faraglioni just off the coast, my camera (along with its brand-new telephoto lens) slipped from my hands, hit the cobblestones that had seemed so romantic only a moment before, and smashed into half a dozen pieces. In a heartbeat, the island that for years I'd been calling "my favorite place on earth" became the one place I never, ever wanted to visit again. And that turned out to be the result. I've never gone back to Capri, and whenever I think of the island now, all I can remember are those cold March winds and my ruined camera on the ground. That image has completely replaced the dozens of delightful experiences, wonderful meals, and beautiful conversations I'd had there in the past. On that single day in March 2007, I came face to face with what psychologists call the *peak-end rule.*

The peak-end rule states that when we look back on a series of experiences, we don't base our feelings on the entire collection of experiences, but rather on the moment in which our greatest pleasure or pain (the peak) occurred, filtered through how we felt during the last event in the series (the end). In the case of my travel to Capri, I'd encountered both components of this principle simultaneously: the peak emotional experience (a bad one) was the last event in the series. The effect was doubled. So it's no wonder that I now have no desire to return. At a simple level, the peak-end rule accounts for why we say things like, "When you fall off the horse, get right back on or you'll never ride again." It's also why we feel strong emotions in situations that range from the trivial (the restaurant we used to love but now avoid because we were disappointed by the dessert we were served there during our last visit) to the life altering (the parent or dear friend we loved so much, but whom it now pains us to recall because his or her final weeks of suffering have become so much more vivid than all our times of joy together).

The importance of the peak-end rule was first suggested by the Nobel Prize–winning psychologist Daniel Kahneman and has been applied to fields as varied as economics, marketing, counseling, industry, and sports (Kahneman, Wakker, and Sarin, 1997; Fredrickson and Kahneman, 1993; Kahneman, Diener, and Schwarz, 1999). To be sure, a number of studies have since found important exceptions to the peak-end rule and situations where the concept doesn't seem to apply at all (Miron-Shatz, 2009; Kemp, Burt, and Furneaux, 2008; Cojuharenco and Ryvkin, 2008). But researchers have also found environments where the peak-end rule can be validated repeatedly for both pleasant and painful experiences (Do, Rupert, and Wolford, 2008; Verhoef, Antonides, and de Hoog, 2004; Nasiry and Popescu, 2011).

In our day-to-day experience as academic administrators, we're likely to encounter the peak-end rule regularly. For example, we've all known researchers who suffer writer's block after a single negative review, faculty members who refuse to serve on certain committees because after a long record of success, they had one bad experience with other members, and students who complain every day while writing their dissertations but later describe it as the best experience of their lives because of all the praise they received from their defense committees. And while it's simply intuitive that extremely positive or extremely negative experiences can color how we view an entire series of events, what about the other part of this rule: those end experiences? If they're neither particularly pleasurable nor decidedly awful, what impact do they have on how we remember events? A number of studies have indicated that three things occur when people recall a succession of experiences:

1. Their memories of the last event are usually far more vivid than their memories of earlier events in the series, even if all the experiences occurred quite recently.

2. Their favorite event in the series tends to be the last one, even if all the events were somewhat similar.

3. These effects are exacerbated when people know a series of events is about to end.

Ye Li and Nicholas Epley produced these results in a set of experiments where subjects were asked to choose their favorite jelly bean in a randomly ordered series, and Ed O'Brien and Phoebe Ellsworth of the University of Michigan drew similar conclusions when they gave subjects a randomly ordered series of chocolates (Li and Epley, 2009; http://www.ns.umich.edu/new/releases/20177-experiences-are-better-when-we-know-theyre-about-to-end). These researchers believe the three tendencies may help explain such occurrences as why jobs are most frequently offered to the last candidate interviewed, Academy Awards so often go to films released later in the year rather than during the first few months, people who use online dating sites tend to rate the last profile they see as "most appealing" if they're told in advance that they're about to be shown the final profile in the series, and people often conclude that the last speaker on the program has been the most persuasive (see http://ideastations.org/npr/146874769-why-best -chocolate-is-one-you-eat-last; Li and Epley, 2009; http://www.ns.umich .edu/new/releases/20177-experiences-are-better-when-we-know -theyre-about-to-end). On a more mundane level, this same phenomenon helps explain the "What have you done for me lately?" syndrome that occurs when gratitude for favors diminishes rapidly or when people start their jobs with a great deal of energy and enthusiasm, only to lose it even as their salary increases and their working conditions improve.

The peak-end rule has a great deal of significance for administrators who are trying to include positive leadership strategies in running their departments or colleges. First, it demonstrates that no matter how difficult the relationship has been between administrators and faculty members in the past, it's still possible to mend those rifts if we decide to make the effort. Over time, academic leaders tend to be judged by their greatest achievements (or worst failures) and their most recent accomplishments rather than the missteps they made along the way. So even if your administrative track record has been a bit bumpy, there's no such thing as a lost cause: you can turn this situation around dramatically. Second, the studies by Li, Epley, O'Brien, Ellsworth, and others tell us how we can bring about these impressive results: we need to shift our focus away from checking tasks off our administrative to-do lists and concentrate more on creating the type of environment where peak experiences of learning, discovery, and maximum collegial flow are likely to occur.

In other words, if we become so goal oriented and task focused that we end up treating students and faculty members as though they were obstacles in our path rather than fellow travelers on our journey, we make our long-term tasks more difficult to complete and our ultimate goals more difficult to attain. It's not that we intend this result; it occurs because our tendency has been to view student credit hour production, increased efficiency, and assessment as goals rather than as ways of achieving the more important goal of improving insight, wisdom, and understanding. Ironically, all our focus on key performance indicators and benchmarks can end up creating an environment where student attrition increases, numbers of applications decrease, and the quality of education and research declines. The lesson we should learn from studying maximum collegial flow and the peak-end rule is this: improve your environment first and document your successes later. If we reverse those priorities, our students and programs will suffer.

Of course, the objection might be raised that the world of higher education today makes such idealistic sentiments impractical. After all, it's one thing to identify and increase peak experiences for individuals; it's another thing altogether to try doing so for an entire department or college. For example, suppose you have a friend who enjoys golf. The way to create an environment in which he or she is likely to have more peak experiences is to schedule more golf outings. If someone in your family loves to read, the way to improve the environment is to make more good books available. But no two people in any program are likely to identify exactly the same type of peak experience when describing how a whole unit could be improved. One person will think all that's needed is an increase in salaries. Another will want reduced teaching loads. A third calls for more research equipment. Is the only way to enhance this environment a matter of pursuing all these goals simultaneously? Well, no. In a famous early study, Howard Baumgartel (1957), then an assistant professor of human relations and business administration at the University of Kansas, studied twenty large research teams and looked for correlations between the manager's personal leadership style (defined for the purposes of this study as laissez-faire leadership, directive leadership, or participatory leadership) and each group's level of satisfaction in four key areas (their sense that they were doing something important, their belief that they were making progress, their level of support for the leader, and overall). Baumgartel discovered that what resulted consistently was a high correlation between greater satisfaction in all areas—what we might call more frequent peak experiences—and a participatory style of leadership. In other words, the factor that mattered most to the satisfaction of people working in an academic setting was their belief that they were informed, consulted, and given a voice in determining the direction of their discipline. Moreover, when that participatory approach was adopted, the most notable result was the group's sense that they were making progress together. So it wasn't assessment and benchmarks that were identified as causes of success; it was positive academic leadership.

Don Chu, dean of the College of Education, Health, and Human Services at the University of California-San Marcos, has underscored the importance of this connection among participatory leadership, more frequent peak experiences, and a group's collective sense of progress. In *The Department Chair Primer* (2012), Chu notes that departments stagnate when everyone within them regards the unit as a closed system, an environment focused on only its most obvious internal stakeholders. In other words, when you ask members of a closed academic system what they're doing and why, they'll respond that the faculty members are there to teach and conduct research, the students are there to learn, and the administration is there to make sure that the doors are open and the lights are on. Where departments are truly flourishing and dynamic, people tend to see themselves as part of an open system, an environment in which our stakeholders and constituents are legion: the upper administration, the local community, our alumni, our professional organizations, accrediting bodies, state and federal governments, the media, parents of students, prospective students, donors and potential donors, and many others. To put these findings in the simplest possible terms, when we become preoccupied with "products," results, and only the stakeholders who are immediately in front of us, we make it harder to achieve the goals we claim to be pursuing. When we treat our full range of stakeholders as active and valued participants, we create environments in which peak experiences become more likely and our goals are easier to attain. If you pay attention only to your immediate problems and the people you see every day, a large number of opportunities won't even enter your field of vision. You will have put on blinders that permit you to see in only one direction. But positive academic leadership requires awareness of the complete picture. Tunnel vision has never been the best way to identify alternative paths to a better future.

The best part of all these studies is that we don't have to assume progress is impossible unless our budgets are increased, new institutional procedures are developed, and additional layers of bureaucracy are created. All we have to do is to change the way we think about what we're trying to do. Engage in the following thought experiment. Open a word processing file or take a blank sheet of paper and answer each of the following questions:

1. Who are the stakeholders who are affected by what I do?
   (Remember to include not just the people who work for or with you. Consider as well those constituents who exist elsewhere within your institution or are not even represented on the organizational charts of your institution.)

2. Look at each group of stakeholders in turn, asking: What do they want from me? What are they hoping for?

3. After you've considered their desires, do the exercise again, this time asking: What do they need from me? What do they require in order to succeed?

4. Continue examining each group of stakeholders a third time, now asking: What do I want from them?

5. As you make your fourth pass through the list, ask: What do I need from them?

6. Then go back to your answers to questions 2 to 5 and try to identify any areas where the needs or desires of different groups (including yourself) overlap or complement one another. It's here where peak experiences are commonly found.

It's important as you conduct this thought experiment always to ask about both needs and desires. Most of the time, you'll find that what each group of stakeholders needs and wants is very similar. But where you begin to gain insight is on those occasions when what a stakeholder desires is different from what he or she requires. Consider the following example. Your president or provost may need your area to produce more student credit hours, but what he or she really wants is for your program to stop wasting so much time with grievances, tenure appeals, and negative stories in the local newspaper. In this case, if you can offer your supervisor what he or she ultimately wants, you may discover that you'll have relieved some of the pressure you're feeling to deliver on what he or she claims to "need." Similarly, you may need your alumni board to become more effective at raising external funds, but want them to become more independent so that they don't have to be led by the hand whenever donor calls have to be made. If you focus exclusively on meeting their needs, you'll deprive yourself of the possibility of creating additional peak experiences because you haven't paid enough attention to how one group's requirements happen to blend perfectly with another group's desires. But effective leadership requires us to recognize where these needs and desires converge (figure 3.4). We'll explore these ideas in greater detail in chapters 9 and 10 when we discuss using a systems approach to help improve our academic leadership. For now, it's enough to conclude that we're more likely to obtain what we need and want when we can describe it to our stakeholders in terms of what *they* need and want. But you can't even begin to do that until you're aware of who all your stakeholders are.

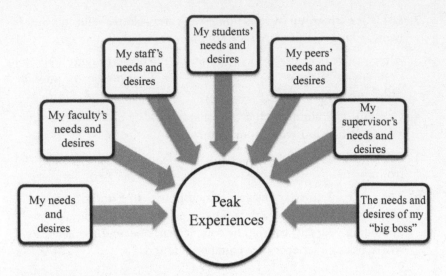

FIGURE 3.4 Maximizing Peak Experiences

When Positive Academic Leadership Is Not Advisable

I've spent so much time focusing on the benefits of positive leadership that it may appear as though I'm suggesting that this approach works in all situations. But as we saw in chapter 1, the positive leader sees different approaches to an issue as simply different tools in a toolbox. Not every challenge is a crisis, and not every unanticipated outcome is a catastrophe. As college administrators, we should expect to face challenges and opposition every day. Those difficulties aren't a crisis; they're just our job. At the same time, however, we can't deny that genuine emergencies occur at colleges and universities. Consider the following:

o The shootings at Virginia Tech

o The tornado that ravaged Union University in Tennessee

o The sex abuse scandal at Penn State

o The sex abuse scandal at Syracuse University

o The bankruptcy (and rebirth) of Antioch College

Those crises were serious, and they called for quick administrative decisions. While such emergencies are rare (thankfully), they do occur, and academic leaders must know how to deal with them. And you can't stop and form a committee when the building's on fire. Nevertheless, true administrative crises usually fall into one or more of the following four categories:

1. Danger to people's health or life
2. Major destruction of property or facilities
3. Lasting damage to the reputation of a program or institution
4. The ongoing viability of a program or institution

Even within this range, there's an important caveat to remember about the fourth category: not every program or institution that's shut down should be saved. In order to develop and achieve long-term sustainability, schools need to close programs from time to time. And if an entire institution has ceased to be needed in order to achieve its primary mission or no sustainable outcome is possible, entire schools occasionally have to be closed. (For a list of American colleges and universities that have closed, see http://www2.westminster-mo.edu /wc_users/homepages/staff/brownr/closedcollegeindex.htm.) But for the most part, the four categories can help us distinguish an actual emergency from a situation that is important but doesn't require us to enter crisis mode.

When true crises occur, we need to adopt a different set of leadership tools. In crisis leadership:

○ *Decisiveness must take precedence over consensus building.* When life or property is at stake, no one has time to build coalitions or consult about possible courses of action. In genuine emergencies, it is frequently better to have *a* decision than the perfect decision.

○ *Action must come first; analysis can be done later.* During emergencies, leaders won't have the luxury of having all the information they need. They have to intervene to alleviate the situation. Figuring out everything that happened—including who may have been at fault—can wait until the crisis has passed.

○ *Leadership roles will be blurred.* Some people who rank high on the organizational chart will not have the skill sets needed to address the emergency as it's unfolding. Although the threat still exists, it's counterproductive to insist on being in charge because of your administrative title. When the building is flooding, the skills of a plumber may take precedence over those of a provost.

○ *Different styles and methods of communication may be needed.* While positive leaders, as Kim Cameron says, tend to focus on positive messages, being in the midst of an emergency changes all of that. It may be necessary to warn people about what they shouldn't do, even when it hasn't yet become clear what they should do. And it may not be possible to communicate one-on-one in a highly personal manner. Even leaders who pride themselves on communicating directly with everyone in the program may not have time to do so and need to send messages through others or as terse instructions conveyed by e-mail or text messaging.

These leadership strategies are vital. But the important lesson is that they shouldn't be our default approach to guiding our programs. One of the best indicators of positive academic leaders is that they can tell the difference between true and illusory emergencies. Developing this capacity is a repeated theme in the chapters of part 2.

Conclusion

Great universities deserve great academic leaders who can produce a positive result even when budgets are tight, enrollments are rapidly increasing (or rapidly decreasing), and change appears to be getting out of control. In the chapters in the next three parts of this book, we'll explore strategies for introducing this type of positive leadership into your own administrative assignment in three key areas:

1. Creating a positive academic environment for yourself
2. Creating a positive academic environment for faculty, staff, and students
3. Creating a positive academic environment for higher education as a whole

References

Baumgartel, H. (1957). Leadership style as a variable in research administration. *Administrative Science Quarterly*, 2, 344–360.

Birnbaum, R. (2000). *Management fads in higher education: Where they come from, what they do, why they fail.* San Francisco, CA: Jossey-Bass.

Buller, J. L. (2007). *The essential academic dean: A practical guide to college leadership.* San Francisco, CA: Jossey-Bass.

Buller, J. L. (2012). *The essential department chair: A comprehensive desk reference* (2nd ed.). San Francisco, CA: Jossey-Bass.

Chu, D. (2012). *The department chair primer: Leading and managing academic departments* (2nd ed.). San Francisco, CA: Jossey-Bass.

Cojuharenco, I., & Ryvkin, D. (2008). Peak-end rule versus average utility: How utility aggregation affects evaluations of experiences. *Journal of Mathematical Psychology*, 53, 326–335.

Csíkszentmihályi, M. (1990). *Flow: The psychology of optimal experience.* New York, NY: Harper & Row.

Do, A. M., Rupert, A. V., & Wolford, G. (2008). Evaluations of pleasurable experiences: The peak-end rule. *Psychonomic Bulletin and Review, 15*(1), 96–98.

Fredrickson, B. L., & Kahneman, D. (1993). Duration neglect in retrospective evaluations of affective episodes. *Journal of Personality and Social Psychology, 65*(1), 45–55.

Kahneman, D., Diener, E., & Schwarz, N. (1999). *Well-being: The foundations of hedonic psychology.* New York, NY: Russell Sage Foundation.

Kahneman, D., Wakker, P. P., & Sarin, R. (1997). Back to Bentham? Explorations of experienced utility. *Quarterly Journal of Economics, 112,* 375–405.

Kemp, S., Burt, C.D.B., & Furneaux, L. (2008). A test of the peak-end rule with extended autobiographical events. *Memory and Cognition, 36,* 132–138.

Li, Y., & Epley, N. (2009). When the best appears to be saved for last: Serial position effects on choice. *Journal of Behavioral Decision Making, 22,* 378–389.

Macdonald, I., Burke, C. G., & Stewart, K. (2006). *Systems leadership: Creating positive organizations.* Aldershot, England: Gower.

Miron-Shatz, T. (2009). Evaluating multiepisode events: Boundary conditions for the peak-end rule. *Emotion, 9,* 206–213.

Nasiry, J., & Popescu, I. (2011). Dynamic pricing with loss-averse consumers and peak-end anchoring. *Operations Research, 59,* 1361–1368.

Twale, D. J., & Luca, B.M.D. (2008). *Faculty incivility: The rise of the academic bully culture and what to do about it.* San Francisco, CA: Jossey-Bass.

Verhoef, P. C., Antonides, G., & de Hoog, H.A.N. (2004). Service encounters as a sequence of events: The importance of peak experiences. *Journal of Service Research, 7*(1), 53–64.

Vygotsky, L. S. (1978). Interaction between learning and development (M. Lopez-Morillas, Trans.). In M. Cole, V. John-Steiner, S. Scribner, & E. Souberman (Eds.), *Mind in society: The development of higher psychological processes* (pp. 79–91). Cambridge, MA: Harvard.

Vygotsky, L. S., & Kozulin, A. (Eds.). (1986). *Thought and language* (rev. ed.). Cambridge, MA: MIT Press.

PART TWO

POSITIVE APPROACHES FOR YOURSELF

CHAPTER 4

POSITIVE LANGUAGE

In their 1968 book *Pygmalion in the Classroom,* Robert Rosenthal and Lenore Jacobson suggested that most students were likely to work at a level that met their teachers' expectations, no matter how high or low those expectations happened to be. Their idea was that if you praise genuine success often enough and demonstrate confidence in your students' ability to produce superior work, those students are likely to begin performing at a higher level. But if you expect failure and compliment those who achieve even fairly minor results, students are likely to begin performing at a much lower level.

Two years later, at the University of Texas at Austin, Jere Brophy and Thomas Good (1970) confirmed Rosenthal and Jacobson's hypothesis through a behavioral study. They demonstrated how important it is for teachers not only to set high standards for students but also to convey these expectations through positive language. Words, it seems, don't merely describe our world; they often create our world, making it become what we expect it to be. That same concept can be seen in a saying, widely (though unverifiably) attributed to Gandhi:

> Keep your thoughts positive because your thoughts become your words. Keep your words positive because your words become your behavior. Keep your behavior positive because your behavior becomes your habits. Keep your habits positive because your habits become your values. Keep your values positive because your values become your destiny. (http://www.spiritual-experiences .com/spiritual-quotes/quote.php?teacher=2 and http://www.notable -quotes.com/g/gandhi_mahatma.html)

Or as Daniel Levin (2009) puts it in *Zen Life,* "What you think today, you become tomorrow" (p. 74). In short, words affect our behavior. For this reason, the first component in positive academic leadership must be a conscious effort to keep what we say as constructive as possible, eliminate negative terms from our administrative decisions whenever we can, and speak in terms of what we'd like to occur instead of what we're hoping to avoid.

The role of positive language in effective leadership isn't just a matter of wishful thinking. Research conducted by Jackie and Milton Mayfield has repeatedly confirmed the connection between positive communication and such factors as the morale, retention, and productivity of employees (Mayfield, Mayfield, and Kopf, 1998; Mayfield and Mayfield, 1998, 2009). Recall Edward Thorndike's observation that we encountered in chapter 1: punishments only teach people what not to do, while rewards and recognitions reinforce the behaviors that we want people to do. Positive language works in precisely the same way. If you tell a faculty member, "Stop making your annual reports so vague I can't decipher them," you're really creating more problems than you're solving. The faculty member will understand from your statement that you don't want imprecise or overly general annual reports, but you've done little to help this person understand what he or she now needs to do in order to make these reports better. In addition, you've probably damaged the faculty member's morale, at least temporarily, and that attitude could hamper his or her work.

It's not that as a supervisor, you can never say that someone's work hasn't been performed up to acceptable standards or that good leadership is all about stroking egos. Positive academic leadership doesn't require you to become satisfied with mediocrity or build self-esteem in non-achievers simply because feeling good about ourselves is valuable for its own sake. But it is about finding effective strategies to achieve the goals you develop for your programs. Causing someone to live in a state of fear or dissatisfaction doesn't take you very far in that direction.

Recall the differences among the client/professional, customer/business, and soldier/officer models of interaction that we explored in chapter 3. As an academic leader, you're working within that client/professional environment; your coworkers are your colleagues, and they both expect and deserve a certain level of interaction with you in order to do their jobs effectively. By reprimanding faculty members over relatively minor matters, you build a wall between you. For reasons of pride or fear, they may not feel comfortable coming to you for guidance any longer on such matters as how to prepare better annual reports. Your negative language could convey an impression, however unjustified, that you'd dismiss any inquiries about improvements as "dumb questions" or matters that "anyone with a Ph.D. ought to know already." So rather than making it more likely that you'll receive better reports in the future, your language has actually made that objective much more doubtful.

A preferable strategy would be to use positive language in such a way that the faculty member understands exactly what you do want. Sit down with the person and offer advice, keeping your tone constructive and forward looking. For instance, you might say:

> Thanks for getting me your annual report so early. It's great not having to track people down and ask them repeatedly for their materials. I was wondering, though, if we could reorganize a few items on it to make it a little easier for me to gather the information I have to report—and ultimately a lot more helpful for you as well. In this part where you mention having two articles appear in print this year, could I have the citations? I always try to be as specific as possible when I list all the achievements of our program. Similarly, where you mention that you had "yet another great year of teaching," are there some data I can provide to support this statement? Perhaps ratings from student evaluations? Graduate school placements? Awards or nominations for excellence in instruction? That sort of thing.

In this way, you act as a helpful and concerned colleague while still making it clear that you need specific changes. As satisfying as it may feel to come down hard on a faculty member who's frustrated you by failing for the fifth straight year to do what you asked, harsh words and reprimands are usually counterproductive in the collegial environment of higher education. It's far more effective to praise what you can (in our example, you praised the faculty member's timeliness because there was nothing else particularly noteworthy about the report you received), provide guidance gently and helpfully, and demonstrate absolute confidence in the person's ability to meet the standards you've set.

That's a perfectly good theory, you may be thinking, *but what do I do if it's not the fifth time the faculty member has let me down, but the fifteenth or even the fiftieth?* In these cases, you may need to explore in greater depth why the problem keeps occurring. After all, not every mistake or failure is alike. Some occur because the person doesn't understand something. Others occur because someone has been negligent. Still others occur for completely unforeseen reasons. Only a very small percentage of mistakes occur because of willful spite or malice. As a result, it's simply poor administrative practice to treat every setback as though it were intentional, preventable, or the result of someone's carelessness.

Have you ever made a mistake on purpose? Have you ever been treated as though you had? A mistake is, by definition, an unintended fault. And yet people in our lives frequently treat us as though we're making mistakes on purpose. The next time someone you know makes a mistake, remember how you felt when you were treated as though the error had been deliberate. Then plan your response accordingly.

The positive leadership approach involves investigating the actual cause of the problem and addressing that source issue rather than beginning with the assumption that someone must be at fault. If a lack of understanding was the root of the problem, people can be trained. If carelessness led to errors, new policies and checklists can be developed. Even in situations where multiple mistakes are caused by a single person who "just doesn't get it," assigning that person a mentor may end up being far more effective—and less costly—than replacing the faculty member, initiating a complex disciplinary procedure, or merely blowing up at that person during a meeting. Keep in mind too that not all mistakes are necessarily harmful. Certain mistakes can lead to better ways of doing things or opportunities that wouldn't have existed if everyone kept doing the same thing over and over. Remember that as an academic administrator, your job isn't to work in a perfectly smooth environment in which nothing ever goes wrong. Your job is to work in the messy, complex, and interesting environment of a college or university shaped by human flaw and error, using your judgment and leadership to make that environment as conducive to success as possible.

How Our Rhetoric Shapes Our Reality

As you walk across campus and greet people, one of the most common questions you're likely to ask is, "How are you?" We often consider this greeting to be little more than a substitute for "Hello," and don't really expect an answer. But next time you pose this question, pay close attention to each person's response. Most people will probably answer "Fine," "Pretty good," or something equally bland. But if your school is like most others, the remaining answers will often be one of the following:

"Busy."

"Hectic."

"Crazy."

"Swamped."

"Exhausted by everything we have to do."

"Overworked and underpaid."

The basic assumption many people seem to have is that if they talk about how hard they're working, others will see them as dedicated, focused, and engaged. What they don't realize is that responses like these often give the appearance that the people who resort to them are frazzled, in over their heads, and out of their depth. That appearance is intensified if the same people who always describe themselves as "busy, busy, busy" don't end up producing very much. Moreover, by describing themselves as overburdened with work, they may actually begin to feel genuinely exhausted and depleted. Their sense of stress will go up even as their productivity goes down.

If you find that you too have lapsed into this habit of describing yourself as busy or hectic when someone asks how you are or how things are going in your area, you might consider the following experiment. For several weeks, in response to people's questions about how you're doing, don't focus on how hard you're working, but try saying one of the following:

"I can't believe how much I'm getting done these days."

"I'm making so much progress; it's incredible."

"I'm excited about all the possibilities that are coming up this week."

"I'm doing things that really matter."

"I'm *so* far ahead of where I expected to be."

If you stick with this approach, you'll probably notice several things. First, you'll begin to feel that you're really accomplishing a lot and experiencing much less stress. Next you'll begin to be aware that you actually are getting much more done than you were before. That old adage of "fake it 'til you make it" usually turns out to be true with regard to productivity and confidence. Third—and this may be the most satisfying result of all—the people around you who used to join in the chorus with you about how busy they are and how hectic their pace of work is these days will gradually stop sharing these complaints with you and may actually even start getting more work done themselves.

If you like the results of this experiment, you may wish to consider changing your rhetoric in other ways too. For example, if you engage in an interior monologue where you constantly describe yourself as "the worst possible administrator" or "not at all suited for this job," you could well be giving off signs to others that your description of yourself has some hint of truth. But if you tell yourself instead that you're up to the challenges of the day and fully capable of making a real difference at your institution, you increase the likelihood that you will meet these very high standards. The idea isn't to become cocky or demean your colleagues. Rather, what you want to do is adopt a positive vocabulary that helps position yourself so that you can achieve your very best. We're all familiar with what's been called the imposter syndrome—that sense that we're really not qualified for our positions and that it's only a matter of time before others figure out what frauds we are. (For research on the imposter syndrome, see Clance and Imes, 1978; Brems, Baldwin, Davis, and Namyniuk, 1994; Parkman and Beard, 2008). The imposter syndrome can sap your confidence and ultimately make you much less effective.

The language of our inner dialogues can affect us as much as or more than what we say out loud to others. Positive academic leadership involves giving ourselves an occasional reminder that we wouldn't have been appointed to our jobs if someone hadn't thought we were up to the task and that the imposter syndrome is a recognized experience that everyone undergoes every now and then.

How Our Rhetoric Shapes Other People's Reality

Just as how we speak can affect the way we see ourselves and feel about our work, so too do our words have a major impact on the people around us. When we hold titles like dean or provost, our rhetoric can take on a force that it wouldn't normally assume if we were someone's peer or employee (Buller, 2010a). As an example of this phenomenon, try this thought experiment:

Imagine that you're the president or chancellor of a university. In the hallway one day, you meet a new faculty member who knows who you are from your state of the university address. Although you say no more than a single sentence as you pass this faculty member, how might you phrase your comments in such a way that

a. You absolutely destroy that person's morale and motivation (at least temporarily)?

b. You have a significantly positive effect on that person's morale and motivation (at least temporarily)?

As part of this experiment, imagine how the person would feel if you said something like, "Don't you have some work you should be doing right now?" or, "Stop wasting time in the hallway; those grant applications aren't going to write themselves, you know." Now imagine your impact if you were to say something like, "Oh, I'm so glad we hired you!" "There's our new superstar!" or even just a warm "Hello!" addressing the faculty member by name. It's not just newly hired faculty members whom we can affect with our words. Try repeating this experiment by imagining an encounter with one of your senior and well-respected researchers, a visitor to campus, or a member of the support staff. It's good to keep these results in mind as we interact with everyone we meet. The comments we make in passing and perhaps never think of again sometimes assume a life of their own. Ultimately they can have a far greater impact than we ever imagine.

We're communicating and sending messages continually even when we don't realize it. When I was in graduate school, my mentor told me a story that stuck with me and guided me through many professional challenges. About twenty years later, I met my mentor again at a professional conference and told him how much that story affected me and changed my entire life. He looked at me puzzled and said, "Really? I don't remember saying that at all." The most insignificant statements we make in our own lives can become the most influential statement in someone else's.

If we multiply the effect of our words across the span of many days and months, it's easy to understand why words really matter, even when we don't think they do. A supervisor from whom one regularly hears criticism and almost never hears a word of praise ends up producing an environment in which morale is low and people begin to doubt their own abilities. A supervisor who finds something positive to say, even in the midst of the most severe problems, creates an environment in which people more readily find solutions to problems because they've been reminded that problems are solvable. Contrast the confident, forward-looking speeches of Winston Churchill during the darkest days of World War II, when the outcome of that conflict was seriously in doubt, to the sour pessimism of the grumblers we regularly meet in higher education. On the one hand, you have a truly desperate situation that people met with determination, optimism, and resilience. On the other, you have minor inconveniences that will be forgotten almost immediately. It's not a matter of whether you feel optimistic on any given day of your administrative work. Some days you'll feel that things are going to work out just fine. Some days you'll feel as though you can't possibly take on even one more problem. But if we want to be effective administrators, it's simply a better approach to describe situations with language that allows those around us to envision potential solutions rather than despair at the hopelessness of it all.

Why Positive Language Is Important in Setting Goals

Colleges and universities of all kinds are constantly involved in strategic planning and the pursuit of ambitious goals. But if we were to set a strategic goal that we immediately undermined because of our language ("In five years, we'll increase our enrollment by 50 percent—though personally I'd be happy if we could raise it more than 10 percent. And I doubt if even that's a realistic target."), no one would ever take our planning seriously, and we would have absolutely no hope of making our vision a reality. Predictions of failure are invariably accurate because they produce an environment in which it seems futile even to try.

While forecasting success is no guarantee that success will be achieved, it's only when we give others the confidence to achieve significant goals that institutions have any likelihood at all of fulfilling their ambitious plans. As Bruce Grube, the former president of Georgia Southern University, was fond of saying, "No institution, no university, ever became great without expecting to be great" (Georgia Southern University, 2009, p. 3). Yet it isn't merely in the area of strategic planning that positive rhetoric is important. Positive language can help us become more successful in day-to-day tasks too.

When administrators come to work each day expecting that they'll be putting out one fire after another, they're setting themselves up for frustration and failure. Describing our jobs, whether to ourselves or to others, as consisting solely of problems waiting to be solved forces us to direct our attention to the past (to identify the source of these difficulties) instead of present opportunities and future possibilities. Constructive goal setting involves what I call the three

Ps of constructive phrasing (for a similar system, see Kirschner and Brinkman, 1999):

Positive Avoid describing a goal in terms of what you don't want to happen. Rather, focus on what you do want to happen. Remove all negative words (*no, not, never*) and prefixes (*un-, in-, non-*) from any goal you set. *Example:* Instead of saying, "I want our department meetings to stop being so unpleasant and disagreeable," say, "I want our department meetings to become more efficient and future oriented."

Present Instead of saying what you're going to do (usually at some unspecified time in the future), declare what you're doing right now in order to make your vision a reality. *Example:* Don't say, "I'm going to get in touch with our alumni to collect a number of our program's success stories," when you can say, "I'm contacting our alumni office this afternoon for an updated list of e-mail addresses so that I can begin contacting our graduates more effectively."

Precise Avoid vague references to when the goal might be achieved. Instead set a specific target date that requires you to work consistently in order to achieve your objective. A dream is just a dream. But remember Harvey Mackay's (2005) dictum: "A goal is a dream with a deadline" (p. 57). *Example:* If you're tempted to say, "I'd like us to double our enrollment," say instead, "By the time the fall semester begins eight years from now, our enrollment will have doubled."

Putting these three principles together, we can see how this type of constructive phrasing might be used to transform everyday problem solving into the transformative style essential for academic leadership. Negative academic leaders might state a goal as follows: "I wish we'd stop getting sidetracked by ancient history and trivia at our faculty meetings." This statement really isn't so much a goal as it is a complaint: it focuses only on what we don't want to happen, not on what we do want to happen. And it doesn't demonstrate the three Ps.

If we were to rephrase this statement to make it more positive, present, and precise, we might say, "This morning I'm going to prepare a more detailed agenda for today's curriculum meeting so that we spend the greatest amount of time on our highest priorities." With this phrasing, we've focused on what we want to occur rather than what we want to avoid, what we're doing right now in order to make our hopes a reality, and what specific deadline we have in mind. We've stopped grumbling about something that bothers us and started taking steps that will make our work better.

Why Positive Language Is Important in Effecting Change

Positive statements bring about change more effectively than does negativity. That idea seems counterintuitive: if we describe everything as positive, where is our impetus to change? Shouldn't we use negative language to identify a clear and threatening problem in order to make others understand why it's essential to try a different approach? After all, that's the advice found in most management books about facilitating change. John Kotter, the author whose *Leading Change* (1996) is perhaps the most widely read guide to organizational transformation, states that the first step in any change process must be to establish a sense of urgency:

> Establishing a sense of urgency is crucial to gaining needed cooperation. With complacency high, transformations usually go nowhere because few people are even interested in working on the change problem. With urgency low, it's difficult to put together a group with enough power and credibility to guide the effort or to convince key individuals to spend the time necessary to create and communicate a change vision. (p. 36)

In fact, that's precisely how negative academic leaders think. They take an approach that may be effective in a customer/business or soldier/officer model of interaction and try to apply it to a client/professional model of interaction. But as we've already seen, that approach doesn't work well because the models are too different.

After all, consider how establishing a sense of urgency would play out in the actual setting of a college or university. Shared governance means that members of the faculty have played a central role in developing the curriculum and may have even shaped the institution's nonacademic policies. For that reason, instituting a change in higher education almost always involves asking the very people who put their hearts into developing a program, policy, or procedure to destroy it. Even suggesting that there may be a better option will be seen by these people as an accusation that they somehow "got it wrong" the first time or didn't know what they were doing. This problem is particularly acute when administrators are hired into an institution from the outside and, in their eagerness to begin making a difference immediately, implement a wide range of changes in their first or second year (Buller, 2010b). These academic leaders may have been specifically advised to do so because someone told them that there's a limited honeymoon period or window of opportunity for new administrators to make significant changes without strong opposition.

But what the honeymoon period theory of college administration doesn't take into account is that creating a sense of urgency doesn't make faculty members embrace change more readily. It makes them become defensive and dig in their heels. A new president or dean who attempts to instill a sense of urgency as a catalyst for change unintentionally (I hope unintentionally) conveys the sense that people at the institution didn't know what they were doing until he or she arrived to "save" them. Members of the faculty and staff will believe, perhaps correctly, that the administrator is simply making a crude attempt to enhance his or her own résumé at the expense of them and the institution. Those who have been at the institution for a number of years feel a sense of ownership toward "the way we do things around here." By creating a sense of urgency in order to promote change, what the administrator is actually doing is threatening people by suggesting they might lose something important to them:

> The phenomenon of resistance to change is not necessarily that of resisting the change per se but is more accurately a resistance to losing something of value to the person—loss of the known and tried in the face of being asked, if not forced, to move into the unknown and untried. Feelings of anxiety associated with such change are quite normal. Another form of loss that leads to resistance can come from one's experiencing a lack of choice, that is, the imposition of change, or being forced to move to some new state of being and acting. Thus, people are not simply and naturally resistant to change. What comes closer to a universal truth about human behavior is that people resist the imposition of change. (Burke, 2002, pp. 92–93)

In another book bearing the same title as Kotter's *Leading Change,* James O'Toole (1995) identifies thirty-three hypotheses for why people resist change. In the field of higher education, seven of O'Toole's hypotheses seem most relevant: inertia, fear, self-interest, cynicism, ego, habit, and the fallacy of the exception (i.e., the assumption that "we're different from other colleges and universities"). Positive academic leaders are aware of the force these factors have on most campuses and understand that creating a sense of urgency will only exacerbate them.

In higher education, positive language is far more effective at bringing about a desired change than are blunt descriptions of yourself as a "change agent" or, even worse, as an "in-your-face" type of academic leader. (And, yes, there really are administrators who use precisely these terms when referring to themselves. I've met them.) Positive language involves demonstrating respect to the people who came before you in your position, even if you personally believe that many of their decisions were ill advised. Remember that even people who cause the greatest harm to an organization almost always act in the belief that they were doing the right thing. It's not impossible that in ten years or less, one of your own successors will look back on a decision that you made and wonder what in the world you were thinking—and then seek to undo the damage caused by your misbegotten policy.

For this reason, positive academic leaders present change in higher education as a natural outgrowth of current developments rather than a dramatic departure from them. They understand that for every person who gets excited about the prospect of innovative change, there will be five to ten who view change with a mixture of suspicion, fear, and a conviction that everything you're doing stems from a conspiracy to make them work harder. Keep in mind, too, that no one at a college or university is ever ready for as much change as they claim to be. Even if during your interview, everyone you met told you that things couldn't possibly change fast enough to suit them, these same people may well resist your initiatives once you become serious about making substantive changes. For most people, a desire for radical change means thinking, *I want other people to change so that they become more like me. I don't want to change myself.*

How then can positive language help you bring about needed reform without causing widespread panic or resistance? First, avoid the unfortunate connotations that tend to surround the word *change* itself. Instead use one of the following ways of describing the initiative you have in mind.

- "An opportunity to build on our solid foundations"
- "A chance to take full advantage of our past successes"
- "A natural development made possible by the achievements that this program has had"
- "The next logical step in our ongoing progress"
- "An occasion to grow that can now occur because of our program's established strengths"
- "Carrying the plans that we've made together to the next stage"

If at all possible, try to avoid the phrase "moving to the next level of excellence." That expression has been so overused in higher education that it's now often greeted with derision, and that's the last reaction you want when you're advocating change.

Second, go out of your way to acknowledge the contributions of your predecessors. Even if the people who held your position before you were universally recognized as failures or scoundrels, it profits you little to focus on their shortcomings. Graciousness to one's predecessors is never inappropriate and helps to maintain a positive tone.

Third, rather than creating a sense of urgency, spend your time laying the groundwork for why this change is necessary. Show people how the change will benefit them by making their job easier or more rewarding. Urgency causes people to act out of fear because they come to believe that a disaster may be imminent. Motivation, however, causes people to act out of enthusiasm because they sense that a great opportunity may be possible. And just as often as fear can rouse people to action, it can immobilize them so that change becomes even more difficult. The standard question any administrator is asked during any change process is, "Exactly what problem are we trying to solve?" Positive academic leaders respond, "Let's not look at it that way. Let's ask instead, 'Exactly what exciting prospect are we hoping to pursue?'"

Being gracious and respectful to your predecessors is particularly important if you've recently joined an institution from the outside. In this case, any rhetoric that makes it sound as though you believe that you're there to "fix" the institution can lead to a great deal of resistance. Members of the faculty and staff may come to feel that they're being treated as problems to be solved rather than as valuable resources to be celebrated. A common habit of positive academic leaders is active listening. (I discuss active listening in greater detail in chapter 7.) Don't be too ready to dismiss out of hand ideas or approaches that run counter to what you have previously experienced. If you're viewed as the sort of administrator who's not open to suggestions from others, it'll become all the more difficult for your initiatives and proposals to get a fair hearing. Your ideas will be dismissed as a sign of your inflexibility or lack of imagination. ("The new provost is just trying to make us more like [insert name of provost's previous institution]. That's all he [she] knows.") Even worse, if you couple the perception that you have a messiah complex to too many references to the colleges or universities where you used to work, your language will be seen as negative and insulting even if you think you're just introducing exciting new possibilities to your new institution. Remember that no matter how successful a policy was somewhere else, you're here now. Using positive language means that you take every opportunity to celebrate that fact and express your gratitude.

The Power and Limits of Storytelling

One final aspect of positive language is that it frequently blends data with a healthy dose of illustrative stories. While some disciplines may find anecdotal evidence an unwelcome distraction, positive academic leaders appreciate the power of narrative in making organizations more unified, illustrating the need for change, and keeping morale high. As Stephen Denning (2007) has observed, leaders use stories to reinforce a sense of shared values and mission, while also emphasizing that change is non-threatening and, in fact, beneficial:

> A simple story about an example showing where the change is already happening can connect with an audience at an emotional level and generate a new story in their own minds that leads to action . . . The object of this kind of story isn't to *tell* the audience to implement their change idea: that would lead to an argument. Instead, the springboard story implicitly invites the listener to imagine a new story of which the audience becomes the hero. (p. 171)

Like powerful seasoning, a dash of storytelling is enough. Administrators who begin each statement with, "That reminds me of something that happened once . . ." undermine the effectiveness of a well-chosen narrative. Either people will stop listening after a while or they'll remember the story even if it runs counter to hard evidence:

> *We prefer stories to statistics.* Since we have evolved as storytelling creatures, our mind naturally gravitates toward stories and away from statistics. As a result, we overemphasize anecdotal information when forming beliefs and making decisions. Our preference for anecdotal data cannot be overestimated . . . The problem is, when we rely purely on anecdotal information in our everyday decision making, we typically disregard the statistics that may conflict with the anecdotes. (Kida, 2006, pp. 233–234)

Most important of all, positive academic leaders never use stories or any other aspect of positive language to manipulate or mislead members of the faculty and staff. Management is not manipulation. But leaders do use positive language to make their ideas seem more accessible, convincing, and exciting than page after page of numbers and charts alone. Best of all, your positive language may someday become the basis for some other academic leader's story of how the faculty, students, and staff came to view their academic community and brought about a widely supported innovation.

Conclusion

Using positive language means discovering ways of communicating with people that motivate them rather than discourage them. Threats, veiled or not, may cause people to act quickly and thus make administrators believe that they're being effective. But the ultimate cost is too high: negative language destroys morale, reduces productivity over the long haul, and cuts administrators off from the bad news they really need to hear.

Positive academic leaders use language to reinforce how much they care about the faculty, staff, and students in their programs. They take time to learn how to pronounce people's names correctly so that the faculty member who's receiving an award, the staff member whose years of service are being celebrated, and the student who's graduating all realize that they are important and that their contributions have been recognized. They view morale building not as a distraction from their "real work" but as an essential component of the position they occupy. And they understand that change in higher education proceeds more smoothly when people understand its benefit rather than simply endure its discomfort.

References

Brems, C., Baldwin, M. R., Davis, L., & Namyniuk, L. (1994). The imposter syndrome as related to teaching evaluations and advising relationships of university faculty members. *Journal of Higher Education, 65*, 183–193.

Brophy, J. E., & Good, T. L. (1970). Teachers' communication of differential expectations for children's classroom performance: Some behavioral data. *Journal of Educational Psychology, 61*, 365–374.

Buller, J. L. (2010a). The authority and responsibility of the title. *Academic Leader, 26*(3), 4–5.

Buller, J. L. (2010b). Rearranging the academic furniture. *Academic Leader, 26*(8), 3, 8.

Burke, W. W. (2002). *Organization change: Theory and practice.* Thousand Oaks, CA: Sage.

Clance, P. R., & Imes, S. A. (1978). The impostor phenomenon in high achieving women: Dynamics and therapeutic interventions. *Psychotherapy: Theory Research and Practice, 15*, 241–247.

Denning, S. (2007). *The secret language of leadership: How leaders inspire action through narrative.* San Francisco, CA: Jossey-Bass.

Georgia Southern University. (2009). *Strategic plan.* Retrieved May 21, 2011, from services.georgiasouthern.edu/osra/councils/spc/stratplan.pdf .http://services.georgiasouthern.edu/osra/fb/fb0506.pdf.

Kida, T. E. (2006). *Don't believe everything you think: The six basic mistakes we make in thinking.* Amherst, NY: Prometheus Books.

Kirschner, D. R., & Brinkman, D. R. (1999). *Life by design: Making wise choices in a mixed-up world.*New York, NY: McGraw-Hill.

Kotter, J. P. (1996). *Leading change.* Boston, MA: Harvard Business School Press.

Levin, D. (2009). *Zen life: An open-at-random book of guidance.* Pittsburgh, PA: St. Lynns Press.

Mackay, H. (2005). *Swim with the sharks without being eaten alive: Outsell, outmanage, outmotivate, and outnegotiate your competition.* New York, NY: HarperBusiness Essentials.

Mayfield, J., & Mayfield, M. (1998). Increasing worker outcomes by improving leader follower relations. *Journal of Leadership and Organizational Studies,* 5(1), 72–81.

Mayfield, J., & Mayfield, M. (2009). The role of leader motivating language in employee absenteeism. *Journal of Business Communication,* 46, 455–479.

Mayfield, J. R., Mayfield, M. R., & Kopf, J. (1998). The effects of leader motivating language on subordinate performance and satisfaction. *Human Resource Management,* 37, 235–248.

O'Toole, J. (1995). *Leading change: Overcoming the ideology of comfort and the tyranny of custom.* San Francisco, CA: Jossey-Bass.

Parkman, A., & Beard, R. (2008). Succession planning and the imposter phenomenon in higher education. *CUPA-HR Journal,* 59(2), 29–36.

Rosenthal, R., & Jacobson, L. (1968). *Pygmalion in the classroom: Teacher expectation and pupils' intellectual development.* New York, NY: Holt.

Resources

Buller, J. L. (2011). Management by manipulation. *Academic Leader,* 27(12), 1–2.

Elashoff, J. D., & Snow, R. E. (1971). *Pygmalion reconsidered: A case study in statistical inference: Reconsideration of the Rosenthal-Jacobson data on teacher expectancy.* Worthington, OH: C. A. Jones. This work is a book-length critique of Rosenthal and Jacobson's study, with particular emphasis on what the authors regard as severe methodological flaws. Although it does not completely repudiate all of the earlier study's findings, it provides an important complementary analysis of the data.

Kahan, S. (2010). *Getting change right: How leaders transform organizations from the inside out.* San Francisco, CA: Jossey-Bass.

Lewis, S. (2011). *Positive psychology at work: How positive leadership and appreciative inquiry create inspiring organizations.* Oxford: Wiley-Blackwell.

Soder, R. (2001). *The language of leadership.* San Francisco, CA: Jossey-Bass.

CHAPTER 5

POSITIVE PERSPECTIVES

In chapter 4, we saw how positive academic leadership begins with a change in rhetoric, a new way of describing and presenting things that emphasizes their overall benefit. That seems eminently achievable. After all, we already know how to control or modify our language. We've all had to bite our tongues in order to avoid saying something harsh or negative. And we've all used euphemisms to phrase our remarks in a more pleasant manner. But when we move from changing our language to changing our perspective, the challenges suddenly seem far greater. How in the world can you choose the point of view you bring to a situation? Don't we simply see things as they are, even when we recognize that our judgment of events is shaped by our own personalities and experiences? Isn't perspective an important part of our identities and all but impossible to change?

The fact of the matter is that we have a lot more control over our perspective than we often assume. To illustrate this point, let's engage in the following thought experiment.

One of your faculty members works in an extremely rare specialty. In fact, you hired this person precisely because her area of expertise was so unusual that you were certain your program would now become highly distinctive. Now, on the very day before classes are scheduled to begin, the faculty member comes to you and informs you that she has been awarded a major, prestigious international award. The award is so well respected that you instantly know it'll make her career and bring an incredible amount of renown to your institution. Unfortunately, in order to meet the terms of the award, she will be required to leave immediately for at least one full year, and you are aware of no one else who is qualified to cover her courses.

What are five reasons that this situation is an absolute disaster?

Think for a moment about all those angry students who'll be in your office, declaring that they came to your school solely for the opportunity to work with this professor and now are going to graduate without having had any chance to take her courses. Think of the parents who will call, e-mail, and even drop in at your office, declaring that you're incompetent for making such substantial changes in the schedule just as classes are beginning. Think of the faculty members who are going to be upset because their workload will increase. Think of your own problems in being forced to address this catastrophe at a time when you're already far too busy doing other things. Think of how your governing board may react since they place so much emphasis on efficiency and productivity, not the convenience of individual faculty members. And then imagine the result if you somehow pull it off and endure all these difficulties but then, at the end of the leave, the award-winning faculty member abandons your institution for a more prestigious opportunity at another school.

A first-class disaster, isn't it? Of course, it is. Well, that's one way of viewing the situation. But let's continue our thought experiment for a moment and approach this situation from a different perspective.

Consider five ways in which the faculty member's award is the best possible thing that's ever happened to you as an academic leader.

Now, instead of focusing on the inconvenience you'll have to endure, think of all the advantages your program and institution will reap when the faculty member completes the project. Imagine the new opportunities you'll have for support from donors and foundations. Imagine how good it'll look for you that one of your own faculty members was recognized in this way. Imagine the benefits that the faculty member's experience will bring to teaching and research in your area. Imagine the new network of important contacts that the professor is likely to develop and how those contacts might help your institution in other ways. Imagine the possibilities for favorable media coverage. Imagine how, even if the faculty member does take another job at the end of the leave, your program was the springboard for this important development. And imagine how your governing board may well credit you for creating the academic environment where all this became possible.

That was a pretty lucky opportunity that came your way, wasn't it? Of course, it was. As this exercise makes clear, the same experience can become a disaster or a godsend, depending solely on the perspective we choose to take on it. Moreover, a long history of research supports what we just experienced. Seligman (2006), for example, notes that the backlash against behaviorism from the late 1950s through the 1990s—including the work of such notable figures as Noam Chomsky, Jean Piaget, and Ulrich Reisser—established the importance of personal control and self-direction over such matters as self-image, preference, and perspective. To this list we might add the work of Richard Lazarus (1966, 1976), whose studies on hope and other emotions demonstrated that the way in which we choose to perceive a situation often determines its outcome, and James Averill (1973), who divided matters of personal control into three types: behavioral (based on action), cognitive (based on interpretation), and decisional (based on choice). As Averill discovered, the amount of personal control we have over each of these areas is much greater than most people initially believe.

The difficulty arises when we seek to apply this theoretical and experimental understanding of personal control over perspective to what we actually do on a day-to-day basis. The numerous pressures we all face as administrators, the competing priorities we encounter, our stress at being pulled in different directions by our supervisors and faculty members, complications in our personal lives, and even our mood on any given day may seem to make it impossible to find the good in all these unexpected and uncontrollable situations. In higher education, choosing to focus on the positive appears a bit too reminiscent of Pollyanna's "glad game," in which even the worst disasters were reframed as strokes of luck. None of us wants to be dismissed as "just a Pollyanna." Nevertheless, it's counterproductive to ignore the role we can have in deciding to interpret our challenges in a different way from our default mode.

Let's consider one famous example, not in higher education but in the even more stressful world of international politics. In Edward Kennedy's *True Compass* (2009), the late senator recounts an episode in the lives of his brothers Jack and Bobby that illustrates how approaching setbacks with a positive perspective is really quite practical. After the Bay of Pigs fiasco, John F. Kennedy was concerned that such a major disaster early in his presidency would doom the rest of his time in office. Robert Kennedy suggested that the president discuss it with their father, who had the experience needed to see this challenge in its larger context. The former ambassador's reaction was,

> "Jack, well done. Well done. You took responsibility. People like that in their leaders. Take my word for it. People like leaders who take responsibility." And then, with almost prophetic wisdom, our father told the president that "this is going to turn out to be one of the best things that ever happened to you." (p. 176)

Later in his administration, during the Cuban missile crisis, President Kennedy's painful experience during the Bay of Pigs disaster caused him to become wary when his military advisors were encouraging him to respond aggressively to the Soviets. That caution, taught by what he had experienced during the Bay of Pigs incident, proved to be an important factor in the successful outcome of the missile crisis. Kennedy realized that what he had once regarded as a terrible catastrophe was in fact one of the best things that ever happened to him—just as his father had told him. If he had chosen to see his failure as a permanent setback, he may have reacted differently. For instance, he may have questioned his own judgment, yielded to the advice of others he viewed as experts, and brought about a world war. But by choosing to see his embarrassment as an opportunity to learn, he discovered how to avoid problems that had implications far worse than personal humiliation.

In much the same way, the perspective we as academic leaders adopt toward our responsibilities has important consequences for the students and faculty members in our programs. Amy Wrzesniewski (2003), an associate professor in the Yale School of Management, observes that how we view the tasks we perform every day affects both our own job satisfaction and the attitudes of everyone around us. As she notes, we approach our profession in entirely different ways if we see it as a job (the way we make money in order to do the things we really want to do) than if we see it as a calling (an opportunity to do the things we regard as truly important):

> It appears that the way in which people see their work is highly predictive of their own individual thriving, and has positive implications for the groups and organizations of which they find themselves a part. In particular, people with Calling orientations toward their work engage with the domain of work in qualitatively different ways than those who have Jobs or Careers. (p. 307)

In order to adopt this type of positive perspective, all that's required is our recognition that we control our reactions to what happens to us. But there's the rub: seeing ourselves as in control of our emotional reactions is a particularly difficult task for many people today.

In the West, our modern understanding of the self has been significantly shaped by the theories of Sigmund Freud. Since the time of Aristotle and intensified by the Age of Enlightenment in the eighteenth century, the dominant philosophical view in Europe and America was that human beings are "rational animals." Logic or reason, in other words, is the quality that distinguishes us from other animals. Unlike creatures that act from instinct alone, we can make rational choices based on the information we receive. In fact, a leading premise of Western education has been that if people are taught how to think logically and critically, they will do so and thus create a happier, better world.

But at the beginning of the twentieth century, Sigmund Freud shattered that view by focusing on the way in which subconscious motivations shape our behavior in almost every situation. Taken to an extreme, Freud's theory can make us feel as though we're helpless victims of forces we don't understand. After all, how can we ever be sure that we're making an objective and rational choice when so much of our emotional state, behavior, and perspective has been shaped by factors of which we're not consciously aware? If an experience that happened to us in childhood—one that we don't even remember—can cause us to react to a situation in a certain way, how much choice do we have over how we feel about anything?

Recent discoveries in neuroscience have intensified this view of the self. Sam Harris in *Free Will* (2012) discusses studies indicating that milliseconds before we "make" a rational decision, the subconscious and emotional parts of our brains have already determined what we'll "decide." In other words, although we may believe we evaluate all the evidence and use our critical thinking skills to draw a valid conclusion, the deep, emotional parts of our brain actually make the decision first, and we rationalize it only later. (For some of the studies that led Harris to his conclusions, see Custers and Aarts, 2010; Wegner, 2002; and Libet, Gleason, Wright, and Pearl, 1983.)

But as with so many other approaches that present the world in stark black-and-white terms, neither Aristotle and the Enlightenment nor Freud and Harris give us the entire story. The truth is that most of us see ourselves as operating somewhere between these two concepts of human behavior. We have complex minds that react emotionally to certain triggers because of experiences—perhaps remembered, perhaps not—that shape who we are. At the same time, we retain a great deal of control about how we respond to our emotions, even if much of that control isn't part of our conscious awareness. In short, both nature and nurture contribute to who we are. We may think, "He made me so mad," or, "She frustrates me when she talks that way," whereas what happens is entirely different. He or she simply did or said something, and we embarked on one of several possible courses. In reality, he didn't make us angry, and she didn't frustrate us; rather these people provided a trigger, and we chose to indulge in the emotion prompted by that trigger. *But that's not at all the way it happens,* you may be thinking. *It's not as though someone does something, and when I start feeling angry or frustrated, I then say to myself, "Okay. I'm going to go ahead and act on these emotions now."* Of course you don't. In everyday life, as Harris and other researchers have found, we respond so quickly to the stimuli around us that our reactions seem automatic and instantaneous. But the key to adopting a positive perspective as an academic leader is to compel ourselves to slow our responses, choose a more constructive vantage point from which to interpret the situation, and only then respond in a skillful manner.

At professional conferences and in administrative journals, much of the advice academic leaders receive tends to focus on the need to be decisive enough to respond to situations that can arise in the blink of an eye. And while it's true that a great deal is changing very quickly at colleges and universities, it's not necessarily true that a rapid response is always the best way to handle the situation. The goal of positive academic leadership, therefore, is to unhook the emotion caused by a situation from determining how we react to that situation. In other words, what we're trying to do is develop a systematic and constructive approach for how to deal with our work most effectively. But separating emotion from reaction takes some practice. It can be very difficult when someone's shouting in your face not to respond in kind. But take it from one who knows: it can be done, even if everyone thinks of you as a hotheaded administrator or the sort of person who leads with your gut, not your head.

The first key to changing your perspective is to force yourself not to react to challenges immediately. Like so much else about positive academic leadership, this advice may initially seem counterintuitive. In a world where information arrives instantaneously and the landscape of higher education can change overnight, it doesn't seem logical to suggest that we should slow our reaction time. But slow reactions result in precisely the sort of behavior that increases the likelihood we'll have a desirable outcome. So when situations that trigger intense emotions occur, pause and try to reframe the experience—for example:

"Oh, this is what it's like to feel anger."

"Right now I'm aware that I'm becoming frustrated."

"What just prompted this strong sensation of fear?"

What you're doing when you go through this mental script is engaging your rational brain to examine the activities of your emotional brain. You're pulling back from your feelings for a moment to study and assess your emotions in the same way you would any other academic issue. This approach works extraordinarily well in higher education because we've all been trained to analyze information, challenge assumptions, and seek underlying causes. As a result, by asking "academic" questions about our emotional responses, we tend to switch from whatever role we're filling at that moment—object of insults, recipient of anger, target of contempt—to a more comfortable and familiar academic role: the researcher who's intellectually inquisitive and skillfully analytical. In short, positive academic leadership involves making a conscious decision to shift our instinctive responses. We're choosing to change our perspective and look at matters from a different vantage point. And once we do that, we have an entirely new set of options about how to respond to the situation. With more tools in our administrative toolbox, we can now select the one that's most likely to produce a positive outcome.

How Changing Perspective Helps Increase Our Options

When we unhook our response to a situation from our emotional reaction to that situation, we significantly increase our options. For example, when someone who reports to us acts in a way that causes us to become angry, that anger may prompt us to think of disciplinary or punitive responses. But other reactions could be more effective. For example, the situation might be better addressed as an opportunity to provide guidance and further training. It might be one in which it's more appropriate to respond out of compassion because what's happening in that faculty member's personal life has prompted an unacceptable behavior. It may be a cause for our own self-reflection since one of our actions may have provoked the other person to act this way. There are dozens of other possibilities as well. The point is that the moment we pause to consider our own emotional perspective, we begin to discover that other perspectives are possible. It all depends on the vantage point we select to view the situation from. Of course, it may well be that our original emotional reaction is the right one after all—there certainly are situations in higher education that call for righteous indignation, fear, or sadness—but we won't know if that's the best, most effective response unless we consider our other options. Developing the habit of slowing down our responses to examine each opportunity and challenge from multiple perspectives becomes a key ingredient in a positive leadership style.

There are also other ways to change our options. In chapter 1, we encountered a brief excerpt from Frederick Ahearn's "A Day in the Life of a Dean." Here are six activities that Ahearn describes as typical of his ordinary responsibilities:

1. Attending meetings
2. Coping with angry students
3. Reducing an already inadequate budget
4. Working with a supervisor who seems to have little concern for or understanding of Ahearn's program
5. Making decisions with regard to faculty appointments and promotions
6. Reconciling or mediating disputes

The result of engaging in all of these activities leaves Ahearn feeling dissatisfied and disgusted. He drives home exhausted, feeling that he hasn't accomplished very much. Now let's engage in another thought experiment in order to determine what other options he might have had.

Read each of the following three perspectives on what your administrative work is all about. Then adopting that perspective as a lens, reconsider the six activities and consider how you might deal with it.

1. "Academic leadership is all about problem solving."
2. "Academic leadership is all about developing and promoting a vision of the future."
3. "Academic leadership is all about helping other people make their dreams come true."

With the first perspective, we're likely to see each challenge we face as a puzzle to be solved. We might bring our skill in examining details to the task, evaluating the advantages and disadvantages of various approaches and considering how we're most likely to be successful. So if having to attend meetings is causing us to lose time for what we regard as higher priorities, we might explore whether we can delegate some of these duties to others, initiate procedural changes to make meetings more efficient, and wonder whether we can get away with a little discreet texting during parts of a meeting that don't relate to us. The advantage of this perspective is that it breaks down all of our responsibilities into manageable and solvable problems that lend themselves a variety of solutions. The disadvantage is that we may begin to view all our stakeholders as problems we have to solve. Our approach to an angry student may simply become, "What's the quickest way to get this person out of my office?" rather than, "What's the best outcome for everyone involved?" For this reason, problem-solving perspectives tend to be most useful in situations where material, financial, or physical obstacles have to be overcome and less valuable in situations where people's emotions, feelings, or interpersonal relations are involved.

The second perspective, looking at our daily tasks in terms of our vision for the future, can help us to see where each of our responsibilities fits into the big picture. The danger is that we might begin thinking of the little tasks that come our way each day as mere distractions from the truly important work we'd rather be doing. We might come to regard the development of long-term plans as our "real work" and feel annoyed whenever we're asked to mediate a dispute among our constituents, read through a stack of job applications, or take a call from a frustrated parent. But those activities are our real work too. Despite the refrain frequently heard from higher education gurus that all academic leaders have to be visionary change agents, constantly seeking to reinvent their institutions, that's not really the world we work in. We all know that things are always changing around us and that higher education must adapt to these powerful forces. And it's obvious too that higher education can't simply respond to external forces when they occur but should assume its rightful place as a leader in matters that have broad public interest. But that still doesn't mean academic leaders are at their best when their eyes are firmly fixed on the future, regardless of current realities. There are plenty of people among the student body, faculty, and staff for whom our expertise is sorely needed right now. Being able to adopt a visionary perspective is a significant—perhaps even vital—skill for an academic leader, but if it's the only skill we ever use, we'll end up creating even more problems than we solve.

The third perspective should be our default approach for every administrative situation we face. We don't talk about it often enough (perhaps because those politicians and trustees who believe higher education exists solely for job creation would regard it as overly idealistic), but the real purpose of colleges and universities is to make people's dreams come true. For all the talk we hear about higher education being an economic engine for our regions and the important role colleges play in helping students become gainfully employed, if we define universities merely as generators of financial benefit, we limit their roles unnecessarily.

No one will deny that many college students today see college as the pathway to their chosen careers, but behind that goal lie dreams—dreams about the type of life they hope to have, the difference they hope to make in the world, and the type of world that they hope to live in. For faculty members too, universities provide a place where their dreams of conducting valuable research, passing their insights on to others, and working with interesting ideas can be realized. Those dreams are what motivate all the constituencies in higher education, from the parents who send us their children to the donors who want to see their names on a building. For this reason, if you approach your work not as a dull series of "job responsibilities," but as a range of opportunities to help fulfill someone's dream, you'll bring an entirely different attitude to your work. If we adopt the perspective that academic leaders exist to fix problems or produce lofty vision, we become fixated on the future, missing all the incredible things that are happening in our programs right now. Even the most curmudgeonly academic leader has to admit that despite endless budget cuts and the rise of incivility among the faculty, we still have students graduating from our programs, still conduct important research, still serve our community, and still have an amazing opportunity each day to talk about meaningful ideas with other intelligent people. All that is part of an astonishing dream that's fulfilled every day before our eyes. We just need to shift our perspective from the future alone to both the present and the future simultaneously in order to see it. And the best news is that we can do that, despite all the buffeting we receive from our emotions, hormones, and neurons. As Jill Bolte Taylor (2008) reminds us, "Fortunately, how we choose to be today is not predetermined by how we were yesterday . . . You and you alone choose moment by moment who and how you want to be in the world" (pp. 176–177).

All you have to do is change your perspective.

Reframing Choices

Perhaps the greatest limitation of the thought experiment we conducted earlier in this chapter was that for each perspective, I asked you to reflect on the notion that "academic leadership is all about" one thing or another. In reality, academic leadership is never all about any one thing.

Colleges and universities are extraordinarily complex enterprises, and positive academic leaders require a multitude of perspectives in order to deal with this complexity. To continue our metaphor of the administrative toolbox, the more complex a situation is, the more advanced tools we'll need to keep the machinery running. In their influential work *Reframing Organizations* (1998), Lee Bolman and Terry Deal discuss the four frames we need to adopt in order to understand how any organization actually operates:

1. *Structural frame,* which includes institutional policies and procedures, the organizational chart, and the strategic plan
2. *Human resource frame,* which includes agendas (both open and hidden), individual motivations, and fundamental human needs
3. *Political frame,* which includes alliances, coalitions, and conflicts
4. *Symbolic frame,* which includes organizational culture and traditions, institutional memory, and "the way we do things around here"

But due to the complex way in which colleges and universities are structured and interact with the broader world of higher education, we can add a few other frames to this list as well. Although we didn't use these terms, our thought experiment caused us to adopt what we might call the (5) *problem frame,* (6) *vision frame,* and (7) *dream frame.* But even these three additions don't exhaust all our possibilities. Let's add these:

8. *Stakeholder frame,* through which we view various situations in the way they might be interpreted by students, parents, faculty, staff, donors, the governing board, and others
9. *Practicality frame,* through which we balance expenditures with resources and establish clear priorities
10. *Idealism frame,* through which we view our programs in terms of the benefits they bring our stakeholders, institution, community, and world
11. *Mission frame,* through which we view each situation in terms of how it relates to our core values, institutional mission, and strategic direction

If you reflect on your own position for a moment, you'll be able to add several more frames to this list. The lesson to be drawn from this exercise is that once positive academic leaders begin to see the many different ways to view each opportunity and challenge, their options for developing more creative solutions dramatically increase, and they are thus more likely to choose the solution that maximizes benefits while limiting undesirable consequences. They can derive a positive consequence from a negative situation, and that's what positive leadership is all about.

Strategies for Shifting into a Positive Perspective

If positive academic leadership is possible even for pessimists, grumblers, and grouches, how do you do all this if you're not naturally an optimist? You certainly shouldn't pretend to feel differently than you do, and you shouldn't encourage others to act in ways you yourself can't imitate. The goal for pessimists who wish to adopt a positive perspective is to rely on the strengths they have and then use those strengths to compensate for what they lack.

Suppose one of your administrative talents is your ability to analyze situations and identify the relevant issues others often overlook. In fact, you've discovered that this tendency of yours often prevents you from feeling overly optimistic about situations since you can quickly spot a number of potential problems that others, in their enthusiasm, usually miss. A good strategy then would be to supplement your regular habit of identifying possible challenges with the insights gained from asking the following question: "I know how *I* normally respond to this type of situation. But what would an optimist do?"

You may be tempted to answer, "That's just the problem. All optimists ever do is hope for the best and forget about the problems that inevitably arise." But that's not really what optimists do. Genuine optimists aren't foolhardy; they merely identify multiple possibilities for success in much the same way that you identify multiple possibilities for failure. So apply those same analytical skills you use to identify difficulties but look instead for ways of drawing a positive outcome out of troubling or unfortunate circumstances.

In a similar manner, if your talent is for reflection and deriving lessons from experience, use that natural tendency to develop a positive leadership frame through which to interpret current challenges. One way of doing so would be to reflect on the following prompt: "Identify five good things that happened during [identify a time period]."

The time period you select should be appropriate for the type of issue you're confronting as well as your own administrative experience. Naturally if you're relatively new to your position, thinking in terms of weeks, months, or semesters is going to be more relevant to your work than trying to consider entire decades. But this exercise is also most effective when you select a time period commensurate with the significance of the opportunity or challenge you're currently confronting. Considering the five best things that happened today is likely to produce a list that seems trivial when you're trying to establish a positive mind-set to deal with the loss of an entire facility because of a fire. Conversely, reflecting on the five best achievements of your career can be a bit of overkill when your current problem is that you're frustrated because someone's late for an appointment.

Properly done, this technique allows you to approach both opportunities and challenges from a more positive perspective, put setbacks into their proper context by reminding you that truly wonderful things regularly occur in your work, and make you aware of successful strategies you've adopted in the past. This type of positive reflection can even be a good technique to adopt when approaching the end of an activity. Concluding your day with a review of five good things that happened that day can give you a sense of accomplishment during even the most frustrating or disappointing times. Concluding each semester or academic year with a review of five good things that happened that term can give you the energy to move forward in a more constructive manner. (Besides, it's a wonderful source of information to use when preparing your summary of annual activities.) And concluding your work in a given administrative assignment with a review of five good things that happened during your tenure there can help create a sense of your legacy as an academic leader and the conviction that you're leaving your academic programs better off than you found them.

Dealing with Negativity Around You

Perhaps our greatest challenge to maintaining a positive perspective as academic administrators is the sheer amount of negativity we encounter almost every day. Our universities teach students and faculty members to identify problems and refuse to accept the notion that the flaws we encounter are unchangeable. As a result, we frequently hear that our most cherished initiatives are impractical, poorly designed, misguided, ill conceived, or irrational. In part 3 of this book, we'll explore ways in which you may be able to engender more positive perspectives in your colleagues. At the moment, however, it's important to consider a few techniques you can use right now to help prevent other people's negative attitudes from ruining your own positive perspective:

o *Examine the effect of the negativity, not the negativity itself.* We have seen that each of us has more control over how we respond to situations than we sometimes believe. That same degree of control exists in how we respond to other people's negativity. We can simply decide not to play their games and refuse to get sucked into the same counterproductive activities we see going on around us. We can consider the actual impact the person's pessimistic attitude has on the operation of our programs. In other words, if someone is merely venting and no actual damage is being done, then go ahead and let the venting proceed. That may be how that particular person processes new information and, after grumbling and protesting for a while, he or she will calm down and the work can move ahead. But if the person's negativity is causing demonstrable harm, then address the harm that's being done and the specific behavior that's causing that harm, not the person's beliefs, behavior, or negativity itself.

o *Establish boundaries for the unproductive attitude.* Faculty members who become annoyed by the negative attitude of one of their colleagues can sometimes just avoid that person. As academic leaders, we don't have that luxury. We're the supervisor of everyone in our programs, not merely those we happen to like or agree with. But that doesn't mean we have to let someone's negative attitude run rampant. If a particularly negative person is coming into your office repeatedly to complain about various matters or criticize your policies, set limits to when this can be done; book regular gripe sessions with this person for fifteen or thirty minutes every other week, and then declare your office to be a complaint-free zone at all other times. Or post an online message board for all objections, concerns, and annoyances, and then consult the message board only when you're in a mood to deal with it, not whenever the negative person decides to appear in your doorway. If negativity is a regular factor in meetings, set the agenda so that there's a limited time for complaints to be expressed or require that all objections be submitted in writing before the meeting so that relevant information can be gathered in advance. Remember that people do have a right to express their opinion, even if that opinion is often frustrating or depressing, but you also have the right to establish reasonable time, place, and manner restrictions on how these opinions can be expressed.

o *Use the negativity as a springboard for finding positive solutions.* The primary purpose of positive academic leadership is to find constructive possibilities in difficult situations even when you're not feeling all that positive yourself. So adopt that same attitude in these situations. Challenge people who bring negativity into discussions to propose solutions to problems, not merely to throw up obstacles. If you encounter statements like, "It's my job to identify the flaws in the administration's plans; it's your job to fix them," remember the positive strategies discussed in this book. Tell the person that that's simply not your administrative philosophy; you find a more inclusive, collegial approach to be better at developing effective ideas, and that's why you're encouraging the group to work together on issues of shared interest. See if you can enlist others to begin proposing improvements to the plan or stating reasons why the objections that have been raised aren't really very significant. Keep the following rule in mind at all times: negativity is never overcome by more negativity. Rather, it's dispersed by being countered with a positive perspective and a refusal to accept the belief that mutually beneficial outcomes are impossible. Judy Orloff (2004), an assistant clinical professor of psychiatry at UCLA, refers to consistently negative people as "energy vampires": they can suck the vitality right out of you. But it's important to remember one other quality traditionally associated with vampires: they're destroyed by the light. Negativity too can be destroyed by the positive energy generated in meetings. So use the support provided by other people with positive perspectives to counteract the gloom and pessimism generated by the grumps in your area. If you do, those grumps may eventually stop spewing their gloom and pessimism as a result.

o *Trace negativity to its origin.* Just as our initial impulse may have been to assume that we can't control our own perspective, so we might assume that negativity is merely part of someone's personality. But whether that person realizes it or not, he or she is actually choosing a negative outlook, just as you've now decided to choose a more positive point of view. What's the real origin of the other person's negativity? He may have felt unjustly treated by you or another administrator, thus reacting with cynicism to everything proposed by an academic leader. He may have troubles at home or feel unappreciated at work, and those troubles are hindering his ability to react to new ideas with enthusiasm. He may have a health issue or just be having a bad day. And there are countless other possible causes for the person's attitude. While these feelings may be directed at you because of something you've done or a personality conflict between the two of you, it's premature to assume that an irreparable breach in your relationship has caused the other person to act this way. If you're able to do so, trace the negativity (which is, after all, a symptom of some other problem, not the root problem itself) back to its origin and see if it may be possible to solve that problem instead of focusing on the way in which the member of the faculty or staff is manifesting a negative perspective.

o *If the person's negativity appears to be particularly severe or ongoing, consider the resources that you have available.* As you trace the person's attitude to its source, keep in mind that certain causes of chronic or extreme negativity reside far deeper than what you can reasonably address. If your institution has an employee assistance program or trained counselors available through a health center or office of human resources, consider the options available to refer that person to these opportunities. At least recommend that he take advantage of the institution's resources. Negativity and hostility may be signs of problems that can't be resolved at the administrative level, so identify all the means available to help the person if you believe the problem is extremely serious in nature.

Conclusion

When administrators adopt a positive perspective, they often begin to see possibilities where earlier they saw only problems. They bring new ideas to their programs and restore the energy of colleagues who may have been experiencing burnout from all the negativity around them.

The perspective we bring to an issue isn't an inevitable result of the situation itself. It's the product of a choice. By adopting the techniques outlined in this chapter, you can decide to lead your programs in a constructive, morale-building manner. But aside from these individual techniques that are useful in specific situations, are there any more comprehensive strategies administrators can use to redefine their entire approach as academic leaders? To, explore the answer to this question, we apply the concept of positive leadership to strategic administration in the next chapter.

References

Averill, J. R. (1973). Personal control over aversive stimuli and its relation-ship to stress. *Psychological Bulletin, 80*, 286–303.

Bolman, L. G., & Deal, T. E. (1998). *Reframing organizations: Artistry, choice, and leadership* (4th ed.). San Francisco, CA: Jossey-Bass.

Custers, R., & Aarts, H. (2010). The unconscious will: How the pursuit of goals operates outside of conscious awareness. *Science, 329*(5987), 47–50.

Harris, S. (2012). *Free will*. New York, NY: Free Press.

Kennedy, E. M. (2009). *True compass: A memoir*. New York, NY: Twelve.

Lazarus, R. S. (1966). *Psychological stress and the coping process*. New York, NY: McGraw-Hill.

Lazarus, R. S. (1976). *Patterns of adjustment* (3rd ed.). New York, NY: McGraw-Hill.

Libet, B., Gleason, C. A., Wright, E. W., & Pearl, D. K. (1983). Time of conscious intention to act in relation to onset of cerebral activity (readiness-potential). The unconscious initiation of a freely voluntary act. *Brain, 106*, 623–642.

Orloff, J. (2004). *Positive energy: Ten extraordinary prescriptions for transforming fatigue, stress, and fear into vibrance, strength, and love.* New York, NY: Harmony Books.

Seligman, M.E.P. (2006). *Learned optimism: How to change your mind and your life.* New York, NY: Vintage Books.

Taylor, J. B. (2008). *My stroke of insight: A brain scientist's personal journey.* New York, NY: Viking Press.

Wegner, D. M. (2002). *The illusion of conscious will.* Cambridge, MA: MIT Press.

Wrzesniewski, A. (2003). Finding positive meaning in work. In K. S. Cameron, J. E. Dutton, & R. E. Quinn (Eds.), *Positive organizational scholarship: Foundations of a new discipline* (pp. 296–308). San Francisco, CA: Berrett-Koehler.

CHAPTER 6

POSITIVE STRATEGIES

In chapter 5, we saw that although we may not be able to control every aspect of our programs, we still have a lot more control over our perspective than we sometimes believe. In this chapter, we build on that approach to positive academic leadership—what we might call a tactical approach because it deals with changes we make in our day-to-day behavior—by adopting a broader and more strategic method. In other words, we're going to explore ways in which positive leadership can become your default leadership style over the long term, the standard way you deal with your administrative responsibilities. This method has five steps:

Step 1 Identify your core values as an academic leader.
Step 2 Develop a philosophy of leadership based on those core values.
Step 3 Distinguish areas in which this philosophy of leadership aligns particularly well with the mission of your institution and the programs you supervise.
Step 4 Move from theory to practice by transforming those areas of alignment into specific goals and projects.
Step 5 Break those goals and projects into discrete tasks, each of which can be evaluated on its progress and degree of success.

In order to understand why these five steps are important in the development of a positive leadership strategy, let's explore each of them individually.

Step 1: Identify Your Core Values as an Academic Leader

Your core values are the principles that define you as a person. All of us have a number of different core values, some of which may complement one another and some of which may at times conflict with one another. For instance, we may believe that the use of deadly force is universally wrong but justify it when we have to protect someone dear to us. Or we may believe that complete transparency is the key to administrative success but be less than candid when we're trying to spare someone's feelings.

We're complex creatures; absolute consistency is rarely possible or desirable. Yet even when our set of values may be hopelessly self-contradictory, these core principles still play an important role in our happiness, optimism, and success. One entire area within leadership studies, the emphasis known as authentic leadership, suggests that the effectiveness of leaders correlates strongly with the degree to which they're aware of their core values and act in accordance with them (Erickson, 1995; Harter, 2002; Kernis and Goldman, 2005). Moreover, it's long been established by researchers such as Edwin Fleishman and David Peters (1962) that there's a significant relationship between a leader's strong commitment to a set of core values and his or her likelihood of success (Fleishman and Peters, 1962). In a cross-cultural study of Japan, India, Australia, and the United States, George England and Raymond Lee (1974) demonstrated that this phenomenon transcends national boundaries. More recently, William Gentry and Taylor Sparks (2012) confirmed that with globalization, the correlation between leadership success and commitment to core values (particularly the values of resourcefulness, the importance of building and restoring interpersonal relations, and a commitment to change) has become all but universal (Schwartz and Bilsky, 1987; Sadri, Weber, and Gentry, 2011; Galford and Drapeau, 2002).

Even so, not all values are alike. For instance, we have personal core values, such as never wishing to do harm or striving to be the best in everything we do. We have relationship core values, such as never trusting a partner again after that person has violated our trust or always putting the needs of our partner ahead of our own. In a similar way, we can all identify our own set of spiritual core values, community core values, and academic core values. But many university leaders, even those who have many years of experience, find it much harder to articulate their administrative core values—the principles that define their fundamental beliefs as chairs, deans, or provosts. Obviously it's impossible to adopt a positive strategy based on your most important administrative principles if you have only a vague idea of what those principles are. So in order to make sure we're all aware of these principles, we'll practice three common methods of identifying core values or beliefs: structured brainstorming, mind mapping, and responding to uncompromising statements.

Structured brainstorming takes the familiar creativity technique of brainstorming and carries it one level further. In other words, you begin by brainstorming as you would for any other creative or problem-solving project: recording your thoughts as they come to you without judging or editing them. In this case, brainstorm your answers to the following question: "What are the principles I regard as most important to the way I approach higher education administration?"

That's the brainstorming part of this exercise. The structured part occurs in two ways. First, impose on yourself some limit to this activity. For example, you could decide that you'll stop brainstorming when you've completely filled both sides of a single piece of paper with ideas. Or you could decide that you'll devote precisely thirty minutes to this exercise—no more and no less. If you find yourself running out of ideas to record while you still have space or time remaining, keep adhering to the limit you've set. Force yourself to continue until you've met your established limit. Similarly, if you reach this limit with many more ideas still in your head, force yourself to stop anyway. If this exercise continues too long, you'll have such an unwieldy list that you'll never be able to organize your thoughts into any sort of clear outline.

Second, put these thoughts in order by using the *paired comparisons method*. This method is widely used to rank a list of random items into a clear order of priority. You start by taking the first two items on your list and asking yourself, "If I had to choose which of these two values was more important to me, which one would I choose?" Be as structured as you were in adhering to your self-imposed limit. Don't allow yourself to conclude that both values are equally important. Imagine that for whatever reason, you could live by only one of these two principles for the rest of your academic career. Which alternative would you choose? Once you've established which value is more important to you, compare it to the next item on the list and go through the same process. Keep making these comparisons until you've completed your entire list. What you'll end up with is your single most important value as an academic leader. Mark it with a big 1, and then start over. After the second iteration of this process, you'll have identified your next most important administrative value. Mark it with a big 2, and go through the process again. Don't stop making these paired comparisons until you have ranked three to five core values in priority order. These are the most important principles in defining who you are as an administrative leader.

The paired comparisons method works well for administrators who find analytical approaches useful. For those who tend to be a bit more visual in their problem-solving strategies, *mind mapping* may be a better technique to adopt. Mind mapping is a way of representing the relationship among different thoughts or concepts in a graphical manner. To create a mind map of your core values, start with a blank sheet of paper just as you would if you were brainstorming. Since what you'll be producing is a fairly large diagram, you may wish to use paper that's legal size or larger. In the center of the paper, write the words "Core Values" and draw an oval around the words. Then engage in a brainstorming session rather similar to the one described earlier. But instead of writing down principles in a list, record each one with a few key words, enclose those words in an oval, and go on to another blank section of the paper. For instance, if one of the values you support strongly is, "Our ultimate focus must be, 'What's best for the students?'" abbreviate this idea with a phrase like "Students First" and enclose it in an oval. Once again set a time limit to this process so that you can focus on your first thoughts (which are usually the best thoughts anyway). When your initial diagram is complete, it should look something like figure 6.1.

Now look at all the ovals you've created, and try to identify relationships among them. For example, if you have one oval containing the words "Students First" and another with the words "Teaching over Research" (reflecting your belief that teaching should be more important than research at your institution), you've probably found a connection between these two ideas: the reason that you value teaching so much is that you regard students as your school's most important stakeholders.

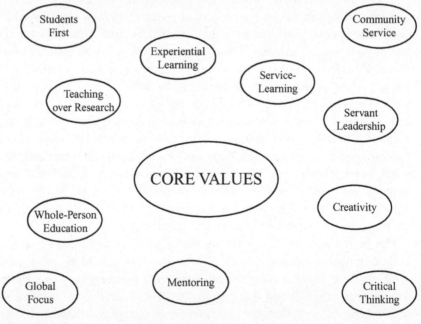

FIGURE 6.1   Sample Mind Map, Phase 1

Try to find relationships among your phrases until all (or nearly all) of them are linked to another core value. Then in each set of linked values, mark the one that seems to drive the others. In our hypothetical example, we might notice the line we drew between "Students First" and "Teaching over Research" and then ask, "Which of these two principles is important to me because I support the other one?" When you've identified three to five values that seem to explain the rest, draw lines directly from these principles to the phrase "Core Values" at the center of the mind map. Your page should now look something like figure 6.2. The principles that connect directly to the center of the diagram are your core values.

If you find that mind mapping is extremely valuable to you, you may wish to explore mind mapping software. These programs automate this process and allow you to export your results to a word processor or a presentation that you create with PowerPoint or Keynote. These products—with names like Mindjet, Inspiration, and ConceptDraw—can speed this process by making it easy to experiment with clustering your thoughts in different ways until you find one that seems to be most effective.

As widespread as structured brainstorming and mind mapping have become, some people discover that these methods don't work well for them. They find it difficult to generate thoughts while staring at a blank

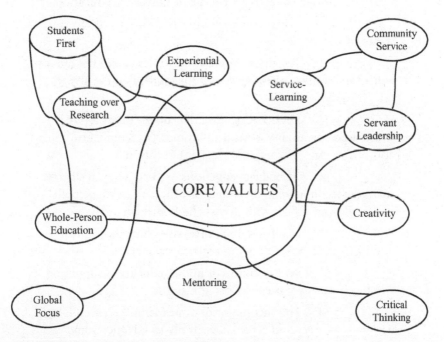

FIGURE 6.2 Sample Mind Map, Phase 2

page and prefer approaches that jump-start their creativity. For these administrators, *responding to uncompromising statements* may be a better method of identifying core values. With this approach, you look at a series of sentences that present extreme positions on various issues and rate the degree to which you agree or disagree with each statement. Since each sentence is phrased in stark black-and-white terms, the items with which you vehemently disagree (or wholeheartedly agree) can suggest to you areas in which to conduct a further inquiry into why you feel so strongly about those particular issues.

The following list is a set of uncompromising statements that relate to higher education. For each item, enter a 0 if you completely agree, a 10 if you vehemently disagree, or a number between 0 and 10 to indicate the degree to which you agree or disagree:

_____ A.   As Winston Churchill observed, "To improve is to change; to be perfect is to change often."

_____ B.   Higher education today does an extremely poor job of preparing students for the world in which they'll actually live and work.

_____ C.   Every student who successfully completes high school is entitled to receive a college or university education.

_____ D.   Most committee meetings are a complete waste of time.

_____ E.   When the interests of students and the faculty come into conflict, the interests of the students must always take precedence.

_____ F.   Higher education that doesn't develop the values and spirituality of students is merely technical training and not worthy of the name "higher education."

_____ G.   If budget reductions are necessary, it's better to eliminate individual programs or offices than weaken all programs and offices with across-the-board cuts.

_____ H.   Colleges and universities have far more administrative layers than are really necessary.

_____ I.   An institution of higher education should be run like a business because it *is* a business.

_____ J.   The vast majority of academic research is useless to society and is pursued simply to advance some professor's career.

_____ K.   Colleges and universities should strive for genuine excellence in a few academic areas rather than simply being good at a wide range of academic disciplines.

_____ L.   If a choice has to be made between lowering standards of admission and laying off faculty because of low enrollments, standards have to be upheld even if people lose their jobs.

_____ M.   No matter how we look at it, colleges and universities are basically vocational institutions: their primary purpose is to prepare students for jobs.

_____ N.   Students today merely want their diplomas as a credential; they're not really interested in getting an education.

_____ O.   The labor-management distinction is a good model for the faculty-administration distinction in higher education.

_____ P.   In a world where so much information is available electronically, learning facts, figures, and formulas is far less important than it once was.

_____ Q.   Tenure is essential for the protection of academic freedom.

_____ R.   Faculty members at my institution are severely underpaid.

_____ S.   Almost all governing boards really don't understand how higher education works.

_____ T.   As Machiavelli said, "One would like to be both loved and feared, but since it is difficult to combine the two it is much safer to be feared than loved."

_____ U.   Although they have different goals and styles, everyone I work with is really trying to do what's right for the institution.

_____ V.   Achieving consensus is a vital factor in effective academic leadership.

_____ W.   Parents these days are far too involved in the education of their college-age children.

_____ X.   Online programs provide an education of no less quality than traditional classroom-based programs.

_____ Y.   Single-gender institutions have a valuable place in today's higher education market.

_____ Z.   On-campus residence halls make a significant contribution to higher education, and so commuter students aren't as well prepared by college as are residential students.

Look over your responses and give special attention to statements that you rated either between 0 and 2 or between 8 and 10. These are the ideas that somehow resonated with you or, at the other extreme, struck a nerve. Reflect on why you had that reaction, and try to develop a value statement based on what you discover. For example, you may find yourself strongly disagreeing with any statement finding merit in nontraditional modes of teaching, such as online courses and independent study programs for commuter students. What does it say about your fundamental concept of what a college or university is that you responded in this way? You might end up with a conclusion like this: "A university education has to be about more than training the mind alone. Conveying facts and formulas simply isn't enough." That conclusion is then one of your core values.

Step 2: Develop a Philosophy of Leadership Based on Those Core Values

If, as we've seen, your core values define who you are as an administrator, then your statement of leadership philosophy helps you clarify those ideals for yourself and explain their significance to others. It has almost become a matter of course for faculty members to develop written philosophies of teaching, research, and service, often including this information in their CVs. But it's far less common for administrators to describe their philosophies as leaders, and so it's not surprising that those around them often don't know what the ground rules are.

As part of your strategy to adopt a positive academic leadership style in everything you do, build outward from the core values you just identified and draft a brief summary of your administrative philosophy. You'll end up with a much more useful document if you adhere to these guidelines:

o Keep your statement between 100 and 150 words in length. If it's shorter than that, you've probably been overly general. If it's longer than that, you probably have a statement too cumbersome to guide you on a daily basis.

o Avoid any first-person forms (*I, me, my, we, us, our*). Writing in the first person usually creates a statement that's not sufficiently condensed. For example, it's unnecessary to say something like, "I believe that . . ." in a statement of philosophy; by definition, the entire statement *is* what you believe. Also, writing in the third person as much as possible will give you the distance you need to scrutinize the statement as though you were an external observer, eliminating whatever strikes you as trite, hackneyed, or insincere.

If you're still having trouble crystallizing your thoughts at this stage, you have a number of options that can help you break through your writer's block. First, if you found mind mapping useful, you can adopt that method again now. But this time, start each diagram with the phrase that summarizes one of your core values and build the map outward from that. The other ovals on your page should represent the ideas that occur to you as you consider what that principle actually entails. Consider questions like these:

o What does this particular core value suggest I should be doing?

o How would I recognize this value if I saw it demonstrated by others?

o What goals in my professional work would be appropriate if I were to base all my actions on this value?

Figure 6.3 illustrates how this diagram might look for an administrator who decided that one of her core values was to be as accessible as possible to the faculty and staff.

Another way of drafting your statement would be to approach it in a freeform manner. Simply write down your ideas as you think of them, and then keep polishing the statement until it is concise, focused, and clear to anyone who might read it. Many people find this "system without a system" liberating; they can just let their thoughts flow. But if you're the type of writer for whom the tyranny of the blank page is intimidating, neither mind mapping nor free-form writing is likely to produce meaningful results. In this case, you can jump-start your statement of administrative philosophy by using a modified Mad Libs approach. The original Mad Libs is a word game created by the television producer Leonard Stern and the humorist Roger Price in which one player asks another for a series of nouns, verbs, and adjectives. The first player then inserts those words into a predesigned template, resulting in a humorous and often bizarre story. For the modified Mad Libs method, you won't be inserting words into a template at random, but rather reading through the template and filling in the first word that comes to mind. At the end of the exercise, you'll have a rough draft of a statement describing your philosophy of leadership that you can then polish and adapt

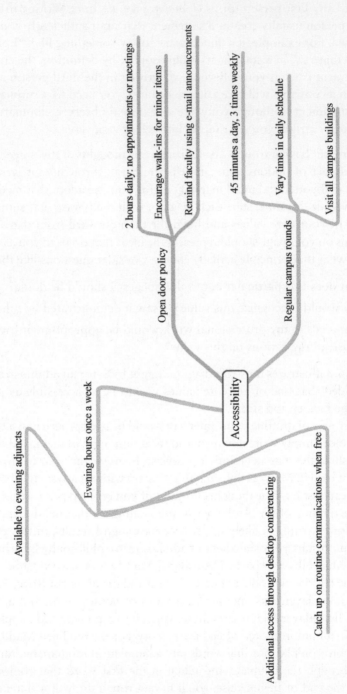

FIGURE 6.3 Mind Map for a Philosophy of Leadership Statement

as you see fit. Remember that first thoughts are usually your best thoughts for this kind of activity, and don't worry about editing your responses until you've filled in every item in the template. Here's an example:

Philosophy of Academic Leadership

Based on my core values, the things I want most for my program and institution are _____, _____, and _____. In order to obtain
                        [NOUN] [NOUN]   [NOUN]

those things, I will need to be _____ with regard to my plan-
                               [ADJECTIVE]

ning, _____ with regard to the faculty and staff under my
     [ADJECTIVE]

supervision, and _____ with regard to my own supervisor(s).
           [ADJECTIVE]

Currently I am least satisfied with my performance in _____
                                   [VERBAL

_____, but I believe that my strengths include my
NOUN ENDING IN -ING]

ability to _____ and to _____ extremely well. I will consider my
       [VERB]   [VERB]

work as an academic leader to have been particularly successful if I achieve this major goal: _____. And I will be most disappointed
            [PHRASE]

if the following occurs: _____.
            [PHRASE]

Once you've completed this entire template, go back and see which responses now seem at odds with the core values you identified earlier. Revise your responses until you're satisfied with the result, and then use the completed template as the basis for a more formal statement. You'll notice, for instance, that the template is filled with first-person forms. How would you express these ideas without reference to yourself? How would you put into your own words some of the phrases you were given in the template?

Keep editing and revising your statement until you end up with a summary of your philosophy that flows smoothly from the core values you identified in step 1. Then place your completed statement in a location where you'll encounter it frequently. Ask yourself regularly what you've done that day to embody the values you've outlined. Some people find it useful to place their statement of administrative philosophy on the inside of the door to their offices. Others prefer to use it as a heading to their list of administrative accomplishments in their résumé. You could also include it as the background or wallpaper of your computer, save it as a note in your mobile phone, or put it anywhere that you'll look at frequently as a reminder of why you do your work as you do.

Step 3: Align the Philosophy of Leadership with Your Programs and Institution

We can describe the statement of leadership philosophy you just created as something like your personal mission statement. It defines who you are (at least professionally) and helps you to determine where you need to go. Of course, your institution and, unless you're a president or chancellor, the individual programs you supervise probably all have mission statements of their own. They may even have developed vision statements as part of a strategic planning process intended to guide them in setting priorities and making choices about the future.

For this step in our process, read these institutional and program-specific statements alongside your own and try to identify clear areas of congruence as well as divergence. For example, if your institution defines its mission as predominantly one of service to the region, nation, and the world and you've also indicated that a call to service and servant leadership characterizes your core beliefs as an administrator, you now have a recognizable direction that can guide you to be even more effective professionally. (For more on servant leadership and its relationship to positive academic leadership, see chapter 2.) This point of convergence will lead you to greater job satisfaction since what you like to do and what your institution needs you to do now harmonize well. But if your statement of leadership philosophy focuses on building research capacity and developing cutting-edge technology while the statement of your college or university describes the school as a "teaching-first" institution, you'll need to work harder to uncover ways in which your professional values align with those of the school as a whole. Even when the disagreement is this extreme, however, the task is by no means impossible. You may be able to direct your research emphasis toward the scholarship of teaching or consider ways in which new technology can be used as valuable pedagogical tools. And just as you reflect occasionally on your own philosophy in order to determine whether you're actually living up to the principles it outlines, so does your effort to compare your leadership principles to the mission and vision statements of your institution help alert you when your individual path appears to be diverging too far from that of your program.

At this point, some readers may be wondering, *Why does this discussion on positive strategies keep returning to a discussion of core values and philosophies? Isn't the best way to achieve positive results simply to act rather than waste time in reflection?* The fact of the matter is that it's almost impossible to sustain a positive leadership approach over the long haul if you feel you're violating your fundamental principles. Each of us can give lip-service to values that we think sound good to others for a few days or even a few months. (Consider the number of times the faculty member who showed up for work in the fall appeared to be a completely different person from that collegial, team-oriented candidate you interviewed the previous spring.) But maintaining a facade month after month and year after year is draining. Even if you feel compelled to act in ways contrary to your core values and administrative philosophy over relatively minor issues, in time you may feel that your job no longer represents who you are or what you believe in. When that occurs, it becomes increasingly difficult to preserve that positive perspective we discussed in chapter 5 and focus on strengths instead of weaknesses. For this reason, it's important to uncover the ways in which your values as a leader correspond well with your assigned responsibilities. By doing so, you'll find it easier to understand how you're making a difference in the long-term success of your institution and why that difference is important.

Let's consider a situation in which an administrator develops this statement of leadership philosophy:

> The key to successful academic leadership is consultation. Administrators who wish to build their programs must regularly build consensus among the faculty, consider their opinions, and recognize that no one ever has a monopoly on being right. A second ingredient vital to all academic leaders is a commitment to the whole student. Universities do not merely add to the knowledge of students; they also must develop each student into a well-rounded human being. For this reason, the best academic leaders view their responsibilities broadly, preparing students for their careers, of course, but also guiding them to become fully engaged citizens, creative and critical thinkers, skilled communicators, and principled members of a global society.

Imagine, too, the administrator works at a university that has adopted this mission statement:

> From its inception, [name] University has demonstrated its ongoing commitment to workforce development through its emphasis on experiential learning, practical and applied knowledge, training students to solve real-world problems, and contributions to applied research. The university serves the community by producing leaders who are capable of meeting the needs of the local economy while actively contributing as citizens of a multifaceted society.

It might initially appear that the administrator's values deviate sharply from those of the institution. Although he or she devotes a great deal of attention to the importance of educating "the whole person" and preparing students for a global society, the university's mission statement appears to be far more career focused and concerned with the local community.

By adopting a positive leadership strategy, the administrator can find several areas in which the two sets of values align. For example, both the administrator and the university emphasize the need for a student's education to be about more than learning information, and both address the relationship between the institution and society. From this point, rather than becoming frustrated by the university's focus on economic development over more broadly based educational goals, the administrator can begin to explore how critical and creative thinking, strong communication skills, and building consensus can be seen as integral parts of preparing future leaders and workforce development. The key in this step is always to find the points of possible unity, not to become caught up in the obvious differences. Doing so is, after all, the essence of positive academic leadership.

Step 4: Move from Theory to Practice

While identifying your core values and mission is a critical component of positive academic leadership, it still doesn't tell you much about your long-range goals for the programs you supervise. Values and mission are about who you are right now; goals and direction are about where you hope to go in the future. Institutions often recognize this distinction by following their mission statements with vision statements, and you should do the same. Since it's easier to imagine the future from your own perspective, we'll start this process with statements that include first-person forms. Imagine how you would end each of these sentences, and record the first thought that comes to your mind:

o In my professional life, five years from now I would like to be

_____.

o Looking slightly further, ten years from now I would like to be

_____.

o The legacy I'd like to leave at the end of my career is to have been

_____.

The value of constructing goal statements in this way is that they can be completed with noun phrases *(a university president, a system chancellor, the most effective department chair in my college)*, adjectives *(energetic, more confident, less anxious)*, participles *(retired, encountering new and interesting challenges, respected for my initiatives)*, and several other structures. The exercise leaves you free to visualize the future in any way that makes the most sense for you. Once you've completed each sentence, ask yourself why that goal matters. What difference would it make to you personally or to other people if that aspiration were never achieved?

After completing your three statements and reflecting on their importance, select the one you regard as most significant and use it as the basis for your personal vision statement. Then rephrase that statement by using as many different words as you can think of to say essentially the same thing. By forcing yourself to keep selecting different vocabulary, you are asking yourself continually, "Exactly what does my goal mean?" At the end of the process, you'll understand your goal far better than you do right now. More important, you'll identify how you'll know when that particular goal has been achieved.

There's an old rule in physical training that says, "Do each exercise as many times as you possibly can. Then do it once more." Follow this same procedure in rephrasing your vision statement. Use different words to say the same thing as many times as you can until you can't possibly think of another way to rephrase it. Then force yourself to say it differently one more time. For instance, an administrator whose goal is to lead an institution might come up with variations like these:

o Ten years from now, I would like to be a university president.

o My goal for a decade from now is to serve as the chief executive officer at a major institution of higher education.

o Seven years after receiving promotion to full professor, I want to be appointed to lead an organization dedicated to postsecondary education.

o For at least twenty years before I retire, it would be personally rewarding to head an organization devoted to advanced learning, research, and community service.

And so on. Each iteration becomes more and more difficult, but it also compels you to explore in greater depth what you really hope to achieve, what your time frame is, and why you care about that goal. For instance, in the example, the administrator gradually has to think through such issues as what it means to be a university president, what a university actually is, and why that ten-year time frame is appropriate for this goal. If the series of statements were to continue, it would also probably be necessary for the writer to reflect on precisely what it means to lead a university and what the administrator expects to achieve by doing so.

The final activity in this step is to break your long-term goal into a series of projects. In other words, what will you need to do along the way in order to make that goal a reality? In the case of our hypothetical administrator who wishes to become a university president, those projects may include participating in the Fellows Program of the American Council on Education (ACE), volunteering for a leadership role in the institution's next major reaccreditation, attending a workshop for future college presidents, interviewing several current presidents about their own experience, and similar activities. Projects help to crystallize your goal from a vague dream into recognizable objectives you can use to transform your hope into a plan. (On the difference between hopes and plans, see the section on administrative resilience in chapter 2.) Most important, from the prospective of positive academic leadership, seeing a goal move closer to reality is an effective strategy for keeping your focus future oriented and directing your attention toward worthwhile purposes instead of daily frustrations.

Step 5: Break the Goals and Projects into Discrete Tasks

It can be highly motivating to establish a clear goal such as, "Ten years from now I would like to be a university president," and pursue that goal through identifiable projects. But even having your goals refined into projects doesn't always tell you what you should be doing today. In other words, what can you do right now—before the day is over—to get yourself closer to that ACE fellowship or all the insight and praise you'll gain from a successful reaccreditation? Just as we broke your goals into projects, the final step in implementing a positive leadership strategy is to break your projects into tasks. The key tests of a suitable task is that it's

o Able to be accomplished in a single setting

o Easily identifiable in terms of whether it has been fully accomplished

o An activity that makes possible either a further task or the completion of your project as a whole

The reason that tasks should be capable of being finished in a single sitting is that you're more likely to begin something you know you can complete than an activity that may not pay off for several weeks or even months. In addition, the satisfaction you receive in checking that item off your to-do list may well give you the energy you'll need to go on to the next task, and your sense of accomplishment could easily become contagious to those around you. (Our goal is positive academic leadership, after all.) It should be clear whether the task has been completed so that you don't waste time redoing something you've already done. And that achievement should carry you further into your project, ultimately taking you to the point of attaining the entire goal. For this reason, "Think about what it would take to apply for an ACE fellowship" is a poorly conceived task. How will you be able to tell when you've finished thinking? How much closer to your goal will you be after you've given the matter some thought? "Visit the ACE website to determine the deadline for applications to the fellows program" is a far better task because you can do it in a single sitting (in fact, you can do it in less than five minutes). In addition, you'll know beyond any shadow of a doubt when the task has been completed. Best of all, it carries you toward the next task in your project: starting your application, securing a nomination, investigating your institution's internal procedure for selecting nominees, or something similar.

For certain projects, identifying the tasks that'll lead to their completion is fairly easy. But for others, it may be somewhat harder to know where to begin or how to prioritize the tasks. If you find yourself encountering problems of this sort, several approaches can help move this process forward. First, use structured brainstorming or mind mapping to come up with as many possible tasks as you can. Keep in mind throughout the process that no activity is too small or insignificant to be included on your list. It's often much easier to cluster a few very minor activities into a single task than to divide what appears to be one continuous process into a series of discreet steps. Second, look at the list you've developed and ask yourself, "Which of these actions can't be begun until one of the other actions has already completed?" For instance, you can't read an article about a certain topic until you've identified the article you need to locate. So if these activities are on your list, move, "Identify ten significant articles to read," ahead of, "Find the full text of an article online or in the library," and move both of those items ahead of, "Read an article." When you've organized as many tasks as possible into a time line of this sort, you may find that you still have several activities that can be pursued at any point in the process because they don't need to wait for anything else on the list to be completed. For these activities, use the paired comparisons method to prioritize them. Then work them into the other items on your time line.

You now have a well-developed list of tasks, carefully structured in terms of priority and time requirements, that'll help you reach your goal. Third, choose the first item on the list, and do it. *Now.* Even before you finish reading this chapter. (Go ahead. I'll wait.) If you allow even a day to go by, you may find your enthusiasm flagging, and it'll be easy to begin putting off accomplishing that first task on the list until tomorrow, and then the next day, and then the day after that. You've worked hard to develop a strategy of positive leadership. Don't let another day go by without applying that strategy to a goal that's important to you.

Conclusion

One way of looking at positive strategies for academic leadership might be to see them as methods for replacing negative or unproductive habits with more skillful practices. Jan Chozen Bays (2011) speaks of a similar idea when she talks about how she teaches students to substitute forward-oriented approaches for the backward-oriented habits of self-reproach and excessive remorse:

> I point out to students that they would never rent and watch the same painful movie two hundred and fifty times. And yet they allow their mind to play painful episodes from the past over and over. "Remember when you made that stupid mistake? Let's run that mind movie again, and again, and again." We need to tell the Inner Critic that we aren't stupid. We only need to review our past mistakes once or twice, then move on with determination to change. (p. 35)

Academic leaders can also get locked into "watching the same painful movie" over and over again. They resort to familiar but negative strategies that haven't worked in the past. They act out of habit rather than seeking more effective solutions. But academic leaders can benefit from replacing those old strategies with an awareness of the core values that should be guiding their decisions and defining who they are as administrators. Consistently acting in accordance with these values helps academic leaders see what's possible for the future, not merely what's on their agenda for that particular day. In addition, feeling that everything you do has reflected the principles you hold most dear makes it easier to leave the office each day with a sense that you've accomplished something significant. Over time, that sense of satisfaction may begin to translate into higher morale and, yes, an increased sense of optimism. But feeling that you're often required to act in opposition to your core values or go to work simply to earn a paycheck quickly leads to frustration, pessimism, and negativity—and that's no way to lead a college or university.

Nevertheless, the leadership of your college or university isn't limited to you alone. In order to be most effective, positive academic leaders should serve as a model for others who can also begin identifying their own core values and acting in accordance with them. For this reason, adopting positive approaches for the benefit of others is the next major topic we address.

References

Bays, J. C. (2011). Getting to know your inner critic. *Buddhadharma, 9*(4), 34–35.

England, G. W., & Lee, R. (1974). The relationship between managerial values and managerial success in the United States, Japan, India, and Australia. *Journal of Applied Psychology, 59*, 411–419.

Erickson, R. J. (1995). The importance of authenticity for self and society. *Symbolic Interaction, 18*, 121–144.

Fleishman, E. A., & Peters, D. R. (1962). Interpersonal values, leadership attitudes, and managerial "success." *Personnel Psychology, 15*, 127–143.

Galford, R. M., & Drapeau, A. S. (2002). *The trusted leader: Bringing out the best in your people and your company.* New York, NY: Free Press.

Gentry, W. A., & Sparks, T. E. (2012). A convergence/divergence perspective of leadership competencies managers believe are most important for success in organizations: A cross-cultural multilevel analysis of 40 countries. *Journal of Business and Psychology, 27*(1), 15–30.

Harter, S. (2002). Authenticity. In C. R. Snyder & S. Lopez (Eds.), *Handbook of positive psychology* (pp. 382–394). New York, NY: Oxford University Press.

Kernis, M. H., & Goldman, B. M. (2005). From thought and experience to behavior and interpersonal relationships: A multicomponent conceptualization of authenticity. In A. Tesser, J. V. Wood, & D. A. Stapel (Eds.), *On building, defending, and regulating the self* (pp. 31–52). New York, NY: Psychology Press.

Sadri, G., Weber, T. J., & Gentry, W. A. (2011). Empathic emotion and leadership performance: An empirical analysis across 38 countries. *Leadership Quarterly, 22*, 818–830.

Schwartz, S. H., & Bilsky, W. (1987). Toward a universal psychological structure of human values. *Journal of Personality and Social Psychology, 53*, 550–562.

Resources

Buller, J. L. (2008). Developing a philosophy of administration. *Department Chair, 18*(3), 8–10.

Miles, M. A. (2011). Cultivating a consultant culture. *Academic Leader, 27*(7), 1, 6.

Morrill, R. L. (2007). *Strategic leadership: Integrating strategy and leadership in colleges and universities.* Westport, CT: Praeger.

PART THREE

POSITIVE APPROACHES FOR FACULTY, STAFF, AND STUDENTS

CHAPTER 7

THE ACADEMIC LEADER AS COACH

Throughout this book thus far, we've seen that positive academic leadership is possible even if you're a grouch and all the people around you are confirmed pessimists. I certainly won't go back on that premise now. But I also won't deny that it's easier to be a positive leader if you and your coworkers share at least some elements of forward-looking, hope-based leadership. As we've seen, it's possible to adjust how you yourself approach your work through applying the concepts we explored in the first five chapters of this book and by practicing what Martin Seligman calls learned optimism. (See chapter 1; for Kaye Herth's hope-based leadership and how it relates to our central topic, see chapter 2.) But how in the world can you make other people act more positively if their natural disposition is to be cantankerous, glum, cynical, or gloomy? We touched on this topic a bit in chapter 5 when we considered how to deal with the negativity that sometimes surrounds us at work. Now we carry these ideas further and discuss not merely coping with negativity but actually increasing other people's positive tendencies.

In this and the next two chapters we're going to explore specific approaches that can help students, faculty members, staff members, and other administrators develop a more positive approach toward their role at the university. These approaches are easy to remember because they all begin with the letter C:

o Coaching

o Counseling

o Conducting

Since these approaches are not mutually exclusive (in fact, they work much better if you practice all three simultaneously), you'll notice a bit of repetition and cross-referencing as we go through them. But I'm hoping that in this way, you'll come to see these ideas as aspects of a single, unified type of leadership, not three discrete management tips you can use to stifle the complaining and interpersonal conflicts that are rife in the academy. With this idea in mind, let's begin with the very first approach to encouraging positivity in others: the academic leader as a coach.

The Difference Between Coaching and Teaching

My first encounter with the difference between coaching and teaching—at least as that difference is widely perceived by the public—came early in my professional career. I had just begun teaching in my academic field, classical languages and literature, and I suggested (privately and quite gently, or so I thought) that a student who was consistently having trouble in Latin might find another foreign language easier for him. The very next day this student's father appeared in my office. It was my first experience with what we'd all soon be calling helicopter parents, the sort who continually hover over their children and manage their lives. Now, of course, since the time *helicopter parents* was coined by Foster Cline and Jim Fay (2006), we've witnessed the emergence of "stealth bomber parents" (who appear without warning, do a great deal of damage, and seem impervious to your defenses), "predator drone parents" (those you never see at all since they do their damage indirectly by complaining to your president or board chair), and "SEAL Team Six parents" (who show up when you least expect it, take no prisoners, and leave your "compound" in ruins) (see Taylor, 2006; Marsh, 2007; Buller, 2009). But because this was my first experience with what struck me as a strange phenomenon—my father never even knew who my professors were, much less felt comfortable appearing in their offices—I've never forgotten it.

The student's father proceeded to critique my teaching style based on what his son had told him, characterized my sincere attempt to be helpful as an insult, accused me of failing to support his son's self-esteem, and compared me unfavorably to the college's football coach who continually harangued his son, "got in his face, kicked his butt, refused to accept any excuses, and forced him to stop being such a crybaby and start acting like a man." Even as I pondered the sheer anatomical impossibility of accomplishing all those tasks simultaneously, I was confused by his logic. Here he was, offended that I had destroyed his son's ego by suggesting that—possibly, just *possibly*—Latin wasn't his best choice of an elective, while the coach was held up to me as a paragon of virtue because he'd engaged in practices I personally would've regarded as abusive. I mentioned this discrepancy to the parent as soon as I could get a word in edgewise, only to be told, "He's a coach. You're a teacher. You really don't get it, do you?"

I must admit that I didn't get it then, but I think I do now. The outcome of that confrontation was a valuable lesson I'd use again and again as an administrator. (Okay, just let me be clear: the lesson isn't to call your faculty members "crybabies" or to kick them in the butts, either literally or figuratively. Bear with me for a moment, and I'll clarify what I mean.) Compare the great teachers who are depicted in the movies—figures such as Charles Edward Chipping from *Goodbye, Mr. Chips,* John Keating in *Dead Poets Society,* and Glenn Holland in *Mr. Holland's Opus*—to the great coaches in movies—Ken Carter in *Coach Carter,* Herb Brooks in *Miracle,* and Herman Boone in *Remember the Titans*—and you'll notice several important differences.

- Teachers often work with those who have little or no prior knowledge of the subject. Their goal is to guide the students to a proper point of understanding.
- Coaches often work with those who already know the sport quite well. Their goal is to guide the athletes toward greater excellence in execution.
- Teachers must sometimes bend the rules in the interest of cultivating the individual. Although they work with groups, the personal growth of each student is the ultimate objective.
- Coaches must be strict in enforcing the rules in the interest of cultivating the team. Although they sometimes work with individuals, the team's success is the ultimate objective.
- Teachers view high self-esteem as a necessary prerequisite for achievement.
- Coaches view achievement as a necessary prerequisite for high self-esteem.
- Teachers seek to develop knowledge and a love of lifelong learning.
- Coaches seek to develop motivation and a love of lifelong winning.
- Out of concern for the student, teachers sometimes reduce pressure when someone is struggling.
- Out of concern for the athlete, coaches sometimes increase pressure when someone is struggling.

o Teachers see their job as providing an environment in which learning is most likely to occur. Nevertheless, they understand that students are ultimately responsible for their own success: a student's failure does not reflect badly on the teacher.

o Coaches see their job as making sure that everyone shows up for the game on time and is mentally and physically prepared for the competition. Nevertheless, they understand that their own success is ultimately a result of how well the team succeeds: a player's failure reflects badly on the coach.

Okay, okay. This list is a gross oversimplification, and we can easily find exceptions to every statement on it. Here are just a few:

o Not all sports are team sports.

o Not all coaches are athletic coaches. (Think for a moment of music coaches, personal trainers, financial coaches, and life coaches.)

o Not all teachers believe that building self-esteem has to occur before true learning begins.

o Not all coaches ratchet up the pressure when an athlete is clearly suffering either physically or emotionally.

Moreover, the line between teachers who coach and coaches who teach is very blurry indeed. In films alone, witness Mark Thackeray in *To Sir, with Love,* Jaime Escalante in *Stand and Deliver,* and Kesuke Miyagi in *The Karate Kid.* Nevertheless, like any other oversimplification, this contrast between coaches and teachers offers a useful, if imperfect, model that we can apply to a number of situations. With that in mind, let's recognize that every positive academic leader knows there's a time when a good administrator needs to stop teaching and start coaching.

The Positive Qualities of the Academic Leader as Coach

Most coaches see their role as improving each athlete's level of knowledge, but they don't stop there. They regard it as one of their fundamental responsibilities to develop in others the motivation and will to succeed. That's one of the primary reasons the father I mentioned earlier tolerated how the football coach treated his son, even if I regarded that treatment as demeaning. Since I was a teacher, the parent had classified me as someone whose sole purpose was to provide his son with an education without harming his self-image. The coach, in contrast, was free to plead, cajole, harangue, shout, bargain, intimidate, inspire, or use any other technique he wished if it had any chance of motivating the young man to play better.

I have all kinds of reservations about the way in which the distinction I'm making here appears to restrict the task of professors to little more than information transfer. Moreover, as an administrator and trainer myself, I have a profound distaste for the negative coaching style that uses threats and insults to spur people on to greater achievement. But the parent's perspective, flawed though it may have been, made me see my role differently. It's not that positive academic leaders should act like drill sergeants, berating and browbeating faculty members in order to get things done. An academic environment isn't boot camp. To the contrary, it should be a place where administrators see it as part of their jobs to motivate and inspire, not just monitor and evaluate. It should be a place where faculty, staff, and administration alike hold themselves to high standards, see that positive outcomes can result even from challenging or disappointing situations, sincerely believe that they're capable of achieving extremely ambitious goals, and derive satisfaction from the achievements of the institution, not just from their own time in the spotlight. When administrators make it a priority to develop this type of work environment, that's when they become academic leaders as coaches.

Consider for a moment all those positive qualities attributed to coaches in the movies I mentioned earlier or to legendary coaches like Knute Rockne, Ara Parseghian, and Vince Lombardi. These coaches didn't just give their players greater skills. They also gave them the confidence to believe they could do great things. They inspired others to be their best. They recognized the difference between explaining failure and providing an excuse for failure. They accepted responsibility, not just for their own actions, but also for the performance of their teams. And they cared about their players as individuals, not merely as cogs in a machine designed to produce high scores. Those are the same qualities that we find in superb coaches outside the field of athletics as well. Think for a moment of how the speech therapist Lionel Logue interacts with George VI in the 2010 film *The King's Speech* or (with some notable exceptions) the coaching provided by Maria Callas in Terrence McNally's play *Master Class*. Applying these practices to higher education, we can identify six aspects of how positive academic leaders view their role as coaches:

1. They inspire confidence even in troubling times.

2. They motivate others to achieve the highest possible standards.

3. They recognize when an excuse is being used to justify a lack of effort.

4. They take responsibility for the group as a whole.

5. They provide criticism in a constructive manner.

6. They don't just delegate; they empower.

Inspiring Confidence Even in Troubling Times

It can be challenging enough to maintain high morale among members of the faculty and staff when an institution is flourishing, enrollments are stable, employee turnover is minimal, and the budget is secure. But take away any of these positive factors, and the difficulty can seem almost insurmountable. A vicious circle ensues: budget cuts due to a poor economy lead to reductions in programs; reductions in programs lead to declining retention; declining retention leads to still more budget cuts; and so on. If that goes on for long enough, the vicious circle becomes a death spiral. As a result, one of the goals of all academic leaders must be to keep morale high so that an area can move forward. But how do you do that when things seem to be falling apart all around you? How do you make members of the faculty and staff focus on the future and feel appreciated when raises are minimal or nonexistent, operating budgets are being slashed, and combating student attrition is a continual struggle?

Invest in People

Morale problems in any organization tend to increase when people feel unappreciated or sense that their contributions don't matter. Studying schoolteachers in several countries, Doria Daniels and Elmien Strauss (2010) and Linda Evans (1998) discovered this principle clearly applied to a wide range of academic settings. In their aptly titled article, "Why Professors Hate Their Jobs" (2008), Jim Parsons and William Frick suggest that this same principle is rampant throughout higher education as well. Troubling times at a college or university mean that administrators must redouble their efforts at recognizing groups and individuals. Positive academic leaders set aside time at meetings to single out members of the faculty and staff who have gone the extra mile. They look for opportunities people can use to develop their skills and pursue activities they find interesting and rewarding. They work with the office of human resources to reclassify staff members whose responsibilities justify assignment to a higher position. They greet new faculty members as they arrive on their first day of work or have a gift waiting for them in their offices. They're generous, to an extent that's fair to everyone and permissible within their institutions, about allowing people to take off work a lit-tle early or extend their lunch hour slightly when they have a personal appointment, must tend to members of their families, or even just need to recover from a particularly hard day.

Explore Alternative Rewards

Although financial challenges frequently make it impossible to reward employees through raises or bonuses, it sometimes becomes possible to find other ways of acknowledging the contributions people make. If ongoing funding isn't available, you may be able to use one-year, expendable money for a bonus or other type of reward. For instance, suppose you can't give someone a raise because you don't have access to money that'll continue from year to year. You may still be able to allocate some of the salary savings resulting from a sabbatical or a leave of absence as a temporary increase to your budget for sup-plies, equipment, or travel. That one-time windfall could be used to upgrade an employee's computer or purchase a new type of software that makes work easier and improves morale as a result. Funding a workshop or conference can allow an employee to enjoy a brief res-pite from day-to-day responsibilities. In fact, some employees actually prefer an increase in travel or research funding to a salary increase because income carries tax obligations that other types of recogni-tion don't. Depending on the individual, even small gifts you purchase yourself can be very welcome.

Find out what each person likes, don't wait for Administrative Assis-tants Day to arrive, and thank the person with a gift certificate to his or her favorite restaurant, a massage or spa day, flowers with a thank-you card, or anything else that's both professionally appropri-ate and meaningful to the recipient. Finally, if no other alternative is possible, consider whether you can relieve someone of a duty that this person finds particularly unpleasant. Excusing a faculty member from a committee or reassigning a task from a full-time staff member to student workers can make an immediate difference in the quality of an employee's work experience.

Convey Realistic Confidence

Everyone expects authority figures to be calm in the face of difficult situations and provide others with the strength they need to surmount impending challenges. In a time of crisis, the president of the United

States frequently uses the media to demonstrate an air of quiet confidence. Airline pilots speak in measured tones when announcing that turbulence is ahead. Parents calmly reassure their children during storms. And academic leaders typically assuage their employees' fears and improve morale by demonstrating that although the current challenges may be great, the talent of the faculty and staff is even greater; together they can overcome any obstacle in their path. These leaders not only express a sincere conviction that the current troubles are only temporary but also cite specific examples of how the faculty and staff have worked together to triumph over similar obstacles in the past.

As always, however, optimism shouldn't be false, foolhardy, or presented as though the academic leader is unaware of actual threats. Merely saying that things will get better rarely makes them so. It's important for academic leaders to acknowledge genuine risks, express a willingness to deal effectively and decisively with these issues, and note that hard work and sacrifice will be required in order to improve the situation for everyone. In short, positive academic leaders must display the type of academic resilience that we explored in chapter 2. Unrealistic confidence can come across as callousness toward anyone who's already suffering from the current problem or ignorance of just how dangerous the situation is. But a combination of confidence and practicality can help others see how the problem is solvable and why their efforts to improve the situation matter.

Communicate Frequently and Openly

It can be tempting for academic leaders to immerse themselves in solving problems during difficult times, spending every minute of every day working on these challenges rather than devoting precious hours to public meetings and informational sessions. But members of the faculty and staff need more information during a crisis, not less. When people don't have access to clear and accurate information about what is happening, they yield to fears that are almost always worse than reality. Rumors become mistaken as facts. Rather than acting as part of a unified effort, employees begin taking action on their own—efforts that are usually well intentioned but can turn out to be counterproductive. And the administrator's desire to focus exclusively on the problem becomes misinterpreted as a bunker mentality. Those who "barricade themselves in their offices" are frequently perceived as shutting out those who could help them or, worse, secretly preparing job applications for what they hope will be less stressful institutions.

During troubling times, it may be necessary for monthly faculty and staff meetings to be held weekly, weekly e-mail announcements to be sent daily, and daily updates to be given hourly. Simply knowing that something is being done can cause people to relax and begin solving the problem rather than just worrying about it.

Motivating Others to Achieve the Highest Possible Standards

Positive academic leadership involves raising the bar—not in such a way that makes faculty members feel it's always a moving target but as part of the administrator's confidence that great people are able to do great things. Successful leaders aren't bean counters. Positive leaders don't say things like, "Last year our area produced ten refereed books of research. So this year, let's produce twelve!" or, "Now that we've reached our goal of bringing in $10 million in sponsored research, our new target is $15 million." Statements like these convey the message that goals are being established for their own sake and that fulfilling them will become more difficult all the time.

Positive academic leaders don't confuse getting bigger with getting better. Goals always have to make sense within a coherent vision for the future. Nevertheless, positive leaders do recognize the value in encouraging people to stretch a little, trying to achieve goals that seem just a bit beyond their reach. As we saw in chapter 3, working within Vygotsky's zone of proximal development can help bring about maximum collegial flow—the esprit de corps that draws a group closer together and transforms a mere collection of individuals into a high-performing team.

Rather than focusing on how many publications an area has produced or the level of external funding it has achieved, turning these targets into goals for their own sake, positive academic leaders discuss how the group's achievements will help students learn better, improve the world through its scholarship, reach a larger number of deserving applicants because of expanded access to the curriculum, and enrich the lives of those in the community. Most important of all, positive leaders express confidence that although these goals are difficult, they are achievable. They regard raising the bar not as a way of creating more work for everyone, but as a reflection of the fact that yesterday's standards are no longer challenging enough for today's highly talented faculty and staff. In short, whereas a negative academic leader's attitude is, "Do this or else!" a positive academic leader's attitude is always, "I know we can do this!"

Recognizing When an Excuse Is Merely a Barrier

There are two common situations in which we tend to justify our lack of success: when we truly aren't able to achieve a goal and when we simply don't want to try. Positive academic leaders know how to tell the difference. They're not the sort of coaches who say, "Just walk it off!" even when a player is seriously injured. At the same time, they're also not the type of overly protective parent who, when a child doesn't have complete success the very first time an activity is attempted, never encourages further efforts because "it's just too hard."

Distinguishing between an explanation and an excuse isn't always easy, and there are no clear guidelines that allow us to determine whether any individual faculty member needs to be pushed harder or allowed more slack. To a great extent, developing that type of insight comes only with experience. Even then, you may find that you still get it wrong occasionally. So while the following two suggestions shouldn't be construed as invariable laws, they can help you improve your insight into how best to help members of your faculty and staff.

First, observe how the person behaves in other situations. One factor that can indicate whether we should increase or decrease the pressure on someone is a result of that individual's personality. Some of us just naturally rebel at being told what to do. The biographies of Frank Sinatra frequently report that the singer was fond of saying, "Don't tell me what to do! *Suggest!*" (Kelly, 1986, 255; Sinatra, 1985, xix; Turner, 2004, 109), while others flourish when "given a mission."

If you notice that someone tends to become defiant, angry, rebellious, or passive-aggressive when being told what to do in relatively minor situations, then try making indirect rather than direct commands. Couple a suggestion with some well-chosen flattery, and relate the goal to something important to that person. As we saw in chapter 3, seek a connection between what you want and need and what the other person wants and needs. And if you're working with someone who seems to take pride in overcoming obstacles, then make it clear you know the person can do better and set the bar higher. There will always be people who love a challenge. When given a deadline, they regularly beat it, talk about how easy they find tasks that others describe as difficult, don't complain about how busy they are, and have résumés that run on for pages and pages because they regard almost everything they do as important. You know who they are: they're the ones you turn to repeatedly whenever you need something done and whom everyone else in the program hates (but secretly envies) because "they're just a showoff!"

Second, compare the benefits of succeeding to the costs of failing. In physical training, "working through the pain" is useful advice when you're slowly increasing the amount of resistance or adding a few more repetitions. But it's terrible advice when someone is actually suffering because it can lead to heat exhaustion, torn ligaments, angina, or strained rotator cuffs. In a similar way, if you think someone's just making excuses but can actually do better, ask yourself, *If I push harder, what's the best thing that can happen if this person succeeds? What's the worst thing that can happen if this person fails?* If failure would result merely in a minor inconvenience or a temporary setback, then it's probably useful to ignore the person's excuse and keep your level of pressure high. If failure could result in a promotion being denied because you encouraged the person to take on something difficult when an easier task would have led to greater success, then it's probably best to back off a little. Similarly, if you have reason to believe that failure could damage someone's self-esteem so severely that he or she would find the consequences unbearable, then the best type of coaching is to demonstrate compassion. In short, always try to be aware of how close you are to someone's breaking point, either physically or mentally, and avoid any approach that could easily put that person over the edge.

Taking Responsibility for the Group as a Whole

Perhaps the most important difference between teachers and coaches is how they approach failure. Teachers, since they both instruct and grade students, have to maintain a certain degree of distance and objectivity when judging how well a student has succeeded. They have to think, *No matter how well I teach this material, ultimately it's up to the student to master it.* But coaches know that each player's success or failure is really *their* own failure or success. They don't have the luxury of telling themselves that although they coached superbly, it was the team that messed things up.

Positive academic leaders don't have that luxury either. They consider themselves responsible not just for everything that happens on their watch, but also for their unit's growth, development, harmony, and level of achievement. It's not that they take credit for the work of others or attribute accomplishments to their "outstanding management," but that they see it as their function to create an effective working environment. They're neither possessive nor paternalistic; they don't speak condescendingly about "my unit" or "my people." Nor do they create artificial barriers between "us" (administrators, academic leaders, and supervisors) and "them" (faculty, staff, and students). They see everyone in their programs as working together in a shared enterprise. By their example, they encourage others to adopt this view as well. Most important, they derive a genuine sense of satisfaction when their colleagues receive honors and never regard it as "someone else's problem" when a member of their unit is struggling, disengaged, or unable to contribute to the common enterprise.

Providing Constructive Criticism

Criticism can be hard to provide and even harder to listen to. Many administrators end up on one extreme or the other, either pulling their punches and failing to get at the crux of the matter or coming on too strong, overstating the case, and making the other person feel awful. Providing criticism in a constructive manner is something of an art, but academic leaders can develop their skills in this art by practicing eight important coaching practices:

1. *Pick your battles.* Not everything that annoys you is worth criticizing. In fact, if you start providing criticism, even constructive criticism, about every little thing, your advice will soon start falling on deaf ears. Always be sure to ask yourself, *What real harm is being done here?* If you can't come up with a compelling answer, it's better to leave the issue alone.

2. *Be discreet.* Dressing someone down in public often backfires. To preserve their pride, people may feel a need to dig in their heels and justify a behavior that they would readily have changed if you had discussed it in private. The vast majority of criticism should be given in a private setting, the only exception being when you have to intervene immediately in a true crisis or when it's important for others to know that a problem is being addressed. At all other times, allow the person to save face by dealing with the issue when witnesses aren't around.

3. *Prepare your remarks carefully in advance.* While you don't want to read your criticism from a script, you certainly want to know what you'll say—and, even more crucial, what you won't say—before you begin expressing your criticism. Failing to prepare your ideas adequately can lead you to make remarks you hadn't intended or leave a major point unexpressed. Impromptu compliments are always welcome; impromptu criticism can often be disastrous.

4. *Never criticize in anger.* As part of your preparation, allow yourself enough time to calm down if something has angered or offended you. If you're outraged when you criticize, you're more likely to say hurtful things you'll regret later and create a worse problem than the one you're trying to fix.

5. *Focus on the behavior, not the person.* Be careful to avoid phrases that imply you're condemning the individual instead of trying to improve his or her performance. For instance, instead of calling someone a liar, address the impact of his or her untruthful statements. Rather than saying a person is lazy, focus on the standards of performance that haven't been achieved. Positive academic leaders recognize that all people (including themselves) are entitled to their own personalities. While good administrators sometimes need to modify a person's behavior in order to achieve a certain goal, they never resort to attacking anyone's character.

6. *Be future oriented.* What's done is done. The goal of constructive criticism is to make things better for the future, not to punish people for what they did in the past. Even if you find it necessary to insist that a person apologize for a previous action, that apology should be part of a future-oriented plan to create a better environment for everyone. Harping on the past is merely nagging; genuine leadership doesn't waste time talking about what should have been done or saying, "I told you so." When a problem is over, let it go. It shouldn't color every aspect of your relationship with the person. I once worked for someone who, on her very first day in the job, criticized the way I had handled a decision. Every time we met after that, she'd say something like, "So, are you doing any better now with [that issue]?" The problem had long been ago been solved, but she couldn't let it go. Ultimately "that issue" came to define my whole relationship with my supervisor. What could have been pleasant and productive conversations for both of us increasingly became one-dimensional. That experience taught me an important lesson about positive academic leadership: people make mistakes. Even I make mistakes. So fix the mistakes, and then get on with something more productive.

7. *Remember Sinatra's dictum: whenever you can, don't tell people what to do; suggest what they should do.* Even if you're someone's boss and have a perfect right to issue that person a direct order, it's not always the best strategy to do so. People have more buy-in for ideas they regard as their own or at least had some opportunity to develop. In fact, the research shows that Sinatra may have been on to something about the power of oblique commands. Analyzing the behavior of flight crews during severe weather emergencies, Ute Fischer and Judith Orasanu (2000) discovered that even in these potentially disastrous situations, outright commands were less effective in preventing errors than were suggestions or statements of preferences. And anyone who has been a parent knows that with children, direct commands produce defiance; indirect commands produce results. (For the research validating this approach, see Kuczynski and Kochanska, 1990; Kuczynski,

Kochanska, Radke-Yarrow, and Girnius-Brown, 1987; Cahn 1994.) Don't conclude from these studies, however, that you should treat your faculty like a group of two year olds. While it's true that most of us preserve a bit of our toddler mentality, only negative academic leaders use that insight as a management strategy. In chapter 2, we saw the reason that this leadership approach was flawed. There is a strong interrelationship among three factors: a participatory leadership style, a group's sense of progress, and a group's satisfaction with its leader. That relationship means that the best administrative approaches usually involve finding a way for people to work with you in solving any problems that happen to arise. Yet even when those approaches aren't possible, you may still find it advisable to recommend corrective actions, not to mandate them.

8. *Praise what you can.* If all a person hears is criticism, then it doesn't matter how constructive that criticism is: it still feels like condemnation and reproach. Even the worst student or coworker will usually have some positive quality or engage in some behavior that's admirable. Don't overlook these aspects of the person in a rush to deal with the problem. Criticism is often perceived as a form of punishment, and remember Thorndike's dictum: punishment tells people only what they shouldn't do; positive reinforcement tells them what they should do. Mary Poppins understood that "a spoonful of sugar helps the medicine go down," and positive academic leaders apply that principle even when dealing with employees who are causing problems.

In their discussion of how criticism can help create or destroy positive organizations, Ian Macdonald, Catherine Burke, and Karl Stewart (2006) conclude:

> As team members work they may need help to complete their tasks or improve their methods. Leaders are helpers. This is a very sensitive area because the *way* in which you coach will affect whether people will accept your help. First, make sure it is clear whether you are:
> a. *Giving an instruction*—telling someone to do something differently and expecting them to do it.
> b. *Giving advice*—suggesting a person think about using your ideas but leaving it up to them.
> c. *Teaching*—showing/telling someone how to do something because they recognise that they don't know how. This area is critical to a leader as few people like being told how to do something while they are in the middle of work unless they think they are having problems. Consequently do not be afraid to ask.

d. *Asking*—gain information from members: for example, "Why do you do that? Do you want any help?"

Although an important part of the leader's work is coaching, do not forget the leader may well learn from the team. (p. 179)

Moving from Delegation to Empowerment

"Managers delegate; leaders empower." That's the sort of statement that consultants love to make, causing everyone to nod in a knowing fashion and feel that a profound truth has just been expressed. But what does it really mean? Delegation involves the assignment of responsibility; empowerment involves the assignment of authority. When managers tell a subordinate to perform a task they don't want to do themselves, what they're passing on is the responsibility for seeing that the job gets done correctly and on time. However, they often fail to pass on the resources, including the leadership resources, that the subordinate needs in order to accomplish that task successfully.

At most universities, the most familiar example of someone who has responsibility without empowerment is the assistant or associate dean. "Deanlets," as they're often called, are usually under a great deal of pressure to meet tight deadlines, but they have relatively few tools with which to meet these responsibilities other than persuasion and personal charm (Stone and Coussons-Read, 2011). After eight years as a department chair (where I always felt I had a great deal of authority, at least within my own discipline), my first full-time administrative appointment was as an assistant dean. It was my responsibility to collect and process documents from all the departments in the college, including requests for new positions, personnel action forms, curricular proposals, budget transfers, applications for tenure or promotion, and the like. Although there was usually a great deal that needed to be done to these documents before the dean could sign them and submit them to the provost's office, many chairs ignored my pleas to get these items to me a few days before the absolute deadline. They had no reason to take my requests seriously: I didn't evaluate them, recommend their raises, prioritize their requests, or make any decisions that affected them in the least. As a result, some chairs had no motivation at all to make my job easier or even to let me be successful. In time, the dean became annoyed with me because my missed deadlines caused him to miss his own deadlines with the provost. As we were discussing how I could do better during one of my annual reviews, I expressed my frustration about having neither carrots nor sticks I could use with the chairs. The dean simply said, "I see," and that's where the conversation ended.

The next time the dean and I were together with the chairs, having given me absolutely no forewarning about what he'd say, the dean began the meeting in this way:

> Just so we're all on the same page, let me share with you my definition of what an assistant dean is. An assistant dean is just an extension of the dean. The assistant dean does the things I don't have time to do myself. So when my assistant dean asks you for something, that's not just a request for you to follow up on (or not) whenever you get around to it. That's actually *me* giving you a firm deadline. So if you don't let my assistant dean do his job . . . well, that's really your way of saying that you don't care very much about how well I do *my* job. And that sort of thing doesn't make me think you've been very effective as a chair when I sit down to do your annual evaluations or recommend your salary increases. In fact, starting this year, I'm going to ask Jeff for his advice on these matters before I complete your merit reviews. So are we all clear now on exactly what an assistant dean is? Good. Moving on to approval of the minutes . . .

It was at that moment that I went from being responsible to being empowered. And I never had a problem meeting a deadline again.

The way in which this particular dean phrased his remarks worked for him, but it violates some of the basic principles I've outlined in this book. It also doesn't happen to fit my personal style. But it does reveal one important aspect of positive academic leadership as coaching: real leaders give genuine authority to those who report to them; they don't just "manage" them. They're not afraid to surrender some power because they feel it would weaken their position or undermine their influence. They don't believe that "if I give other people in my program more independence and experience, they'll just move on to other jobs, and I'll have wasted my time coaching them." They consider it a compliment when a member of their faculty or staff receives an offer for a higher leadership position. It means that they've coached these people well and helped get them ready for higher responsibility.

DePalma, English, and Sabatine on Department Chairs as Coaches

Although positive academic leaders at all administrative levels can benefit from adopting effective coaching strategies, Judith DePalma, Susan English, and Janice Sabatine (2012) have noted that department chairs are particularly well positioned to serve as coaches and mentors. Their idea is that chairs manage when they ensure the right tasks are being completed properly and on time. They mentor when they guide faculty members (and perhaps other chairs as well) to become even more successful professionally. But they coach when they "elicit greatness and empower their faculty" (DePalma, English, and Sabatine, 2012, p. 13).

DePalma, English, and Sabatine, who have served as faculty members and coaches themselves, conclude that there are two important approaches for department chairs to take if they wish to develop a coaching relationship with their faculty: active listening and powerful questioning. Active listening involves paying attention with your entire body rather than just trying to process information in your mind. As academics, we often revert to intellectual approaches even when emotional approaches would be more effective. In other words, we default to our problem-solving mode at times when other people may simply want us to be sympathetic listeners. We start answering the question even before we've heard it in its entirety. Active listening works differently. It includes awareness of the messages we send through our body language, facial expression, and tone of voice, not merely our words. It includes considering our entire response before we reply. It includes recognizing that others have a right to their own emotions, not merely their own opinions.

Positive academic leaders demonstrate active listening in these ways:

o *Following along.* They make a conscious effort to give their full attention to the person with whom they're speaking. Even if they have other pressing engagements, they make that person feel as though he or she is the only individual who matters to them right now. A few times during the conversation, positive academic leaders make sure that they've understood the issue completely by restating what the other person has said in their own words. (You certainly don't want to do so after each of the other person's statements. Paraphrasing occasionally is great, but constant paraphrasing becomes annoying.) As a way of checking that they've truly comprehended what the other person has said, they periodically begin a reply by saying, "So, let me see if I understand you completely. You feel that . . . ," or, "I just want to make sure that I've grasped all the details. The most important thing that you're concerned about is . . ."

o *Following up.* After the conversation is over, positive leaders find some appropriate means to demonstrate that they've taken the other person's concerns seriously and are continuing to regard these issues as significant. In a formal meeting, this type of follow-up may include a memorandum of understanding that outlines the primary points raised during the discussion, what the administrator intends to do about them, and what the other person has agreed to do. In less formal situations, a personally written note or a second brief conversation may be all that's required. The central goal isn't to create the impression that the positive leader was concerned about the issue only during the conversation itself but, once the other person has left the office, the matter dropped completely from his or her mind.

o *Following through.* Most important, if you've promised to undertake any action as a result of your conversation, positive academic leaders do so in a timely manner. Even if they regard the issue as a fairly small concern, they know that the other person probably considers it extremely important, perhaps the most important issue in that person's life right now. So these administrators act quickly to get the information the other person wants or to report that appropriate follow-up was made. If, for whatever reason, the positive leader can't complete the action within a few days, then he or she lets the other person know why there's a delay and what the new timetable will be.

The second approach that DePalma, English, and Sabatine discuss, powerful questioning, is in many ways an outgrowth of the first. It consists of asking questions that are "empowering rather than threatening." Such questions serve to increase understanding, not to interrogate or cross-examine others. In other words, it involves what David Cooperrider and Diana Whitney in chapter 2 called appreciative inquiry. Although it may seem like a simple thing, positive academic leaders ask questions because they really want to know the answers, not because they want to catch someone in an inconsistency or demonstrate their superior knowledge. In this way, perhaps, administrative coaching begins to part ways from athletic coaching. One of the most familiar statements attributed (widely, although some scholars believe not accurately) to Vince Lombardi is, "Winning isn't everything; it's the only thing." Positive academic leaders care about more than just winning. In fact, they recognize that sometimes it's only when you surrender the need to win that you start to succeed.

Conclusion

Barbara Fredrickson is the Kenan Distinguished Professor at the University of North Carolina at Chapel Hill with appointments in both psychology and business. One of her observations about how people come to regard their work as meaningful has a great deal of relevance to the way in which positive academic leaders serve as coaches:

> Positive meaning at work can be drawn from experiences of competence, achievement, involvement, significance, and social connection. Organizational members might promote such experiences with careful consideration of their organization's practices, ranging from incentive and reward structures and group size, to methods of communication and opportunities for refueling and reflection. (Fredrickson, 2003, pp. 174–175)

Good coaches know how to instill in others this sense of "competence, achievement, involvement, significance, and social connection." Positive academic leaders don't believe that the most effective way to motivate members of the faculty and staff is through fear, intimidation, and threats. They prefer to demonstrate a genuine concern for the success of everyone in their programs, and they strive to inspire others to achieve even greater things. Not every department, college, or university, of course, provides an environment harmonious enough to pursue these goals. In these situations, the positive academic leader must often adopt a different set of strategies, shifting from encouraging coach to caring counselor. As a result, it's the counseling role of the positive academic leader that we need to consider next.

References

Buller, J. L. (2009). The excessively demanding parent. *Student Affairs Leader, 37*(9), 4–5.

Cahn, D. D. (1994). *Conflict in personal relationships*. Hillsdale, NJ: Erlbaum.

Cline, F., & Fay, J. (2006). *Parenting with love and logic: Teaching children responsibility* (updated ed.). Colorado Springs, CO: Piñon Press.

Daniels, D., & Strauss, E. (2010). Mostly I'm driven to tears, and feeling totally unappreciated: Exploring the emotional wellness of high school teachers. *Procedia—Social and Behavioral Sciences, 9*, 1385–1393.

DePalma, J., English, S., & Sabatine, J. (2012). Coaching: A powerful tool for chairs. *Department Chairs, 22*(3), 13–15.

Evans, L. (1998). *Teacher morale, job satisfaction, and motivation*. London: P. Chapman.

Fischer, U., & Orasanu, J. (2000). Error-challenging strategies: Their role in preventing and correcting errors. *Ergonomics for the New Millennium, 1*, 30–33.

Fredrickson, B. L. (2003). Positive emotions and upward spirals in organizations. In K. S. Cameron, J. E. Dutton, & R. E. Quinn (Eds.), *Positive organizational scholarship: Foundations of a new discipline* (pp. 163–175). San Francisco, CA: Berrett-Koehler.

Kelly, K. (1986). *His way: The unauthorized biography of Frank Sinatra.* Toronto: Bantam Books.

Kuczynski, L., & Kochanska, G. (1990). Development of children's noncompliance strategies from toddlerhood to age five. *Developmental Psychology, 26,* 398–408.

Kuczynski, L., Kochanska, G., Radke-Yarrow, M., & Girnius-Brown, O. (1987). A developmental interpretation of young children's noncompliance. *Developmental Psychology, 23,* 799–806.

Macdonald, I., Burke, C. G., & Stewart, K. (2006). *Systems leadership: Creating positive organizations.* Aldershot, England: Gower.

Marsh, J. (2007). *Not a helicopter parent. More like a stealth bomber.* mothergoosemouse.com/2007/10/05/not-a-helicopter-parent-more -like-a-stealth-bomber/.

Parsons, J., & Frick, W. (2008). Why professors hate their jobs: A critique of the pedagogy of academic disengagement. *Culture, Society and Praxis, 7*(2), 30–46.

Sinatra, N. (1985). *Frank Sinatra, my father.* Garden City, NY: Doubleday.

Stone, T., & Coussons-Read, M. E. (2011). *Leading from the middle: A case-study approach to academic leadership for associate deans.* Lanham, MD: Rowman & Littlefield.

Taylor, M. (2006, November). Helicopters, snowplows, and bulldozers: Managing students' parents. *Bulletin of the Association of College Unions International,* 12–21.

Turner, J. F. (2004). *Frank Sinatra.* Dallas, TX: Taylor Trade.

CHAPTER 8

THE ACADEMIC LEADER AS COUNSELOR

It may seem rather hypocritical, after having said in chapter 1 that positive leadership is not about being a life coach and that "it's morally (and often legally) wrong to practice counseling without a license," to present a whole chapter now on how academic leaders should be counselors. But we need to distinguish two important senses of this term. A counselor as therapist is someone who helps people deal with severe personal problems, diagnoses recognized psychological challenges, and goes through an intensive training procedure before becoming licensed. A counselor as mentor is the role we all assume with friends and members of our family who want our advice on an issue we've dealt with ourselves or are looking for a sympathetic ear when they're facing the customary frustrations and disappointments of everyday life. This chapter deals exclusively with the way in which positive academic leaders fit the second of these two definitions. Every good administrator knows when he or she is confronted with an issue that's more appropriate for the employee assistance program, office of human resources, or a professional counselor. But every good administrator also knows that there will be those who will want advice, an opportunity to vent, an objective opinion—in a word, the counseling of a mentor or friend.

Even in this limited sense, however, academic leaders may find the whole notion of acting as a counselor to members of their faculty and staff a bit unsettling. "That wasn't what I was trained to do," they might say, or, "I don't believe in a lot of hand holding." But as all academic leaders discover sooner or later, some degree of mentoring comes with the job. You can be good at it or you can be terrible at it, but you can't avoid it entirely. Whether you want them to or not, people will bring you their problems. Most of those problems are likely to be related to their work, but if you're particularly good at listening to people or offering comfort and advice, you can expect to hear about your colleagues' personal lives as well.

Positive academic leaders understand this inevitability. While they won't get involved in issues better suited for a licensed therapist, they know that members of the faculty and staff aren't divided up into professional selves, family selves, and personal selves. What happens at home often affects what goes on in the classroom, library, studio, and lab, even though faculty members may try to leave their troubles at the doorway. And academic institutions are places where interpersonal relations tend to become quite complex. Colleges and universities hire and train people who care deeply about their disciplines and take great pride in the quality of their work. As a result, egos can collide, feelings can get hurt, and vendettas can result. The academic leader as counselor may be called on to mediate these situations and, even if his or her field has nothing at all to do with counseling psychology or interpersonal relations, understands that these problems will frequently find a way of reaching his or her office. So given the choice between being a good counselor or a terrible counselor, why not be a good one? If you choose to improve your skill, you'll find that your programs will be more successful, your job will be easier, and your level of stress will be lower—not a bad trade-off for a little hand holding.

In an interesting quantitative study performed by Stephane Côté and an international team of scholars, a high degree of correlation was found between people who scored well on standardized tests in emotional intelligence and those who demonstrated high levels of emergent leadership skills in small groups (Côté, Lopes, Salovey, and Miners, 2010a, 2010b). The term *emergent leadership* refers to the abilities that people exhibit even when they're not assigned to a recognized leadership position. In other words, no matter whether they hold a title, effective leaders tend to demonstrate the capacity to recognize and respond to the emotional subtext of a situation. They recognize who's suffering, who's having a good day, who's angry, who's distracted by what's going on elsewhere in his or her life, who's supportive, and who's just going through the motions. If it's then possible to reduce that amount of suffering, anger, distraction, and boredom while building on the happiness and enthusiasm of others, the positive leader can proceed to create an environment in which better work is done and better lives are led. In this way, those who can diagnose and respond to the unexpressed needs of the group become what Fred Luthans and Bruce Avolio (2003) call *authentic leaders:*

> Authentic leaders are guided by a set of end-values that represent an orientation toward doing what's right for their constituency. Central to these end-values is a belief that each individual has something positive to contribute to their group. One of the authentic leader's core challenges is to identify these strengths and help direct and build them appropriately . . . Authentic leaders . . . model confidence, hope, optimism, and resiliency, which inspire others to action. Such "walking the talk" has been shown to be much more effective in influencing others than coercing or persuading . . . They constantly think about developing their associates, building on each psychological capacity and strength. This means that they also constantly work on developing themselves so that the emphasis on follower development is seen as being genuine, or something they expect of themselves. (pp. 248–249)

Of course, not only responding to the emotional needs of the people you work with but also modeling confidence, hope, optimism, and resiliency can seem to be a pretty tall order. But if becoming a positive academic leader is a goal you regard as significant, you can begin developing your counseling skills through small, incremental steps. And the first of these steps is to understand the hunger that people have for gratitude.

Developing the Attitude of Gratitude

In a longitudinal study of employees in a wide variety of occupations, Carolyn Wiley (1997) found that five factors consistently rank at the top of any list about what motivates people to make their best efforts at work:

o Salary
o Appreciation
o Job security
o Opportunity for promotion
o Interesting work

Although the precise ordering of these factors varies according to changes in the economy and other external elements, the consistency with which these same items appear among the top five is amazing. Almost always the first or second most important factor employees cite is "full appreciation of work done," a consideration that far outstrips such possibilities as good working conditions, being in the loop when decisions are being made, and the supervisor's ability to be tactful and constructive when offering criticism. This finding becomes all the more important when we realize just how poor a job most supervisors do at expressing that appreciation. In *1001 Ways to Reward Employees* (2005), Bob Nelson discusses what he calls a "feedback gap" that's common in all types of work environments:

> Bob Levoy, president of Success Dynamics, Inc., reports: "I've asked more than 2,500 doctors to rank on a scale of 1 to 5 (1 = never, 5 = always) the following statement: 'I let my employees know when they're doing a good job.' Their average response is 4.4. I then asked their staff members to rank this statement: 'The doctor lets me know when I'm doing a good job,' and their average response is only 1.7. This response between what doctors say they give and what employees say they get is often the underlying cause of employee resentment, diminished productivity, and turnover. This 'feedback gap' is present in almost every manager-employee relationship." (p. 5)

If we were to conduct a similar study at colleges and universities, it's unlikely that the results would be substantially different. What we need, therefore, are some mechanisms to offer praise and recognition to members of the faculty and staff in a systematic manner because we may believe we're thanking people much more often than we actually are. One way of making a system out of this attitude of gratitude is to create what we might call an appreciation calendar. This type of schedule operates by associating a particular constituency with each day of the workweek. For example, a dean or department chair might develop an appreciation calendar that looks like figure 8.1. In your own case, the constituencies you include on your calendar may be somewhat different. But regardless of which groups you choose to recognize, the goal is always to become consistent about thanking people for their efforts. On Mondays, therefore, our hypothetical administrator would take just five or ten minutes anytime during the day and ask himself or herself, "Is there anyone among the faculty whom I need to thank, praise, or offer recognition for something that person did this week?" If there is, the administrator makes a phone call, writes a note, places a reminder to make an announcement at an upcoming meeting, or does something else that conveys gratitude in an appropriate manner. If not, the task is done for the day. On Tuesday, the same question is asked about members of the staff, and so on.

Monday	• Faculty
Tuesday	• Staff
Wednesday	• Students
Thursday	• Donors
Friday	• Others

FIGURE 8.1   Appreciation Calendar

While the practice of offering appreciation should be regular and ongoing, we shouldn't conclude that everyone needs to be thanked in the same way. Nelson sets out four mechanisms for offering gratitude or praise:

1. *Personal praise:* The sort of gratitude you express one-on-one
2. *Written praise:* A note that expresses thanks or congratulations
3. *Electronic praise:* E-mail notes, posting achievements on the unit's website, or singling out someone's contribution during an interview on the radio or through digital signage
4. *Public praise:* Formal recognition at a meeting

If you're uncertain about which form to use, Nelson cites studies that indicate most employees value personalized, instant praise from their supervisors most of all. In fact, in situations where the use of immediate praise is possible, even a slight delay can be interpreted as a lack of appreciation.

Developing an attitude of gratitude in your unit isn't simply a matter of recognizing your own need to thank others. It's also about creating structures that encourage everyone to offer praise and recognition to one another. In controlled studies, Robert Emmons and Michael McCullough (2003) found that expressing gratitude more frequently increases one's happiness and sense of well-being, while Jo-Ann Tsang (2006) found that thanking others caused people to act in a more prosocial manner generally. For this reason, Nelson (2005) describes the importance of "recognizing recognition" in building effective organizational cultures: remember to thank or reward others who are themselves generous in offering praise and recognition. One very effective way to begin this process is to implement roundtable recognition, which can be incorporated into nearly any sort of meeting. In most situations, you'll get the greatest benefit from roundtable recognition if you use it at the start of the meeting, although it can be effective at any point on the agenda. Here's how it functions.

First, the person in charge of the meeting mentions some recent achievements by other members of the group. While in most cases it's probably best to focus on professional accomplishments, there may be certain circumstances in which personal points of pride—such as the birth of a grandchild or the engagement of a son or daughter—are also appropriate. The committee chair can begin this process by saying something like, "Before we proceed to the next agenda item, I'd like to mention that I heard some great news about a few of our own members. Professor X's most recent book has just appeared from Distinguished University Press, Professor Y has had a large grant funded by Major Government Agency, and Professor Z has been recognized as Outstanding Teacher of the Year by the National League for Significant Awards. Isn't it wonderful to be working with such talented colleagues?"

Second, the person in charge invites other members of the group to talk about each other's achievements: "I know that I sometimes get so caught up in what's going on in my area that I don't hear about all the terrific things going on elsewhere. Do any of you know about a recent achievement by another member of this committee that you'd like to share with us?" Encouraging the members of any group to brag about each other both promotes esprit de corps and means that you're not the only one who will start bringing in good news to share.

Then, because no one should feel left out, the person in charge of the meeting invites members of the group to talk about any of their own recent accomplishments that haven't yet been mentioned and to discuss significant achievements by other people in his or her area: "That's all fantastic. Are there any other recent activities we've missed, things going on in your area, or other good news you personally may have had?" From the perspective of positive academic leadership, this section of the recognition roundtable is an important time to keep an eye out for who speaks repeatedly. If the same person feels a need to bring up his or her achievements at several meetings in a row, then this is probably someone who feels that his or her good work hasn't been sufficiently recognized. Before the next meeting, make a special effort to discover several new achievements for which you can recognize this person in step 1 of a future meeting's recognition roundtable.

Finally, bring the process to a close by thanking the members of the group for the hard and impressive work that led to these achievements, and then move on to the remaining business of the meeting.

One of the reasons that recognition roundtables are so useful at the start of an agenda is that they create a positive, mutually supportive atmosphere that can continue throughout the rest of the meeting.

The challenge some administrators find is that it can be difficult to discover all the important accomplishments that occur throughout a college or university, particularly if the institution is large, complex, and not located on a single campus. But positive academic leaders aren't content merely to wait until good news comes to them. They take active measures to make sure that they have access to good news as soon as it happens:

o *Automatic alerts.* Search engines, such as Google and Yahoo! allow users to set up automatic alerts that will notify them by e-mail, text messages, or instant messaging that a new posting has occurred on the Internet relating to some specific subject. By setting up one of these alerts with the name of your department, college, or university, you can be notified as soon as one of your faculty members is quoted as an expert by the media, has a publication appear, or is mentioned in the press release of a funding agency. In small units, it may even be possible to establish an alert based on the name of each member of the faculty or staff.

o *Newspapers.* Even as traditional newspapers are increasingly replaced by online news sources, it can be valuable for academic leaders to receive a hard copy of all publications serving the towns in which members of the faculty tend to live. Notices of births, weddings, and engagements or (less happily) deaths and funerals tend to appear in these sources as a matter of public record. Having the hard copy allows the administrator to clip the item and, when appropriate, send it to the person with a note saying something like, "What a charming new granddaughter! I was delighted to see this announcement in the paper and thought you might like an extra copy to share with your family."

o *Thank a professor.* It's easy to create an online form that students can use to report something impressive one of their faculty members has done. The form would be part of your unit's website and include fields like the instructor's name, the reason that the professor should be regarded as having done something special, and an optional field for the student's name. (For a sample of one of these forms in actual use, see http://tinyurl.com/thankprof.) When the student clicks "Send," an e-mail message to the faculty member's dean or department chair is generated, guaranteeing that the positive experience is shared with that person's supervisor.

Administrators can keep a supply of cards in their desks, and when good news comes their way through any of these means, write a personalized note to the person responsible, thanking him or her for doing such superb work and mentioning how wonderful it is to have that individual as a colleague. In most cases, generic "Congratulations!" cards are appropriate as a medium, but don't just sign the card without including a personal note. Some administrators may prefer to purchase custom-made cards containing the unit's logo and perhaps a printed message—for example, "Here's yet another reason why it's so great to work here!" or, "I heard some good news about you, and I was too proud of you to keep it to myself."

Thanking People Appropriately

A key aspect of positive academic leadership is not merely thanking people, but thanking them appropriately. In light of the importance we've just assigned to praise, thanks, and recognition, it seems reasonable to ask, "How can you ever thank a person inappropriately?" Perhaps a personal example might help answer this question.

In my office I keep three framed certificates, signed by three different presidents who served at different times at one of the schools where I worked. The printed part of each certificate is the same—"Thanks for all you do for" the university—and, while the signatures are, of course, different, the documents also share another feature: my name is spelled wrong on every single one of them. That's thanking someone inappropriately. So what's wrong with the gesture these presidents have made?

- o The printed statement, "Thanks for all you do," is so generic that it could easily have been said (and probably was) by someone who had absolutely no idea what I do for the university.

- o The misspelling of my name suggests that the person who signed the certificate either doesn't know me very well or doesn't care about me enough to find out.

- o The fact that my name is misspelled identically by three successive presidents suggests that each president had very little involvement in the production of these certificates. The task was probably assigned each year to the same staff member who, since we don't work closely together, doesn't know my name very well.

In other words, thanking someone can be done in an inappropriate manner if the expression is insincere, vague, and delivered more in an attempt to manage an employee (i.e., make that person feel appreciated enough to keep working hard) than to express real gratitude for a significant contribution. Have you ever seen a president, chancellor, or member of the governing board completely undermine his or her attempt to thank someone by mispronouncing that person's name, stumbling over the title of the faculty member's research topic, and then trying to make a joke about the difficulty of saying scientific terms, foreign words, or technical jargon correctly? Depending on the honoree's level of sensitivity, what was intended to be a positive act of recognition may end up being perceived as an insult or, at best, an indication that the speaker is so apathetic about the faculty member's work that he or she couldn't even be bothered to ask in advance for some help with pronunciation.

As a framework for discussing the appropriate way of expressing gratitude to someone, I offer my grandmother's five simple rules for writing thank-you notes.

1. Thank-you notes should always be handwritten, not typed.
2. They should mention exactly what the present was and not speak generically about "the gift" or "what you gave me."
3. They should mention how the item will be used or why it's valued.
4. They should fill the entire card, not simply be dashed off as a way of fulfilling an obligation.
5. They should be sent as soon as possible after the gift has been received.

We can extrapolate from Grandma Buller's five rules for writing thank-you notes a valuable set of principles for how positive academic leaders can thank others for the work they've done (see also Buller, 2012).

Make the Gratitude Personal

Thanking people with plaques, generic notes, preprinted cards bearing nothing more than a signature, or brief e-mail messages may make administrators think they're doing something meaningful for the faculty and staff, but the actual impact may be quite different from what they intended. A handwritten note, personal office visit, invitation to lunch for either just the two of you or in a very small group, or warm, carefully chosen remarks in a public address will have much more impact. Remember too Alessandra and O'Connor's platinum rule that we encountered in chapter 1: "Do unto others as *they'd* like done unto them." The most meaningful way of saying thank you to one person may be something totally different from what would please someone else. If you can manage to do so, a gift certificate to someone's favorite restaurant, an evening of free child care so that the person can go out to a movie or spa, an opportunity to leave early each Friday for a month, or free membership to the faculty club will say, "I appreciate what you did," far better that a dashed-off e-mail reading, "Thanks!" If you don't know exactly what would most please the person, try making a confidential inquiry to his or her spouse, supervisor, or close friends on campus. If all else fails, ask the person directly or provide a menu of options to choose from.

Make the Gratitude Specific

Saying, "Thanks for all you've done," or, "Thanks for another great year," is far too vague to provide the person who hears it with a particularly warm and fuzzy feeling. Be sure to mention exactly what the person did, and do so in a manner that makes it clear how important you regard this person to the institution's overall operation. If you're addressing a group, for instance, instead of saying, "Oh, and I'd like to thank Jennifer for that great curriculum proposal. Good job, Jennifer!" say something like this:

> Before we adjourn today, I'd like to say a few words of appreciation about how absolutely incredible Jennifer's work has been in developing the new curriculum proposal. You all know how valuable Jennifer has been to this committee, but what you may not know is what an effort writing this proposal has been. Jennifer is teaching a full load, still organizing her research so that she'll have an excellent portfolio for tenure in two years, and serving on far more committees than should be allowed for any member of the junior faculty. Despite all that, she still took it upon herself to study best practices at more than a dozen universities, consulted with every single one of you, and then brought us a proposal that was very well written, thoughtful, and visionary. Jennifer, I frankly don't know how you do it, but I want to thank you for the care and creativity that went into this proposal.

If you were Jennifer, which statement would make you leave the meeting feeling that your efforts had truly been valued?

Make the Gratitude Clear

Just as in a thank-you note you should always include a line about how you'll use the gift or why it was appropriate for you, so should any expression of gratitude make the importance of the person's effort clear.

For instance, in the case of the curriculum proposal we just considered, the committee chair could have said something like this:

> We've all seen the numbers, and we know that both our majors and our graduation rate have been declining for several years. The next time we come up for accreditation, I think we could've been in severe trouble if we didn't do something dramatic and innovative. That's why Jennifer's curriculum proposal is so significant. It's no exaggeration to say that the students in our program will be better served once this program is in place and that due to Jennifer's hard work, we'll probably be able to keep a few faculty lines that would otherwise be cut during the next round of budget reductions. Remember: her hard work translates into *our* jobs.

Making the importance of the person's action clear in this way indicates that the administrator "gets it." He or she has the right set of priorities, valuing people for the impact of their efforts.

Make the Gratitude Sincere

By filling a thank-note completely, the writer indicates that he or she is not merely going through the motions, sending a card simply because it was expected (or, worse, because he or she had gone to a management workshop and picked up a few useful tips). Talking about the gift and how much it's appreciated lets the person who receives the note understand that his or her act of generosity was truly appreciated. In a similar way, when our expressions of gratitude are terse, pro forma, or simply dropped into the middle of the conversation ("Oh, yeah. Thanks for coming in over the weekend to finish this."), they come across as insincere. People feel that you've thanked them just because you've learned somewhere (such as this book!) that administrators are supposed to do these things. As a result, they end up feeling manipulated, not rewarded. And the last thing the positive academic leader wants people to feel is that they're simply being used.

Even if you're not the sort of person for whom the language of emotion comes easily, give some thought as to how you'll convey why you valued and benefited from the other person's work. If you can't find any other way to get a grasp on this issue, ask yourself, *How is my life or work now better, easier, or richer because of what this person has done?* Then tell *that* to the person you want to thank. Also, this is one area of your work where it's okay to exaggerate a little or use language that's different from what you'd ordinarily say. Phrases such as, "You're terrific," "You're the best," and "You're absolutely unbelievable" have much more impact than do blander statements like, "You did a good job," or hackneyed phrases like, "You went above and beyond the call of duty." For truly outstanding accomplishments, ask the president or the chair of the governing board to write a thank-you note to the person or make a personal call. A note or phone call from someone high in the institutional hierarchy tends to make a lasting impression.

Make the Gratitude Timely

Every second that elapses between the time a positive deed is done and when that person is thanked is perceived as a measure of how long it took you to notice that the person exists. If you're going to thank someone by means of a written message or reward, do it quickly. If you're going to recognize a person's efforts publicly, do so at the first available opportunity. We all hear stories periodically about dedicated workers who give forty years of their lives to an organization, were barely noticed for most of that time, and have the full weight of their contributions understood by others only at their retirement parties. People who give of themselves and keep giving year after year can be found in practically all organizations; they're the stalwarts of every college or university. But most people find it difficult to sustain their morale and motivation for very long without periodic expressions of appreciation. The academic leader as counselor understands this need and thanks others in a timely manner, not just at the end of the academic year or, worse, that person's career.

Making Conflict Positive

Resources for academic leaders are filled with advice on how to reduce, manage, or avoid conflict. Far less common are discussions about how to make conflict beneficial to a program or make disagreement a positive experience for faculty, students, and staff. That oversight is unfortunate because there are many occasions when avoiding conflict is far less desirable than channeling it toward a positive end. In fact, although one may not think that colleges and universities can ever have a surplus of harmony, units that avoid issues completely because they're regarded as too sensitive or that become mired in groupthink ("going along to get along") are often less dynamic than those that have a little constructive disagreement. The goal of the academic leader as counselor therefore should be to foster an environment in which conflict is neither avoided nor destructive. Moreover, when tensions occur, positive academic leaders should guide the process effectively so that the disagreement itself serves to reinforce the department's collegiality, respect for individual differences, and team spirit.

Making conflict positive requires developing ground rules that govern how disagreements will be handled and what the expectations for collegiality and civility are going to be. Members of the institution need to know that it's okay to disagree. It's even okay to disagree publicly, loudly, and emphatically. What's not okay is disagreeing in a way that reasonable people would regard as demeaning to others or inconsistent with higher education's standards of mutual respect among colleagues (i.e., collegiality). If a discussion about how to approach conflict hasn't yet occurred in your area, it's often refreshing to discover that the very act of developing mutually acceptable ground rules for debate can be a powerful team-building exercise. Each unit will want to establish its own guidelines, of course, based on its individual history. But I've found nine general policies to be helpful when programs decide to explore collegial ways of encouraging the free exchange of opinions:

1. *Always focus on the issue, never the person.* Conflict can be positive when it involves debate over the merits of alternative ideas. But it quickly becomes negative when participants in the discussion begin to call into question the personalities or characters of other people. At conferences in our disciplines, we know perfectly well how to distinguish between someone who disagrees with our method or conclusions and someone who has lapsed into making a personal attack. Yet in the hothouse atmosphere of faculty debates at our own institutions, this distinction is all too frequently overlooked. An institutional code stating that all disagreements will be based on issues rather than personalities gives you an opportunity to remind someone who seems to be in danger of violating this principle why it's essential to disagree constructively and that vitriolic denunciation "isn't the way we've decided to approach our differences in opinion here."

2. *If criticism does become too personal, it can often be reduced by deflecting certain statements toward yourself.* For instance, if one of the participants in the discussion appears to become preoccupied with a mistake another individual has made, the hostile atmosphere can be diffused if someone says, "Well, I think we've all made mistakes from time to time. I know that I've been guilty of the very thing we've just been talking about, and aren't there plenty of others here who have done the same thing? But I believe that the more pressing issue is . . ." Positive academic leaders aren't afraid to make such statements and aren't concerned that their status will suffer by admitting to having made an error. It's negative

academic leaders who believe that if they admit to an error, it'll be perceived as a sign of weakness. They lose sight of the fact that this very insistence on always being right is itself a weakness.

3. *Participants in a disagreement should periodically paraphrase what they believe people are saying and provide context for their own remarks.* As a conflict unfolds, it sometimes becomes apparent that it's people's vocabulary, not a fundamental difference of opinion, that lies at the heart of the disagreement. When faculty members care deeply about an issue, it can be easy to become caught up in one set of terms, while others are saying essentially the same thing but using different words. When language appears to be getting in the way, the positive academic leader can make an important contribution by paraphrasing the discussion and providing the appropriate context, using such expressions as, "I think one theme that keeps recurring through everyone's remarks here is that . . ." or, "But by saying X, aren't you really also suggesting Y, or have I misunderstood the point you're trying to make?"

4. *When objecting to an idea, state your reasons.* Constructive debate occurs when all participants in the discussion have the information they need to weigh the strength of different positions. Nevertheless, considering various alternatives is difficult or impossible if participants in the discussion dismiss an idea without offering compelling reasons for doing so. Merely saying, "Well, that won't work," or, "What a waste of time!" without clearly and collegially offering the reasons for such an assertion is unhelpful at best. At worst, it can cause communications to break down completely. At a professional conference, no scholar would openly condemn a new idea without being able to offer the reasons for taking such a stand. Professionalism requires us to extend the same courtesy to colleagues when discussing policies, curricula, pedagogy, and other matters at our own institutions.

5. *When objecting to an idea, offer a better alternative.* It can be easy to criticize almost any proposal since in an imperfect world, plans will never be perfect. What's far more difficult is to develop a reasonable alternative that can withstand the scrutiny of others. As colleagues, we all owe it to one another to propose viable substitutes for flawed plans. In a way, that is the very foundation of constructive conflict: offering practical alternatives moves the issue forward by replacing unworkable approaches with more effective strategies and introducing new ways of meeting goals.

6. *Speak in your own voice.* In difficult or heated discussions, it can be tempting to hide behind the shield that "there's a perception some people have," or, "Others have been saying that . . ." But a speaker with a valid

objection has an obligation to own up to it. Perceptions are impossible to debate since no one can refute what some nameless group of observers is alleged to believe ("I mean, your ideas are all terrific. I'm just saying there's a perception out there that . . ."). So the goal of the participants in a conflict should be to discuss only what *can* be debated (Buller, 2010). As David Frohnmayer (2010), former president of the University of Oregon, says in his "Dave's Rules of Order," "Never try to escape responsibility by adopting the passive voice."

7. *Remind others of their need to reiterate their mutual support even in the midst of a conflict.* Another important role you can play in a conflict is to make sure that the participants come away from the experience with a clear understanding that although there may still be disagreement about individual strategies and ideas, everyone retains a high level of support for one another as individuals and as scholars. If that focus is in danger of being lost, try to reestablish it by saying something like, "I understand how adamantly opposed you are to X's position on this issue, but you're not saying that you have any less respect for X as a teacher and scholar, are you? I personally value X as a colleague, and I just don't want us to have any misunderstandings on this issue." It's then possible to encourage faculty member X to say something similarly supportive about the person you were just addressing, and thus to conclude the discussion on a note of mutual support and professional respect. If, however, the person says that he or she *does* have less respect for the other party as a result of this conflict, revert to guidelines 1 and 2 above.

8. *Always end a debate or disagreement by reaffirming support for the people on the other side of the issue.* As we've seen, it's not necessary for strong, supportive colleagues to see eye-to-eye on every issue. But strong, supportive colleagues always value one another's professional integrity and respect each other's right to hold different opinions. When a disagreement is particularly intense, this fundamental level of mutual respect has a tendency to become overlooked. So it's useful to make a regular practice of ending tense discussions with explicit statements of mutual respect and support. In fact, it's probably a wise plan to end every major meeting with such a statement. That way no one ever has to decide which debates qualify as being particularly acrimonious.

9. *Move forward.* Perhaps the most important action positive leaders can take to make sure that conflict remains a positive process is to insist that a meaningful product or plan results from it. Without developing a plan to move forward, conflict will remain a source of

upheaval and contention rather than a mechanism for developing new ideas. People will continue to ask, "What good came out of all that controversy? We seem to have argued quite a lot but decided very little." Positive academic leaders can be effective in seeing that some concrete product—perhaps something as simple as a memo of understanding or as complex as a complete revision of the entire graduate program—emerges from the process. Even what feels at the time like a difficult and agonizing process may come to be regarded as worthwhile if the outcome is meaningful enough. Moreover, moving forward will help eliminate any misconception that opposition and tension exist among the faculty merely because of a lack of collegiality. The product, in other words, is concrete proof that real issues have been debated and that the faculty has used the controversy to move forward.

The pre-Socratic philosopher Heraclitus notes that what gives the bow its strength and the lyre its beauty is the harmony and balance that comes from a balance of opposing tensions. Positive conflict is like Heraclitus's bow and lyre: it doesn't eliminate tension; rather, it balances it and takes full advantage of it by using it for a constructive purpose. In this time of increased faculty incivility and challenges to collegiality, leaders have a vital role in developing an environment in which as much conflict as possible leads to positive results.

Dealing with Grief and Suffering

Perhaps the most challenging arena in which the academic leader may be expected to serve as counselor occurs when someone is struggling with grief or another type of personal anguish. If a member of the faculty or staff is truly suffering rather than simply being down temporarily because of some specific event, the best thing the academic leader can do is to put the person in contact with professional help. There are times when even the most positive academic leader possible should no longer act as counselor but should call on the resources of the institution's employee assistance program, health center, or office of human resources. Most schools have specific policies about how to make a referral to one of these programs. If the person doesn't seem to be clinically depressed but rather going through a brief period of sadness due to the death of someone close or the breakup of a relationship, then the best approach is usually to make it clear that you're available to help if your assistance is needed but that you're also willing to give the person some space if that seems preferable.

Processing grief occurs over time, and no two people recover on the same timetable. Some heal by sharing their story with others; if this approach would be useful, be there to listen. Others heal by processing their grief themselves; if you try to play too active a role, you can hinder this process. Just as people have a right to their own personalities, they also have a right to their own emotions. Not everyone who's sad needs or wants to be cheered up or treated as if the bad thing never happened. When I was starting out as a teacher, one of my students was not herself for a few days because of something I regarded as a relatively minor matter. I thought it was my role to make her feel better and did everything I could to lighten the mood. A wise administrator who noticed what I was doing gently pulled me aside and said, "People have a right to be happy, but they have a right to be sad sometimes too. We have to honor that." And letting her deal with her sadness in her own way turned out to be the best solution. Within a few days, she was her jovial self again.

The academic leader as counselor understands that when people experience setbacks, it's often the wrong time to try to dispel the gloom through humor or upbeat platitudes. When you're feeling disappointed, pep talks can seem superficial, even callous. Trying to distract people may deprive them of the time they need to work through the issue in their own way. In order to be a good counselor, the positive academic leader knows when to be optimistic and when to back off, when to bring on the motivational speeches and when just to be there for the person. One of the secrets of positive leadership is that sometimes the best possible action isn't an action at all. It's just silently watching and caring.

Conclusion

Like good coaches, good counselors support people both when things are going well and when things are going poorly. They criticize constructively when criticism is warranted and provide a willing ear when listening seems the better approach. They motivate others to do their best by offering what people need, not what the leaders themselves would want in a similar situation. So coaching and counseling often go hand in hand. The third ingredient in taking positive approaches with others is to see your role as a conductor—not, I hasten to add, in the sense of taking tickets on a train or facilitating the flow of an electric current (although those can sometimes be useful metaphors too), but in the sense of leading a great and complex orchestra. It's that approach we turn to in the next chapter.

References

Buller, J. L. (2010). The perception problem, *Academic Leader*, 26(4), 1–2.

Buller, J. L. (2012). *Best practices in faculty evaluation: A practical guide for academic leaders.* San Francisco, CA: Jossey-Bass.

Côté, S., Lopes, P. N., Salovey, P., & Miners, C. T. (2010a). Emotional intelligence and leadership emergence in small groups. *Leadership Quarterly*, 21, 496–508.

Côté, S., Lopes, P. N., Salovey, P., & Miners, C. T. (2010b). Corrigendum to "Emotional intelligence and leadership emergence in small groups." *Leadership Quarterly*, 21, 684–685.

Emmons, R. A., & McCullough, M. E. (2003). Counting blessings versus burdens: An experimental investigation of gratitude and subjective well-being in daily life. *Journal of Personality and Social Psychology*, 84, 377–389

Frohnmayer, D. (2010, November 3). *Major concerns of university leaders in the twenty-first century.* Presentation at the annual Saudi Rectors' Workshop, Yanbu, Saudi Arabia.

Luthans, F., & Avolio, B. (2003). Authentic leadership development. In K. S. Cameron, J. E. Dutton, & R. E. Quinn (Eds.), *Positive organizational scholarship: Foundations of a new discipline* (pp. 241–258). San Francisco, CA: Berrett-Koehler.

Nelson, B. (2005). *1001 ways to reward employees.* New York, NY: Workman.

Tsang, J.-A. (2006). Gratitude and prosocial behaviour: An experimental test of gratitude. *Cognition and Emotion*, 20(1), 138–148.

Wiley, C. (1997). What motivates employees according to over 40 years of motivation surveys. *International Journal of Manpower*, 18, 263–280.

Resources

Buller, J. L. (2007). Interpersonal survival skills for department chairs. *Department Chair*, 18(1), 4–6.

Haynes, J. M., Haynes, G. L., & Fong, L. S. (2004). *Mediation: Positive conflict management.* Albany: State University of New York Press.

CHAPTER 9

THE ACADEMIC LEADER AS CONDUCTOR

In a now-famous presentation at the 2008 TED (Technology, Entertainment, Design) conference in Long Beach, California, Benjamin Zander (2009), music director of the Boston Philharmonic Orchestra, described a moment that entirely changed the way he approached his job. He noted that not until after he had been at the podium for twenty years did he realize that the conductor is the only person in the orchestra who "doesn't make a sound. He depends for his power on his ability to make other people powerful." In other words, great conductors aren't those who demonstrate their creativity through skill on an instrument or the beauty of their own performances. Rather, they are judged by their ability to produce an environment in which the artistry of others may emerge and the quality of that performance may be experienced. Of course, conductors should also be fine musicians themselves. Many of them have studied numerous instruments, performed in a variety of venues, and become virtuosi in their own right. But we appreciate conductors as conductors, not on the basis of the music they create as individuals but on their skill in inspiring others to provide fine performances.

There's a strong parallel between what Zander is describing and the goal we're trying to attain as positive academic leaders. Administrators frequently have had highly successful careers as instructors, researchers, and academic citizens. What's more, they were often encouraged to pursue administrative careers precisely because of their achievements in these areas. But once they become administrators, academic leaders start to be judged less on the quality of their own teaching, scholarship, and service and more on the quality of what their programs achieve. Presidents, provosts, deans, and chairs may be among the very few people at their institutions who hold academic rank but teach no classes, write no grant proposals, publish no books or articles, and are elected to no committees. And yet without them, none of those activities can occur.

How does it change the perspective of administrators when they begin to think of themselves as conductors? Zander describes his sudden awareness of his true function in the orchestra as a life-altering event. When a performance was not going well, he could no longer see it primarily as the fault of the musicians. Rather, he began to ask what it was he was conveying, intentionally or not, that prevented the orchestra from performing well. In a similar way, administrators who view themselves as conductors ask wholly different questions from those of negative academic leaders. When something goes wrong, they don't ask, "Who's fault is it this time?" Instead they ask, "What am I doing wrong that's not motivating people as well as it should? What am I expressing that's not inspiring the level of excellence I know we can achieve?"

The academic leader as conductor is someone who recognizes the truth of the seventeenth verse of the *Tao Te Ching* (Lao Tzu and Le Guin, 1997, p. 24):

> True leaders are hardly known to their followers.
> Next after them are the leaders
> the people know and admire;
> after them, those they fear;
> after them, those they despise.
> To give no trust
> is to get no trust.
> When the work's done right,
> With no fuss or boasting,
> Ordinary people say,
> Oh, we did it.

Positive academic leaders rarely get thanked for what they do, even though they thank others often. When superb books of research are published, grants are received, students are graduating on time, and admission is increasing, no one's going to stick their head in the door of the provost, dean, or department chair and say, "Hey, good job administrating this year!" Students, faculty, and staff will attribute this success to themselves, and that's exactly the way it should be. Positive academic leaders want their stakeholders to say, "Oh, we did it!" In fact, if the administrator's the one who's always in the limelight, something has gone wrong. Either the administrator's ego has gotten in the way or a paternalistic leadership style has made everyone far too dependent on the direction provided by just one person.

Positive academic leaders don't need fanfare to know that they've created the environment that made all those books, grants, successful students, and high admission levels possible. The leader has "conducted" a complex "orchestra" that produces beautiful "music," even if he or she "doesn't make a sound." To put it another way, being a good administrative conductor means understanding how to make everyone perform well as part of a system.

The Systems Approach to Positive Academic Leadership

Every orchestra is a system in the sense of the term that we saw in chapter 1: a collection of distinct individuals who are connected in such a way that they affect and are affected by other members of that system. The resulting synergy is a key reason that systems are so beneficial and yet so difficult to understand at times. After all, you can't learn everything about a computer system just by studying the keyboard, you can't learn everything about your body's circulatory system just by studying the heart, and you can't learn everything about an orchestra simply by studying the flute. In a similar way, positive academic leaders recognize that progress is achieved not by focusing on this particular faculty member or that specific part of the curriculum but by considering the system as a whole.

Systems thinking influences our approach to academic leadership in many ways. First, it causes us to consider how a change we make in one part of our system is likely to affect components elsewhere in the system. Do the following thought experiment:

A faculty member comes to you and complains about his salary. "I know we're all underpaid," the faculty member says, "but it bothers me that I'm the lowest-paid faculty member in my rank and the lowest paid in our entire unit. I could've jumped from school to school as a way of raising my salary like other people have done. But I've been loyal. When you consider how many years I've served this institution, my low salary just isn't right."

Since you first need to verify some of the claims the faculty member has made, you begin by checking where this person's salary falls relative to others at the institution. In doing so, you discover that he really does have a case: his salary is inexplicably low when you compare it to others in the discipline, no matter how you interpret the evidence. Even by controlling for years of experience, merit, market factors, rank, and every other explanation you can think of, this employee's salary still appears to lag significantly behind that of others. You check with your supervisor and, although it's uncommon, receive permission to make a special salary adjustment. The faculty member's happy, and you're happy: you've just taken a step closer to positive academic leadership.

But then something odd happens. In keeping with the time-honored tradition that no good deed goes unpunished, another faculty member makes an appointment to see you. Now she is the lowest-paid member of your faculty and wants an adjustment. (After all, the precedent's been set.) You now see what your future will be like: every time you make a special adjustment to one person's salary, another person becomes the lowest-paid member of your program and demands the next special increase. You envision the line of "unjustly treated faculty members" who are going to appear at your door as stretching to infinity. How might seeing the first faculty member's issue as a system issue rather than as a discrete problem have resulted in a better outcome for everyone?

In this thought experiment, you may have regarded your original solution as a good example of systems thinking. After all, you did look at part of the system: you took market factors and years of experience into account; you compared the faculty member's salary to that of others in the system; you even expanded the system by working in cooperation with your supervisor. But those actions didn't provide you with the whole story, and so your solution ended up "introducing an exotic species into your ecosystem." Just as this faculty member's salary wasn't just low but also low relative to what other people were making, so did your attempt to solve the problem affect not this person alone but everyone in the system. The average salary for the entire unit has now changed, and a faculty member who may have been content to be above average in income yesterday may suddenly become angry or demoralized for being below average today. By helping one faculty member, your decision may result in salary compression or inversion for a dozen others. If this scenario seems far-fetched, it really isn't. This type of problem occurs all the time when administrators operate in silos and don't take account of how their systems are interrelated.

This doesn't mean that you should never raise the salary of an individual faculty member or do anything else that helps one person but not another. But it does indicate the importance of considering all the ramifications of each decision. Most people, when they use the word *ramifications*, treat it as a synonym for *implications* or *consequences:* "I got into trouble because I never considered the ramifications of my actions." But this word is actually derived from the Latin words *ramus* (branch) and *facio/facere* (to do or to make). So the origin of our English word *ramifications* relates to how branches are made as they spread out from a single trunk or source. For this reason, the ramifications of your actions are not just the implications or consequences of those actions, but all the resulting occurrences that branch off from it as part of the system in which that action occurs.

To switch metaphors for a moment, adopting a systems approach means looking at each decision as though it were a chess move. A chess player can't think solely in terms of a single piece and a single move but has to consider each piece's relationship to all the others on the board, all the possible moves his or her opponent may make, and all the possible results of each decision ten or fifteen moves further into the game. Positive academic leaders work in this way as well. They consider the potential impact of their choices in order to select their best possible alternative, and what may appear to be the best solution now isn't always the best solution in the long run.

In the case of our hypothetical situation, a better approach would have been to respond, "Salaries are such an important issue that we can't ever look at just one person's situation in isolation. We always have to examine the larger issue. Give me a few days, and I'll get back to you with my specific plan." Then, after verifying the faculty member's claims and receiving your supervisor's approval, don't make a separate deal with this one faculty member; rather, speak to the faculty as a whole:

> I've been reviewing salaries in our area, and it appears that we have at least one serious case of inequity that we can't remedy through our ordinary salary process. I want you to appoint a group of representatives [at this point, you'd state a specific number, based on the size of your program] who will work with me to develop an approach to salary equity that will guide us for the foreseeable future. We'll take a look at such factors as years of experience, market value, and the results of annual evaluations. And then we'll come as close as we possibly can to achieving consensus with you about the best

way to proceed. Once that plan is in place, we'll follow it, and there will be no equity adjustments outside of that plan. That's why it'll be important for you to make your views known. We probably won't be able to incorporate every opinion, but we will consider them all carefully. In that way, everyone will know how we're proceeding, what the ground rules are, and how the plan relates to his or her individual situation.

By taking this approach, you'll have reduced the length of the line of petitioners forming outside your office in the future. And when someone does plead an individual case, you'll have a clear policy in place that addresses the needs of the entire system, not just the claims of an individual faculty member.

Platonicity, Reification, and the Lorenz Butterfly Effect

The idea that academic leaders benefit from using systems thinking and identifying the various ramifications that result from their actions seems to violate a key principle we encountered in chapter 1: although you can't plan for everything, you can prepare for anything. In other words, positive academic leaders recognize that higher education is such a complex system that it's an illusion to think, "If we plan strategically enough, we can develop a reliable notion of where our institutions will be twenty or thirty years in the future." Nassim Taleb, author of *The Black Swan* (2010), calls this type of thinking *Platonicity* because it bears such a striking resemblance to Plato's concept of ideal forms. As Taleb outs it, Platonicity is "our tendency to mistake the map for the territory" or, in higher education, to believe that strategic plans can be complex enough to become accurate road maps to the future. They can't. It's not that we should never plan for the future, but rather that we should see even our most elaborate planning models for what they really are: nothing more than models. They're not reality itself. No matter how hard we try, we can't identify every independent variable in a structure as complex as real life. Our tendency to "mistake the map for the territory," as Taleb puts it, or to confuse the model with reality is also sometimes known as reification—the habit of treating mental constructs as though they were actual physical objects. *Why can't I get my business to turn a profit?* someone may think. *I've done everything right and planned for every contingency.* The truth of the matter is that it's simply not possible to plan for every contingency. There are factors we aren't even aware of that affect what happens to us. And we can't incorporate a possibility into a model if we don't know it exists.

In 1972, Edward Lorenz, one of the pioneers in the field we now know as chaos theory, spoke to the American Association for the Advancement of Science on the topic of "Predictability: Does the Flap of a Butterfly's Wings in Brazil Set Off a Tornado in Texas?" (Lorenz, 1993, pp. 181–189). The concept Lorenz introduced in that presentation has since come to be known as the *Lorenz butterfly effect,* and it sums up where we go wrong when we resort to Platonicity and reification. Models and plans inevitably overlook any cause that isn't known. You can study your system all you want, but you can't master every detail. So where do all these ideas leave us in our administrative efforts to think like chess players and look ten or fifteen moves into the future? The answer comes in the second half of the principle articulated earlier: although you can't plan for everything, *you can prepare for anything.* Simply because the future is unknowable and, beyond a certain point, uncontrollable doesn't mean that we should simply be fatalistic and let come what may. We may not be able to determine every possible outcome in the complex systems of our academic programs, but we can identify the most likely ones. And it's precisely here that positive academic leaders depart company from their negative counterparts.

Through systems thinking, effective administrators realize that power doesn't just flow in one direction: down the organizational chart. They understand the fragile ecosystem of the academic department, college, or university and realize that although they may be nominally in charge, power, influence, and causality flow in many different directions at once. (On the nature of the academic department as a complex system, see Beswick, Watson, and De Geest, 2007, 2010; Tinto, 1997; Hackman, 1985; Currie and Galliers, 1999.) For example, you can order a faculty member to sit down and shut up if he or she says something you don't like in a faculty meeting, but you'll burn a lot of administrative capital in doing so. As we saw in chapter 3, command and control does not work as well in client/professional models of interaction as it does elsewhere. The faculty member may be quiet *this* time, but you'll have demonstrated your inability to work effectively in a system of shared governance, mutual respect among professionals, and collegiality. For this reason, our goal shouldn't be to try to dictate what happens within our systems; it should be to improve the systems themselves. Keeping this truth in mind, positive academic leaders devote a great deal of effort to learning as much as possible about the systems in which they work, even though they recognize that they'll never learn everything. Somewhere out there, a butterfly is flapping its wings, and we all know what *that* means.

Exploring Your System

Learning as much as possible about the system in which you work means trying to view everyone in your area both as an individual and as a member of an organic structure. In order to begin this process, let's start exploring your system from three different perspectives:

1. What contribution does each person make to the group?
2. What role does he or she play in the group?
3. What connections does this person tend to have with others?

For the purposes of this exercise, it's best to focus on just one system in which you work, although you may see yourself as a member of many different groups simultaneously. Concentrate, for instance, on only one of the following: a single department, the faculty assembly or senate, your college or division, or (if you work at a very small school or serve as the president or chancellor) the institution as a whole. For each part of exercise 9.1, identify all the people you believe to be best described by the phrases and questions found in that section. You may find that for certain sections, you have three or more names. For others, you may have none at all. If you can't think of anyone who really fits that description, don't try to force the issue. Just leave it blank or write "none," and go on to the next section. Remember to think in terms of an open rather than a closed system. In other words, consider everyone who's a stakeholder: staff members and even long-term student workers, as well as the faculty. In addition, don't forget to include your own name if you find that that part of the exercise applies to you. Wherever the word *system* appears in this exercise, feel free to substitute *department*, *college*, *division*, or any other word that best represents the actual network you have chosen.

Exercise 9.1 Seeing Your Program as a System
Part 1: Contributions

In part 1, consider the way in which each member of your system adds value to your area over and above his or her individual job description.

Contribution	Person(s)
Technology: Whom do people turn to in your system when they have a question about a computer or smart phone? Whom do people tend to ask when they're trying to figure out how to use new software?	_____ _____ _____ _____ _____

Contribution	Person(s)
Precision: Whom do people count on when a document has to be proofread or a column of figures correctly totaled? Who never forgets a deadline?	
Budgeting: Who has the best sense of how academic budgets work? Who could easily serve as the de facto budget manager of the system?	
Vision: Who tends to see not merely what exists right now but what may be possible someday? Whom might you ask about exciting ideas for the future?	
Diplomacy: Whom would you want to represent your system to other units (either inside or outside of the institution)? If you had to nominate a member of the faculty or staff to serve as a liaison from your discipline to the rest of the institution or to an external group, whom would you choose?	

Part 2: Roles

Next, we'll consider how, in addition to the contributions we all make to a group, each of us also adopts one or more parts to play. We may be the departmental whiner, the cheerleader, "dad" or "mom," or any one of numerous others. Once again, you may have several people (or you may have no one) in a given role, and don't forget to include yourself where that's appropriate.

Roles	Person(s)
Who is your system's *parent figure*, the person to whom others go when they have a problem or are feeling down?	
Who is your *party planner*, the person who hosts more social events than anyone else or always seems eager to celebrate some occasion?	
Who is your *caregiver*, the person who keeps track of everyone's birthdays, remembers the names of everyone's spouse and children, or immediately senses when others are dealing with a personal difficulty?	

Roles	Person(s)
Who is your *outsider*, the person who prefers to be a loner or has to be encouraged much more than others to participate in group events?	
Who is your *devil's advocate*, the person who often seems argumentative just for the sake of being argumentative or spots the flaw in every idea?	
Who is your *gerbil*, the person who's always "running on the wheel but getting nowhere," always rushing, always frazzled—but who somehow doesn't accomplish as much as others?	
Who is your system's *defense attorney*, the person who will always stick up for the underdog and wants to make sure that no one's rights are violated?	
Who is the *class clown*, the person who always sees the humor in situations (and may sometimes become even a bit too much of a joker)?	
Who is your *windbag*, the person who always takes too long to say what he or she wants to say and whom other people wish would sometimes contribute a bit less to conversations and meetings?	
Who is your *braggart*, the person who takes more pride in his or her achievements than may be warranted or continually brings the conversation back to himself or herself?	
Who is your *drama monarch*, the person who tends to overreact and make every situation a big deal or crisis? Remember that there are drama kings as well as drama queens.	

Part 3: Networks

Finally, for the last part of this exercise, shift your perspective yet again and consider how all these parts fit together. In each section, list several names that fit into a common group. Again, remember to include yourself where appropriate and to list any staff members or other major constituents that are relevant. Since you're likely to have multiple groups or "cliques" for each section, this part is structured a bit differently:

Who are the pairs of people who tend to get together? Who always goes to lunch with whom? Who is often found talking in someone else's offices? Which pairs of people in your system are probably "friends" with each other on social media?

_____
_____
_____
_____
_____
_____

Who are the groups of three or more who tend to get together, perhaps going to lunch with one another often or talking in one another's offices? Who are probably "friends" on social media?

_____
_____
_____
_____
_____
_____

Who tends to vote or side with whom on most issues?

_____
_____
_____
_____
_____
_____

Who tends to vote against or oppose whom on most issues?

_____
_____
_____
_____
_____
_____

Who tends to be jealous or envious of whom? What rivalries exist?

_____

_____

_____

_____

_____

Who has baggage with whom?

_____

_____

_____

_____

_____

_____

Now that you've looked at your system and its components in these three ways, it's time to draw some conclusions:

1. Are there any members of the system whose contributions or talents don't align well with their official duties? If so, what type of assignment might be more appropriate for them?

2. Are there any members of the system whose contributions or attributes are being underused? If so, how could you make better use of the talents these people have to offer?

3. Are there any negative qualities that are overrepresented in your system? For instance, most units can tolerate at least one braggart, gerbil, or windbag, but having too many people in these roles can be highly destructive. These terms, and perhaps a few others in this exercise, will strike some readers as unnecessarily negative, possibly even offensive; I chose them because they reflect the anger or frustration we may often feel when we encounter individuals playing these roles. As a further venture into positive leadership training, how might you rephrase these terms to make your characterization of these roles less distasteful?

4. What alliances and coalitions currently exist in your system? How could these relationships be better directed to the overall advantage of the system? Are there ways in which these relationships are detrimental or counterproductive? If so, are there strategies you might adopt to improve the situation?

5. What hostilities and competitions currently exist in the system? How could these relationships be better directed to the overall advantage of your area? Are there ways in which these relationships are clearly detrimental? If so, are there strategies you might adopt to improve the situation?

6. What do you now have to keep in mind about your interactions with individual members of the system? In other words, if you do something to one individual's advantage or disadvantage, who else might be affected or concerned?

By viewing your unit in this way, you may more easily understand why processes that should be simple sometimes become overly complex and why people occasionally react strongly to issues that don't seem relevant to them at all. As we saw earlier, we'll never be able to uncover every connection or interrelationship that affects a department or college. But by approaching our work units as systems rather than as collections of discrete individuals, we can be much more effective in building an environment that produces positive and constructive results. Systems thinking affects our hiring decisions, since it makes us aware of how the entrance of a new factor into an existing system is likely to change the chemistry of how people interact. It affects how we approach challenges because as we progress in positive academic leadership, we become much less likely to mistake symptoms for the disease itself. And it allows us to tap in to the networks that are already present rather than imposing a new hierarchical network, usually with ourselves at the top of the pyramid.

Moreover, just as it's important for you to understand how your system operates most effectively, it's important to explain this concept to your other stakeholders as well. Particularly those who are new in the job and have come from another institution may find that the various relationships lying just beneath the surface are something of a mystery, different in so many ways from all the other places they've worked before:

> Too often systems are in people's heads. This is why knowledge as well as experience may leave with a person. People need to know what they are meant to do, what authority they have and how they fit in to the whole picture. They need to know what they will be held accountable for. The process of system documentation in itself may reveal anomalies and errors. A note of caution here is that system documentation is a descriptive process. Be careful it does not become a bureaucratic rulebook limiting discretion. It should contain the flowchart and methods of recording the information flow of the system including control and audit information. (Macdonald, Burke, and Stewart, 2006, p. 221)

Sharing this knowledge certainly helps newcomers to be effective, but it helps you as well. The default understanding others bring to a new environment is usually that the administrator is the boss and that the boss makes all the decisions and instructs everyone else in what to do. Since positive academic leadership is more about building environments than about ruling from a position of power, those who aren't familiar with this approach sometimes interpret it as anarchy or weakness. It's in your own best interests to explain what you're trying to do, why you think it's important, and what benefits you expect to result.

The Catalyst in the System

Since we seem to be surrounded in this chapter by so many metaphors—the academic unit as orchestra, as ecosystem, and as a chessboard—perhaps it won't cloud the landscape too much by adding just one more: the positive academic leader as catalyst. A catalyst is a substance that promotes and intensifies a reaction without itself being consumed. Another way of understanding this concept is that when a catalyst is introduced into a system, it changes the environment in such a way that speeds up an activity, but it doesn't become expended in the process. Contrast, for instance, the difference between putting gas in your car and installing a catalytic converter. In order for the engine to run, the gas has to be consumed. That's why you have to refill the tank so often. But the catalytic converter uses platinum and palladium to change some of the harmful compounds in the car's exhaust—carbon monoxide, nitrogen oxide, and hydrocarbons—into less harmful substances—carbon dioxide, nitrogen, oxygen, and water. Throughout this process, the platinum and palladium aren't affected themselves, so you rarely, if ever, have to replace your catalytic converter.

This distinction clarifies two different ways of approaching higher education systems: some administrators are "fuels," and others are "catalysts." The fuels are often people who take pride in being change agents. They come to their positions with a strong desire "to shake things up" and "get things moving." Since fuels are highly combustible, these administrators generate a lot of heat and—give them their due—cause a great burst of activity to occur almost overnight. But they also consume a large amount of energy, produce significant quantities of "harmful by-products," and often "burn out" very quickly. The "catalysts" are the quiet leaders referred to in that passage of the *Tao Te Ching* earlier in this chapter. They promote change not by explosion, but by fostering subtle improvements in the environment that lead to growth and progress. Since they're not consumed by the process, catalytic leaders tend to last longer and cause less "collateral damage" than do "fuels." Initially, "fuels" may seem a bit flashier than "catalysts" and appear to be having a greater impact, but in the end it's the "catalysts" who create more meaningful and lasting improvements. In other words, catalysts don't view their role in the system as fueling an exciting but explosive process. They see their function as promoting organic change throughout the program. They work collaboratively with the faculty senate, the union, and student government to create an ongoing partnership, not a short-lived nonaggression pact.

The results of these two approaches can be dramatic. For example, a fuelish university president may bring energy to an institution by inciting, provoking, goading, threatening, or stirring up the faculty. A catalytic president works to increase energy by encouraging, empowering, revitalizing, advocating for, and supporting the faculty. You may see results of the first approach very quickly because fear is a powerful motivator. But it's not a sustainable motivator. Eventually the president or the faculty, or both, will burn out, and what appeared to be a blazing burst of activity will be reduced to a burned and depleted husk. Conductors have been known to lead orchestras by threatening or badgering the musicians, and this approach has resulted in some memorable performances. But virtuosos tend not to remain in environments where they feel they're treated with disrespect and filled with anxiety, low morale, or self-doubt. Fear simply can't produce an environment conducive to enduring success. The challenge to positive academic leaders is thus to maintain patience long enough for the benefits of their style to emerge. The challenge to supervisors and governing boards is to maintain trust in the leader long enough to give his or her approach a fair test.

Stakeholders who are familiar only with an authoritarian leadership style may be confused at first by the catalytic approach to academic leadership. It may seem to them as though you're not doing anything at all. But creating an environment in which creativity and excellence flourish is hard work. It can be tempting to intervene in a situation and take care of a problem for someone (what's often called the push style of leadership) when the better course of action is to let that person figure things out on his or her own (the pull style of leadership). The positive academic leader often adopts the approach described by Daniel Levin, whose *Zen Life* (2009) I mentioned earlier: "Teach not with words, but with who you are" (p. 30). In keeping with the principle of *wei wu wei*—action without action—found in verse 3 of the *Tao Te Ching*, positive leaders advise through example rather than rule through decrees. People don't fear them; they want to be like them.

Nurturing the System

Once again you may be thinking that this all looks good on paper, but that's not how higher education really works. Supervisors and governing boards get impatient. Administrators are under intense pressures to produce results now. We don't have the luxury of waiting five or ten years for things to change when academic environments have become highly politicized, faculty and staff dissatisfaction is high because salaries are low, public resistance to higher education funding is increasing because many people believe that university salaries are too high, and turnover of faculty and administrators is constant.

Those are all valid concerns, but positive academic leaders answer these objections in several ways. First, they recognize that patience is something that has to be taught. They don't expect people to understand immediately why long-term solutions are preferable to short-term fixes or why the advantages of positive academic leadership are worth the wait. Communicating what they're doing and why is thus one of their highest priorities. Constructive change doesn't happen overnight, and positive academic leaders have to keep reminding others (and themselves) that it'll be several years before a noticeable improvement in any system will occur.

Second, they resist the urge to lapse back into top-down, authority-driven solutions even when the pressure to do so is great. If, for example, two faculty members have had a long history of friction between them, positive academic leaders know that it does little good to address the symptom and ignore the disease. Instructing them both to "knock it off" causes the problem to become less visible for a while but doesn't make it go away. However, by taking a systems approach, positive academic leaders realize that no one sustains a hostile relationship over a long period without becoming invested in it. As much as someone might say, "I hate how much this atmosphere of tension and suspicion affects my work every day," the conflict would've ended long ago if he or she weren't getting something from it. One faculty member or the other would've said at some point, "This is stupid. I'm not going to play this game anymore," and the problem would've faded. But many participants in long-term quarrels begin to define their identities from them. They think of themselves as the person who "won't let so-and-so get away with that anymore" or who "actually *cares* about academic standards, not like so-and-so." In situations like that, you can't nurture the system merely by quashing the product of the conflict when you don't understand the origin of the conflict. Remember that everyone in your system has a role to play. "Angry

Guy" and "the person who hates X" are roles no less than are the parent figure, caregiver, class clown, and all the others we discussed earlier. If you help both participants find new roles to play, gradually the entire system will change.

Third, the positive academic leader understands that he or she is part of the system as well. Truly effective leaders reexamine their own roles by asking from time to time, "What is it that I may be doing that's causing others to act in this way?" We sometimes discover that we're doing something, perhaps unconsciously, that sends a signal indicating to those around us that it's okay to act out, be obstructionist, or fail to do their part. When we catch ourselves behaving in this manner, we can begin to look for ways that make it easier for people to interact positively rather than negatively. Three good questions to ask ourselves periodically are

1. What can I do to make the faculty's job less stressful?
2. What can I do to make the staff's job less stressful?
3. What can I do to make my supervisor's job less stressful?

And remember that all of these activities take place in an open system, so there'll be other stakeholders in addition to your faculty, staff, and supervisor for whom it'll be necessary to ask these questions. It's a reversal in thinking from how negative, "fuelish" leaders view their roles. To paraphrase John F. Kennedy, positive leaders don't ask what others can do for them; they ask what they can do for others. And that very shift in perspective begins to transform the entire system.

Finally, positive academic leaders help their systems thrive because they surrender the notion that they themselves are the linchpin that holds everything together. They distribute credit, responsibility, and authority broadly, encouraging each member of the system to take on leadership responsibilities in his or her own way. Doing so is not a mere matter of generosity; it also helps to get things done more quickly. People never vote against the ideas they generate themselves. When the role of the administrator ceases to be that of selling an idea or vision, and instead is that of creating a fertile environment for ideas to flourish, better ideas result. In a way that flows directly from the principles of the *Tao Te Ching*, the best administrators lead without leading, guide without guiding, rule without ruling, and judge without being judgmental. They trust those around them, a practice that inspires others to trust them in return. Seeing leadership as a type of conducting, they understand that an orchestra's harmony can be destroyed when the voice of the conductor intrudes on the music being performed. In a similar way, at a college or university, harmony is diminished by administrators who insist on being soloists when what they really should be doing is evoking great performances from others.

Conclusion

In the same TED Talk we considered at the beginning of this chapter, Benjamin Zander discusses how excellent conductors know whether their efforts have been successful:

> You know how you find out? You look at their eyes. If their eyes are shining, you know you're doing it . . . If the eyes are not shining, you get to ask a question. And this is the question: "Who am I being that my players' eyes are not shining?" . . . And I say, it's appropriate for us to ask the question [in our everyday lives]: "Who are we being as we go back out into the world?"

On days when morale is low, the entire faculty is upset, and an endless series of disgruntled parents are sending you angry e-mails, if you think of your role as that of a conductor, you won't ask, "What's wrong with these people?" Instead, you'll pull back, take a look at your entire system, and ask, "Who am I being that their eyes are not shining?"

References

Beswick, K., Watson, A., & De Geest, E. (2007). Describing mathematics departments: The strengths and limitations of complexity theory and activity theory. *Mathematics: Essential Research, Essential Practice, 1*, 113–122.

Beswick, K., Watson, A., & De Geest, E. (2010). Comparing theoretical perspectives in describing mathematics departments: Complexity and activity. *Educational Studies in Mathematics, 75*, 153–170.

Currie, W., & Galliers, R. (1999). *Rethinking management information systems: An interdisciplinary perspective.* New York, NY: Oxford University Press.

Hackman, J. D. (1985). Power and centrality in the allocation of resources in colleges and universities. *Administrative Science Quarterly, 30*(1), 61–77.

LaoTzu & Le Guin, U. (Trans.). (1997). *Tao te ching.* Boston, MA: Shambhala.

Levin, D. (2009). *Zen life: An open-at-random book of guidance.* Pittsburgh, PA: St. Lynns Press.

Lorenz, E. N. (1993). *The essence of chaos*. Seattle, WA: University of Washington Press.

Macdonald, I., Burke, C. G., & Stewart, K. (2006). *Systems leadership: Creating positive organizations*. Aldershot, England: Gower.

Taleb, N. (2010). *The black swan: The impact of the highly improbable*. New York, NY: Random House Trade Paperbacks.

Tinto, V. (1997). Classrooms as communities: Exploring the educational character of student persistence. *Journal of Higher Education, 68*, 599–623.

Zander, B. (2009). *Classical music with shining eyes*. Retrieved February 24, 2009, from www.ted.com/index.php/talks/benjamin_zander_on_music _and_passion.html

PART FOUR

POSITIVE APPROACHES FOR HIGHER EDUCATION AS A WHOLE

CHAPTER 10

POSITIVE ADMINISTRATION
THROUGHOUT THE INSTITUTION

Using positive academic leadership to improve a single department or program can be difficult enough. But trying to alter the culture of an entire institution adds a new level of complexity. Of course, if you're a president or chancellor, the initial stages of this process could be relatively easy: you could make positive academic leadership the topic of a retreat for deans, directors, and department chairs; hire a consultant to train them in this new approach to leadership; and then maintain a focus on these strategies by referring to them repeatedly in your public speeches and campus updates. Even if you're a provost, this type of leadership from above may be effective for introducing positive strategies in your division. But if you're a dean, department chair, or full-time faculty member, it can be much more difficult to spread positive academic leadership outside your own area. In this chapter, we explore several methods for achieving this goal, focusing on four primary strategies:

o Leading upward
o Centrifugal leadership
o Lateral leadership
o Environmental or essential leadership

Leading Upward

We saw in chapter 3 that the image most people have of organizational leadership falls into the traditional pyramid structure of authority, a form that's essentially regal or feudal in nature. It's the type of leadership we're all familiar with from the Old Kingdom in Egypt, the early empire in Rome, the Nara period of Japan, France under Louis XIV, and most monarchies throughout history. As P. G. Herbst (1976) suggests, "The basic assumption which generates bureaucratic hierarchical structures is that each member is restricted to a single specialized task. As a result, a single structure of hierarchical linking relationships is established within which the functioning of each level is controlled by the next higher level" (p. 66).

In the Japanese feudal system, for instance, the emperor, shogun, samurai, farmers, and merchants all have their assigned tasks, with relatively little overlap in terms of their responsibilities. Each level is its own clearly identified unit, with power and authority always flowing from the top to the bottom. And yet within the single large pyramid that is the organization as a whole are smaller pyramids. In traditional European feudalism, nobles may report to the king, but each noble is also at the head of a hierarchy that includes many knights, and the knights would have been viewed as ruling over peasants and serfs. On paper, at least, not much has changed. If you look at the organizational charts of most colleges and universities, this regal or feudal leadership structure still exists. No matter whether we call it a leadership pyramid, chain of command, hierarchy, pecking order, or food chain, the person in charge still stands at the top of the structure with his or her influence radiating to the various bureaucratic levels underneath. But it doesn't have to be that way. At least, it doesn't have to be that way for you. In addition to leading those who report to you, you can also lead upward.

The expression *leading up* is probably most familiar through the work of Michael Useem (2003), the director of the Center for Leadership and Change Management in the University of Pennsylvania's Wharton School of Business. Although Useem's focus is primarily on corporate and military structures, his concept certainly has relevance to higher education. All of us who are interested in positive academic leadership have a responsibility to consider how our decisions affect those to whom we report. And just to be clear, leading upward does not mean controlling, managing, or manipulating your boss. It's about viewing your role holistically, seeing your institution as the type of integrated system we explored in chapter 9, and becoming more effective as a leader.

It may be easiest to understand the concept in this way. You probably view various aspects of your program quite differently from those who report to you. Faculty members may see very small classes as the best possible academic environment in which to teach and learn, an opportunity to engage each student more directly in one-on-one activities, and a healthy improvement to your school's overall student-to-faculty ratio. To you, that same situation may look more like a threat to your program's productivity, financial sustainability, and future growth. In much the same way, your supervisor has a view of your program that's not likely to be identical to your own. But you'll need to know and understand what that view is in order to communicate with your supervisor effectively. In this way, department chairs need to consider how decisions look from a dean's perspective, deans need to keep in mind the impact of various choices from the provost's perspective, and so on. Leading upward is essential whenever you want to embark on a new initiative. It helps you forecast what questions you're likely to be asked and what objections those above you in the hierarchy might raise.

For instance, suppose your supervisor believes that the path to success is to be found through increased enrollment and larger grant proposals. That goal now has to become your goal too as you think strategically about your program. If you're embarking on a course that involves absolutely no progress toward achieving your boss's objectives, you're unlikely to receive the sort of support you'll need to make your own initiatives effective. Even worse, if your plans contradict or hinder those of your supervisor, you may well encounter so much friction that even more minor tasks become difficult for you. The alternative is to begin leading upward by asking questions like these:

1. What does my supervisor need from me?
2. What does my supervisor want from me?
3. What do I need from my supervisor?
4. What do I want from my supervisor?

You'll recall similar questions from chapter 2. There as here, I've separated needs and desires; although these two usually go together, sometimes they necessarily diverge. And if you're mindful of only one of these, you won't lead your area as effectively as you could.

In addition, leading upward includes the recognition that your boss has a boss too. Even if you report directly to the chancellor of a large system, he or she probably answers to the chair of a governing board or perhaps the state legislature. Issues frequently look different from that level as well. For this reason, I have added two more questions to the list of what we need to know in order to lead upward effectively:

5. What does my supervisor's supervisor need?
6. What does my supervisor's supervisor want?

The goal, as we try to spread positive academic leadership throughout the institution, is to avoid losing sight of these six important questions as we work. The optimal situation, of course, is to discover some area where the answers to all six questions happen to overlap. That utopian sweet spot may be extremely difficult to identify, but it's not just a myth. Finding an area where what you want is the same as what your supervisors want is sometimes merely a matter of slightly changing your language, the same strategy set out in chapter 4.

In higher education, we're used to these slight adjustments of language whenever we apply for sponsored research. For example, suppose we have a project for which we want external support. The agency to which we apply for funding undoubtedly has its own priorities that are outlined in the request for proposals or their bylaws. Our goal in writing the proposal then becomes finding possible connections between our needs and the agency's interests and then adopting the agency's vocabulary to describe our own goals. In other words, we try to view our project through the lens of the funder's priorities and values.

Leading upward uses this same approach but applies it to our supervisors and other stakeholders. If your needs and desires happen to be exactly the same as those of your supervisor and his or her boss, that's terrific; it's likely you'll be able to count on their institutional backing as you proceed. But if the similarities between your plans and theirs are not immediately obvious, your task becomes discovering ways in which you can relate your goals to their agendas. You'll need to find a way for them to understand that supporting your objective will help them achieve what they regard as important. Consider the question you must ask in this way: What does my supervisor (and his or her own supervisor) need to know in order to say yes to my request? If you can identify that, you can phrase your proposal in terms of this person's priorities, increasing the likelihood that he or she will agree with your plans.

Centrifugal Leadership

Centrifugal leadership takes the concept of leading upward one step further by combining it with Don Chu's notion that higher education functions as an open system, which we discussed in chapter 3. We can visualize centrifugal leadership as something like the diagram that appears in figure 10.1. In other words, the leader views himself or herself as standing not above or below other stakeholders in a hierarchy, but in the center of a complex network of relationships. With centrifugal leadership, the terms *superior* and *subordinate* have a diminished meaning.

Certainly there will be those in the organization who will evaluate others, and there will be those who will be called on to make final decisions. But aside from situations where a chain of command is absolutely essential, centrifugal leadership considers all members of an organization as on roughly the same footing. It's a particularly good approach to use in client/professional models of interaction where each member of the institution has specialized knowledge (and, in the case of higher education, advanced degrees). In this way, centrifugal leadership bears a number of similarities to Daniel Wheeler's concept of servant leadership in higher education, which we explored in chapter 2. Like servant leadership, centrifugal leadership views the leader's role not as dictating from above, but as nurturing and empowering from within.

Notice in figure 10.1 that all the arrows are moving outward. This type of leadership by definition is not focused on the individual who happens to hold a title. It involves energy and attention moving outward from the leader, not reverence, obedience, and subservience moving inward toward the leader. (We might term the latter situation *centripetal leadership,* and it's something that the positive academic leader scrupulously avoids.)

Centrifugal leadership builds on the question we encountered at the end of the previous chapter: What can I do to make each of my stakeholder's jobs less stressful? Or to ask this question in another way, What does this stakeholder need from me, and how can I best provide it? That's a very different question from what we would find in a rigid hierarchy (even when we're leading upward)—"What do my subordinates owe me?" and "What do I owe my supervisor?"—and it results in a very different type of administrative approach.

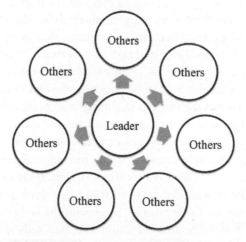

FIGURE 10.1 Centrifugal Leadership

Centrifugal leadership is a bit like throwing pebbles into a pond. The ripples radiate out from the spot where the pebble strikes the water, with each ripple becoming much larger than the pebble itself. In a similar way, bringing positive leadership into your open system offers the opportunity to influence others well beyond the environment of your department or college. But as with so many other approaches we've considered, centrifugal leadership doesn't mean that you're going to change anyone's behavior overnight. As people see the effect that you have on others over time, the improvement in performance and morale that's occurring within your unit, and their own ease in working with you, they'll want to adopt some of the practices that have been effective in your own administration. They may even begin modeling your strategies unconsciously, thus influencing those who aren't even aware of your influence. And it all begins by rethinking your relationship with the staff, students, and faculty members you interact with daily. Your goal becomes not to do something "to" those who report to you, even if that something is as positive as inspiring and motivating them. Rather, centrifugal leadership defines your role as engaging with people at any level of the institution. Once leaders stop seeing others as problems to be managed and begin seeing them as partners in their progress, their true progress in leadership can begin.

Lateral Leadership

A similar philosophy lies behind what is sometimes known as lateral leadership. You can think of lateral leadership as the polar opposite of the management philosophy summarized by the words "stay in your own lane." Lateral leadership suggests that everyone is responsible, at least at some level, for everything that happens throughout the entire organization. When lateral leaders encounter a problem, they never think, "That's not my job," or, "Someone else will take care of that." They're proactive in making sure that everything runs as smoothly as possible, even if the situation is in an area where they have no direct responsibility or authority. But lateral leadership is not the same as meddling: it respects existing structures and policies and doesn't seek to circumvent them. Nevertheless, in higher education, lateral leadership recognizes that colleges and universities are complex institutions where everyone has to be responsible for many activities that don't fall within their own job description. If creative leaders have long been associated with the now-worn phrase "think outside the box," then lateral leaders are those who try to expand the box itself.

Contrast the following two situations. A man tells a group of children in his neighborhood to ignore what their own fathers have told them because he's the best parent in town. In a different neighborhood, a woman asks the Department of Children and Families to look into what's going on at a house where she's seen a group of children who seem to be ill fed, physically abused, and neglected. The man was meddling; the woman was practicing responsible citizenship. The difference is as sharp as that between taking the law into your own hands and the principle of "if you see something, say something." Along similar lines, lateral leadership is a way of bringing responsible citizenship into an academic setting. No one would argue that it's appropriate for one administrator to countermand the instructions or policies of another. But by the same token, it's also never appropriate to let a student lose his or her scholarship because of a small oversight that someone from a different unit can easily fix. Admittedly, knowing when to intervene laterally often becomes a judgment call, but true academic leadership requires frequent judgment calls. We can think of lateral leadership as a useful corrective to a common attitude found throughout academia: "It's not my program, so I don't care." That attitudes builds silos; lateral leadership builds bridges.

Authors such as Fisher, Sharp, and Richardson (2004), Sit and Bundgaard (2009), and Galbraith and Lawler (1993) describe lateral leadership as making a positive difference in situations where you're not technically in charge. As part of a positive administrative approach, lateral leadership can be integrated into your personal administrative philosophy and provide guidance in solving problems or taking advantage of opportunities. It can also go further by helping us think of new ways of structuring an organization so that a culture of positive leadership develops. Roland Deiser (2011) describes how this approach works in the corporate world:

> Creative organizational design is the new strategic weapon. Hierarchical control, functional silos, and an obsession with formalization are obsolete in our connected, fast-changing world. To master the strategic innovation challenge, companies need a culture of agility and learning that supports high performance and reinvention. They need: enabling structures, mechanisms, processes, and policies that encourage and support creative dialogue and experimentation; principles that help to address disruptions and discontinuities with creativity, courage, and intuition, just in time, with a minimum of red tape, across boundaries; and highly efficient processes. (p. 18)

Exercise 10.1 is a thought experiment for judging how comfortable we feel with the principle of lateral leadership when it comes to our own work.

Exercise 10.1 The Principle of Lateral Leadership

Identify two or three peers at your institution, preferably people who hold the same title as you. For example, if you're a dean, think of the deans of other colleges or schools. If you're a chair, think of other chairs both within and outside your own college or division. (If you're a chief executive officer, this exercise will be more difficult to perform, but try to imagine a situation similar to the one described that would involve presidents of peer institutions.)

Assume that each of the following situations occurs in someone else's area of authority. Then consider whether your most likely response:

a. I would intervene immediately without consulting the person in charge of that program.

b. I would inform the appropriate person and let him or her deal with it.

c. I would do nothing since the issue is really none of my business.

The Situations

_____ 1.   A safety issue poses an imminent danger in a building. Although you're not responsible for that building, you do have the knowledge and experience necessary to solve the problem.

_____ 2.   A student received poor information from an advisor and has enrolled in a course she doesn't need.

_____ 3.   Three faculty members who don't report to you are engaging in a heated political argument in the hallway as students and other professors pass by.

_____ 4.   You discover that a public space is littered and unsightly.

_____ 5.   Someone has placed artificially low enrollment caps on courses that your students need for their major. Although these courses are the other administrator's responsibility, you discover that your institution's new computer system allows you to raise those caps yourself.

If you answered c for any of these situations, you would benefit from being more proactive in your lateral leadership. Question 1 is a situation that truly begs for immediate intervention; even delaying long enough to inform the person in charge could cause an injury (or worse) that you could easily have avoided. Question 5 is a situation that almost certainly crosses the line into meddling if you change the enrollment caps yourself; it's a good illustration of the principle, "Just because you can do something, it doesn't always mean you should do something." Talk this problem out with the person in charge of those courses.

The other three situations are all judgment calls. It's probably best to intervene in these three cases, but there are likely to be factors you don't know. The advisor may have had a reason for placing the student in that course. Many people would say that universities, even university hallways, are the very place for spirited political debate to occur and that students should be exposed to this type of discussion. And although the public space is unsightly, we weren't told that it was dangerous, and some colleagues may be offended that rather than mentioning the problem to them, you took it on yourself to clean up their area. For the middle three situations, therefore, your answers may tell you a great deal about your own comfort level with lateral leadership. If you were ready to intervene in each case, you're not unduly intimidated by organizational structures. What you'll need to think about, however, is the possible reactions of those whose boundaries you would have overstepped.

Now see if you can think of other situations that would cause you to intervene immediately, report the problem to the appropriate person, or do nothing since the situation doesn't concern you. What do you learn about your administrative approach from where you draw these lines?

In the academic world, what this idea means is that our traditional vertical divisions (president, vice president, dean, chair, faculty), as well as our traditional horizontal divisions (arts and letters, science, business, education, engineering, medicine, and so on), often hinder us by ignoring the reality of what we do. But those structures are no longer universal throughout higher education. For example, research teams that result from strategic or cluster hiring span disciplinary boundaries. No single college or department can "own" a field like neuroscience, poverty studies, medical ethics, or sustainable urban development (Buller, 2011). In a similar way, cross-functional teams that are organized on the basis of the issue addressed, not the title held, produce better-informed and more realistic decisions. So if the academic calendar were set only by a council of vice presidents or academic deans, it's likely that the needs of certain stakeholders would be overlooked. A cross-functional team of representatives from academic affairs, student affairs, athletics, the alumni office, financial affairs, research, and facilities is likely to produce a better schedule because it can see the impact of each decision from many different perspectives. (For an excellent illustration of lateral leadership in action, see Martin, 2001.)

Environmental or Essential Leadership

The fourth strategy we'll consider is referred to as environmental leadership. This approach to leadership is environmental because it was developed by organizations dedicated to promoting ecological sustainability, the wise use of natural resources, and stewardship of the earth's ecosystems. But it's also environmental in the sense that it builds on many aspects of systems theory we considered in chapter 10: it treats every association, corporation, or institution as a unique and complex organism that must be understood on its own terms or as part of its own environment. In this way, environmental leadership avoids simplistic solutions in favor of more holistic approaches. For example, John Gordon and Joyce Berry (2006) describe the challenges often faced by environmental leaders as requiring

> long times to solutions, complex interactions of components and people, a weak and scattered science base, a need for integration across disciplines to understand or solve them, and an atmosphere that is emotion-charged and contentious. When all of these five characteristics are taken together they imply a sixth: the likelihood of surprises and unintended consequences born of uncertainty. (p. 2)

Sound familiar? Gordon and Berry could be speaking about the issues that administrators in any college, university, or university system face. In fact, as a way of indicating that their ideas have broader applications than in the area of ecology, they suggested renaming their whole philosophy *essential leadership*. Gordon and Berry describe environmental or essential leaders as people who have the capacity to understand how complex systems work, can make trade-offs where compromise is appropriate, and have the capacity to keep moving forward in uncertain terrain:

> All complex problems involve tradeoffs among the values of those who have the problem and those who seek its solution . . . Essential leaders are good at confronting this sort of complexity and at

dealing with uncertainty. Henry Webster (1993, 105) described environmental leaders as absorbers of uncertainty who lead in complex situations through "thinking and cooperation." Ethics, a secure and clear knowledge of right and wrong and how to apply it, are a major and tricky component of leadership under uncertainty. Essential leaders have to be exceptionally sensitive to the values of all those with a stake in their decisions and actions. At the same time, they have to be exceptionally good at separating their own personal values from those of their clients and those for whom their solutions have major effects. (Gordon and Berry, 2006, p. 3, with reference to Webster, 1993)

From this description, we can identify three major strengths of environmental or essential leaders:

1. They understand the complexity of the system in which they work.
2. They can compromise without being compromised.
3. They work successfully even in highly ambiguous situations.

Let's examine each of these three assets in turn.

Understanding the System

We saw in chapter 9 how important it is for academic leaders to use a systems approach when dealing with issues in their department, college, or institution. But Gordon and Berry (2006) also note that leaders must be attentive to the values shared by members of a system and, we might add, the values shared by the various subgroups within that system. In chapter 6, we saw how important it was to identify our own core values. This can be challenging since we need to distinguish between the values we really have and those we feel we should have. But how do you even begin to identify the principles that motivate all the different people, groups, and subgroups in your system? You certainly can't read their minds or peer into their hearts, and people aren't always candid about telling you exactly what they believe. For a variety of reasons, they may tell you what they think you want to hear, keeping their true convictions and principles locked deep inside them.

There is, of course, no foolproof method of seeing through the facades we all encounter, but one way in which you can avoid proceeding blindly is to build on the "need" and "want" questions we considered earlier. In other words, ask yourself what it is that different people and groups need and want from you, and then use those answers to help identify the values that shaped them. Suppose you're a dean in a college of seven departments with 100 faculty members, 25 staff members, and approximately 4,800 students each semester. It's obvious that although it's possible to know the 125 people who are on the payroll in your college (at least, it's possible to know their names), it's highly unlikely that you'll know them all well enough to have insight into each person's core values. It may even be impossible for you to understand that much about all 7 of your department chairs, and no one could possibly do so for all 4,800 students. Rather than attempting a clearly impossible task, think instead about the various needs and desires likely to occur among each group of stakeholders.

One convenient place to begin is with Maslow's hierarchy of needs since that concept is familiar to almost everyone in higher education today. In 1943, the psychologist Abraham Maslow (1908–1970) proposed in *A Theory of Human Motivation* that people have five levels of needs, ranging from the most basic to the most advanced (figure 10.2). The most fundamental needs are physiological or survival needs: food, liquid, shelter, and so on. In our hypothetical college, we can think of these as the basic needs each group of stakeholders has in order to achieve its goals. As this unit's dean, you would ask yourself whether you've done everything you can to provide your forty-eight hundred students with the proper environment in which to learn, your one hundred faculty members with the essential tools they need for their teaching, research, and service; your seven department chairs with sufficient resources to help their disciplines flourish; and your twenty-five staff members with the equipment, supplies, and information they require to do their jobs. Notice that at this point, we're still talking just about needs, not desires. No university in the world has enough resources to provide everyone with everything he or

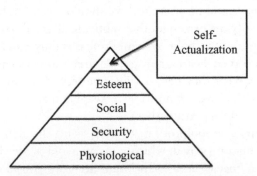

FIGURE 10.2 Maslow's Hierarchy of Needs
Source: Maslow (1943).

she wants, but positive academic leaders have an obligation to advocate for what those around them need.

As we proceed up Maslow's pyramid, we can ask similar questions about the other four categories. In terms of security, what steps have we taken to increase the likelihood that all our stakeholders will be safe, not just physically but also in terms of freedom from harassment, verbal abuse, unnecessary embarrassment, or preventable inconvenience? On the level of social needs, what do our stakeholders need in order to feel truly valued as part of our community and to be aware that they're making important contributions? In the area of esteem, what efforts have we taken to make more of our stakeholders feel that they're respected as individuals and that even when we disagree with them, we've listened to and considered their ideas, opinions, and perspectives? Finally, in terms of self-actualization, what do our stakeholders need in order to reach their full potential? How can we create an environment in which they can use their energy, creativity, and experience to the utmost? As you reflect on these questions, remember that your stakeholders are both individuals and members of a large, complex system. What Dr. Smith needs as a person may not be the same as what she needs as a member of the department, college, or university. At the same time, your stakeholders also function as members of various subsystems, such as the cliques, alliances, and competitions we identified in the previous chapter. Each of these subsystems has its own identifiable needs, and we don't really understand the entire system until we consider how all these needs complement, compete with, and reinforce one another.

Compromising Without Being Compromised

Everyone today seems to have a love-hate relationship with the word *compromise*. In situations where we have nothing vital at stake, we love to see progress being made through negotiation and mutual concessions. "Politics is the art of compromise," we're fond of saying, demonstrating little tolerance when legislators stall progress by stubbornly refusing to come to an agreement. And yet when we're heavily invested in an issue, we look with disdain on all those "compromisers" and describe something that's been reduced in quality as having been "compromised." On one side of the spectrum, we see desirable give-and-take; on the other side, we see only spineless capitulation. Yet between those two extremes exists a large domain where higher education administrators spend most of their time. As positive academic leaders, we know we can't get everything we want for the programs we serve, and we certainly want other disciplines and institutions to prosper as well. But we also feel that if we give up too much too often, we fail in our role as effective advocates for our areas. So if environmental or essential leadership consists of dealing appropriately with situations that "involve trade-offs," how can we ensure that most of them resemble what we'd regard as wholesome compromise and resist what we'd consider wholesale surrender?

It's in answering this question that we see why positive academic leaders place such an emphasis on identifying their core values. Remember that core values are those principles for which there can be no retreat or misunderstanding. If you make concessions in these areas, you'll feel that you've betrayed yourself as both an administrator and a person. So we can compromise when we're dealing with goals or principles that we support but would never go to the wall for. When it comes to our core principles, we become much more entrenched. That's why principled leadership sometimes places us in difficult situations. If we find that our core values and goals differ significantly from those of our supervisors, we have to ask ourselves whether these principles are really ones we support heart and soul or whether they're nice to believe in, but when the real test comes, they're of only secondary importance. When we candidly decide that the issue is one where we can compromise, we should feel free to mold our objectives to those of our supervisors (even as we continue trying to persuade them that our own ideas are really better). But if we discover that we're dealing with an issue about which yielding at all would make us feel that we've been compromised, it's clear we now have a serious choice to make. If we believe we can still function effectively in a system that's moving in a direction away from what we stand for as a leader or as a person, then we still have a valuable contribution to make. But if we don't believe we have valuable contributions to make, it's doubtful we can honorably continue in our positions.

Let's suppose, for example, that you have identified the following three values as fundamental to who you are as an academic leader:

o A college education should not be mere job training. Rather it should broaden and enhance every aspect of a student's life.

o Colleges and universities exist to provide as many people as possible with access to educational opportunities. They shouldn't be just an entitlement of the privileged and affluent.

o While all of a university's functions are important, its instructional mission, particularly at the undergraduate level, has to be given priority over research and service.

With those values in mind, imagine that you're working for a new supervisor who wants to improve the university's research profile through rapid expansion of the school's graduate program. That objective may not precisely fit the values you regard as most important, but it doesn't necessarily contradict them either. You can still design your own programs so that they develop students in the broadest possible sense, provide access to students who may not otherwise have those opportunities, and use the institution's new research emphasis as a way of advancing your area's pedagogical mission. Compromise is possible, and it can be achieved in a way that allows you to be true to both your supervisor and yourself.

But if your supervisor then proceeds to demand that each program pare down its curriculum so as to eliminate any course not directly related to a student's employability, balances the budget through massive tuition increases accompanied by reductions in scholarships, and shifts resources from undergraduate instruction (where nearly all courses must now be taught in large auditoriums) to faculty-led research (which is now evaluated solely in terms of the revenue it generates from grants), you're in a completely different situation. If you yield on these principles, you're violating the very ideals you hoped to protect as an academic leader. In the end, you'll feel that you've given up too much, and you'll be likely to convey an attitude of defeatism and submission as a result. In this case, you're no longer compromising; you're capitulating. And that's diametrically opposed to positive academic leadership.

Leading in the Midst of Uncertainty

Some people are more comfortable with ambiguity than others. They don't need to know the game plan every single moment and are content to move forward even though many issues remain unresolved. These individuals stand in stark contrast to those who need to know absolutely everything that's going on in their areas, have a clear strategy in mind for dealing with every possible contingency, and become nervous when they're unsure about their ultimate destination. If you find yourself falling into this latter category, keep the following observation firmly in mind: as higher education administrators, we're always leading in the midst of uncertainty. Some of us just don't know that yet.

Remember everything I said in chapter 1 about the differences between planning and preparation. As we've seen repeatedly, if you think you can anticipate every eventuality, control everything in your area of responsibility, and create a model that accounts for each possible variable, you're fooling yourself. We can't always predict when budget crises will occur, new academic fields will emerge, game-changing technology will become available, or natural disasters will befall us. Despite all our careful planning, we may get new supervisors who pursue agendas that are different from or even in direct opposition to those of their predecessors. As much as we adhere to the principles of positive academic leadership, we still can't live our lives entirely free from uncertainty. What's more, we wouldn't really want to. *Uncertainty means possibility.* Uncertainty prevents us from doing things the same way we've always done them. It encourages us to explore new options and take advantage of new opportunities. As bad as a major budget cut can be, we can't deny that it gives us the leverage to reconsider our priorities and, by doing so, keep our programs from becoming stale.

People who find ambiguity threatening often say that uncertainty is the biggest cause of their stress. The word *stress* has become so much a part of our daily conversations that we sometimes lose track of its origins. For many years, the term *stress* was used in fields like engineering to describe force when it's applied to a particular area of some material. During the first half of the twentieth century, however, psychologists and biologists began to borrow this word because they needed a convenient way to refer to the tension, anxiety, and strain that human beings (as well as other organisms) experience.

In higher education administration, when we speak of stress, we're usually talking about the negative effects that can arise from our professional responsibilities: anxiety, increased blood pressure, panic, burnout, exhaustion, and the like. In this sense, *stress* is indistinguishable from *distress* because it appears to convey very little benefit and impose a great deal of harm. But that there are also times when we intentionally seek out greater stress because we find it pleasurable, even exciting. Consider, for example, why we might engage in the following activities:

o Watching a horror movie or crime thriller

o Riding a roller coaster

o Telling ghost stories around a campfire

o Bungee jumping or skydiving

o Whitewater rafting

o Extreme sports, such as those featured in the X Games or Ironman Competition

All of these examples involve experiences that people willingly undergo—sometimes waiting in long lines at a theater or amusement park to do so—even though they cause many of the same feelings of fear, tension, and apprehension that result from distress. The difference is that in these situations, we know we're still (reasonably) safe even in the midst of our anxiety. We derive pleasure from the release of additional endorphins and serotonin in our systems. And so we're willing to devote money and time to activities that to other people may seem much more anxiety producing than confrontations with angry parents or grievances filed by a faculty member. As a way of distinguishing this positive, pleasurable type of stress from distress, the endocrinologist Hans Selye (1907–1982) coined the term *eustress* (see Selye, 1956, 1974). Eustress is the "upside of stress," the type of uncertainty that allows us to distinguish thrilling and exciting experiences from nerve-wracking, anxiety-producing ones.

The goal of environmental or essential leadership is thus to transform the stress or distress that arises from our ongoing sense of anxiety into eustress. To a large degree, this goal can be achieved simply by altering our perspective, using the techniques that we explored in chapter 5. By choosing to see ambiguity not as threatening but as exhilarating due to the endless possibilities it presents, we approach matters differently and our apprehension begins to decline as a result. But many other positive leadership strategies that we encountered in this book can also help us replace our stress with eustress. We can start catching ourselves when we're imagining only worst-case scenarios and encourage ourselves to identify more desirable outcomes. The task then becomes to ask not, "What will I do if this disaster occurs?" but, "What can I do in order to make this attractive goal a reality?" In addition, we can review what we learned about administrative resilience in chapter 3, keeping in mind that our departments and colleges are valued not because they thrive in good times but because they can maintain their core functions even in the worst of times. After all, our departments, colleges, and universities are systems. One of the great things about systems is that they're adaptable. If any single member of a resilient system is harmed or eliminated, the other parts reconfigure to make the entire network sound again. In short, resilient systems heal, and so can your academic unit. That thought alone should be enough to help reduce your stress during particularly trying times.

Transforming Upward, Centrifugal, Lateral, Environmental, and Essential Leadership into Positive Academic Leadership

It's apparent that the four institution-wide leadership strategies we've been considering in this chapter have a great deal in common with positive academic leadership. Like leading upward, positive academic leadership recognizes that how you see things depends on your position in an organization or, to put it another way, "where you stand is where you sit." (That last phrase, by the way, is the title of an excellent 2006 book on higher education administration by Bob Smith, the provost at Texas Tech University, a fine example of a positive academic leader. He signs his open letter to his academic community, http://www.depts.ttu.edu /provost/bio/, "Kindly, Bob." How many provosts do *you* know who close their letters with "Kindly"?)

Leading upward involves identifying the needs and desires of others and finding where they share points of commonality with your own. Like centrifugal leadership, positive leadership involves approaching your unit as an open system and avoiding strict hierarchical, chain-of-command reporting structures. It means that although you'll be proactive in keeping people in the loop about issues that affect them, you won't refuse to meet with someone simply because "presidents work only through vice presidents, deans work only through chairs," and so on. You'll empower everyone in your area, giving them sufficient authority to improve their programs. Your door will be open to everyone, no matter where their names happen to appear on the organizational chart.

Like lateral leadership, positive leadership means that administrators never hesitate to intervene where it's appropriate just because "that's not my job." Instead they see themselves as invested in the success of every part of an institution. As a way of making operations more effective, they'll replace existing structures with cross-functional teams, and they'll bring creativity and innovation to the new policies and committees they develop.

Finally, like environmental or essential leadership, positive leadership is committed to a systems approach, based on the belief that colleges and departments are networks of relationships, not mere collections of individuals. Positive academic leaders see themselves as advocates for the needs of everyone who works in their area—and, at times, due to their lateral leadership style—to everyone who works at the institution. They adhere to their core principles, but otherwise they make compromises where a healthy amount of give and take is possible. If all of these choices lead to greater uncertainty, then positive academic leaders embrace uncertainty as a necessary prerequisite for exciting opportunities; they don't avoid it as something to be feared and eliminated.

In short, when working with other levels of their institution, positive academic leaders regard problems as resulting from processes, not people, and attribute the actions of others to their own values about what's right and good, not to malice, corruption, or a conscious intent to cause harm. They accept responsibility for their own actions that led to unsatisfactory results. They interpret their role not as "the decider" but as the catalyst who can help bring about progress throughout the institution as a whole. They recognize that they don't hold a monopoly on the truth. To the positive academic leader, it's not just the system that's open; it's their minds as well.

Conclusion

Tracy Tyree, past associate vice president of student affairs at the University of South Florida, has discussed various ways of using both qualitative and quantitative approaches to measure the effectiveness of nonhierarchical forms of leadership, such as those described in this chapter (Tyree, 2001). Although Tyree's primary focus was on programs aimed at developing student leadership, many of his recommendations are applicable to administrative leadership as well. Tyree bases his assessment process on the social change model of leadership development, which recognizes that meaningful change often occurs not as a result of actions taken by those at the pinnacle of a hierarchy, but as a result of choices made by those not nominally "in charge." The social change model theorizes that positive change occurs when individuals demonstrate seven critical qualities, referred to as the Seven C's:

1. *Consciousness of self:* Awareness of one's core values
2. *Congruence:* Engaging in activities consistent with those core values
3. *Commitment:* Sufficient passion to sustain an effort
4. *Collaboration:* Recognition that leadership is not a solo activity
5. *Common purpose:* Sharing a vision of a better future
6. *Controversy with civility:* Resolving differences with professionalism and collegiality
7. *Citizenship:* Responsibility and active engagement with the larger community

Tyree's recommendation is that organizations should adopt assessment strategies that measure the degree to which a leader's embodiment of these seven qualities results in constructive and desirable change. If these strategies demonstrate a strong correlation between the Seven C's and organizational improvement, we'll have important evidence we can use to persuade critics that alternatives to hierarchical, chain-of-command leadership are effective. (For a further elaboration of this idea, see chapter 12.) But there is one caution. Remember that negative academic leadership produces results quickly, while nonhierarchical methods take far longer. If you begin practicing the approaches described in this book, you're unlikely to see measurable improvements at your institution anytime soon. No one is going to say, "Oh, look! She's engaging in positive academic leadership now. Just look at how much better everything is!" To the contrary, your influence will radiate outward gradually and centrifugally, producing widespread effects only over a period of time. Nevertheless, those effects will emerge. And once you start noticing how positive academic leadership has improved your own college or university, you may want to expand this leadership philosophy throughout higher education as a whole. It's to that topic that we turn in the final two chapters.

References

Berry, J., & and Gordon, J. (Eds.). *Environmental leadership: Developing effective skills and styles.* Washington, DC, and Covelo, CA: Island Press.

Buller, J. L. (2011). Strategic hiring: Aligning personnel decisions with long-term institutional objectives. *Academic Leader, 27*(8), 3, 8.

Dreiser, R. (January 2011). Creative leadership. *Leadership Excellence, 28*(1), 18.

Fisher, R., Sharp, A., & Richardson, J. (2004). *Lateral leadership.* London: Profile Books.

Galbraith, J. R., & Lawler, E. E. (1993). *Organizing for the future: The new logic for managing complex organizations.* San Francisco, CA: Jossey-Bass.

Gordon, J. C., & Berry, J. K. (2006). *Environmental leadership equals essential leadership: Redefining who leads and how.* New Haven, CT: Yale University Press.

Herbst, P. G. (1976). Non-hierarchical forms of organization. *Acta Sociologica, 19*(1), 65–75.

Martin, S. B. (2001). The peer-to-peer context. In C. L. Outcalt, S. K. Faris, & K. N. McMahon (Eds.), *Developing non-hierarchical leadership on campus: Case studies and best practices in higher education* (pp. 99–108). Westport, CT: Greenwood Press.

Maslow, A. H. (1943). A theory of human motivation. *Psychological Review, 50,* 370–396.

Selye, H. (1956). *The stress of life.* New York, NY: McGraw-Hill.

Selye, H. (1974). *Stress without distress.* Philadelphia, PA: Lippincott.

Sit, H. W., & Bundgaard, L. (2009). *Lateral approach to taking charge: Simple principles for new bosses on building authority and partnerships*. Moraga, CA: Lateral Approach Publishing.

Smith, R. V. (2006). *Where you stand is where you sit: An academic administrator's handbook*. Fayetteville, AR: University of Arkansas Press.

Tyree, T. M. (2001). Assessing non-hierarchical leadership. In C. L. Outcalt, S. K. Faris, & K. N. McMahon (Eds.), *Developing non-hierarchical leadership on campus: Case studies and best practices in higher education* (pp. 238–249). Westport, CT: Greenwood Press. 9

Useem, M. (2003). *Leading up: How to lead your boss so you both win*. New York, NY: Random House.

Webster, H. (1993). Lessons from state and regional resource management. In J. Berry & J. Gordon (Eds.), *Environmental leadership: Developing effective skills and styles* (pp. 120–121). Washington, DC, and Covelo, CA: Island Press.

Resources

Berry, J. K., & Gordon, J. C. (1993). *Environmental leadership: Developing effective skills and styles*. Washington, DC, and Covelo, CA: Island Press.

Buller, J. L. (March 2012). Leading upward. *Academic Leader, 28*(3), 1–2.

Van, K. G., Homan, A., & Beersma, B. (2010). On angry leaders and agreeable followers: How leaders' emotions and followers' personalities shape motivation and team performance. *Psychological Science, 21*, 1827–1834.

CHAPTER 11

THE CRISIS INDUSTRY AND HOW POSITIVE LEADERS SHOULD RESPOND TO IT

If we want positive academic leadership to improve the way colleges and universities work, there's one fact we can't ignore: higher education is in crisis. Don't just take my word for it. Glance at the titles of books about higher education that have been published in the past fifteen years and draw your own conclusions. Here's just a sample:

- *The Academy in Crisis: The Political Economy of Higher Education*, by John Sommer (1995)
- *Crisis in the Academy: Rethinking Higher Education in America*, by Christopher Lucas (1996)
- *Higher Education in Crisis: The Corporate Eclipse of the University*, by Samuel Natale, Anthony Libertella, and Geoff Hayward (2001)
- *Grade Inflation: A Crisis in College Education*, by Valen Johnson (2003)
- *Take Back Higher Education: Race, Youth, and the Crisis of Democracy in the Post–Civil Rights Era*, by Henry Giroux and Susan Giroux (2004)
- *The Quiet Crisis: How Higher Education Is Failing America*, by Peter Smith (2004)
- *Declining by Degrees: Higher Education at Risk*, by Richard Hersh and John Merrow (2005)
- *Reconstructing Alma Mater: The Coming Crisis in Higher Education, a Blueprint for Reform*, by Philip Francis (2006)

- *Failed Grade: The Corporatization and Decline of Higher Education in America,* by Albert Soloway (2006)
- *Missing the Boat: The Failure to Internationalize American Higher Education,* by Craufurd Goodwin and Michael Nacht (1991)
- *Crisis on Campus: A Bold Plan for Reforming Our Colleges and Universities,* by Mark Taylor (2010)
- *Academically Adrift: Limited Learning on College Campuses,* by Richard Arum and Josipa Roksa (2011)
- *Higher Education in a State of Crisis,* by Roccio Teixeira (2011)

Crisis. Failure. Risk. Limited. Adrift. Decline. You don't need a Ph.D. to figure out what's happened: American higher education is bad, and it's getting worse. Students have finally come to recognize that going to college in the United States just isn't worth the investment of time and money. Enrollments are plummeting. The number of students in university courses continues to shrink. The portion of the population that chooses to attend American universities is getting smaller and smaller. Everything around us is a mess. It's time for professors and administrators to circle the wagons, adopt the techniques of crisis leadership, and introduce some radical changes—except that *none of the conclusions I just presented is true.* To the contrary, attendance at American universities has been climbing at an accelerated pace:

> Enrollment in degree-granting institutions increased by 9 percent between 1989 and 1999. Between 1999 and 2009, enrollment increased 38 percent, from 14.8 million to 20.4 million. Much of the growth between 1999 and 2009 was in full-time enrollment; the number of full-time students rose 45 percent, while the number of part-time students rose 28 percent. During the same time period, the number of females rose 40 percent, while the number of males rose 35 percent. Enrollment increases can be affected both by population growth and by rising rates of enrollment. Between 1999 and 2009, the number of 18- to 24-year-olds increased from 26.7 million to 30.4 million, an increase of 14 percent, and the percentage of 18- to 24-year-olds enrolled in college rose from 36 percent in 1999 to 41 percent in 2009. (http://nces.ed.gov /programs/digest/d10/ch_3.asp)

In other words, it's not just that more students than ever before are attending American universities today; a greater segment of the population is pursuing higher education. Access to our academic programs is better than it ever has been.

"Well, okay," a skeptic will say. "That may well be true of Americans because they have such limited educational choices. After all, primary and secondary education is a disaster in the United States. Students who want a job have no other options. Elementary and high schools aren't preparing students adequately. People have to attend college to become even minimally qualified for the job market. But that's not the case in other countries. After all, elementary and secondary education is so much better there. You see it repeatedly in how the United States ranks against other countries on standardized tests. Foreign students trounce American students in reading, math, science, geographical awareness, and historical knowledge. It's no wonder that Americans still have to attend the dumbed-down universities in the United States. But foreign students have other options. They're no longer coming to the United States for college. American higher education was once a model for the entire world in how to educate their populations. Now, as the quality of universities in the United States continues to decline, foreign students are fleeing our campuses to enroll in far more demanding institutions, such as those found in the new economic powers like China and India."

You get the drift. It's the sort of thing we hear all the time. Well, unfortunately for the crisis industry, none of those assumptions is true either:

> The number of international students at colleges and universities in the United States increased by five percent to 723,277 during the 2010/11 academic year, according to the Open Doors report, which is published annually by the Institute of International Education (IIE) in partnership with the U.S. Department of State's Bureau of Educational and Cultural Affairs. This represents a record high number of international students in the United States. This is the fifth consecutive year that Open Doors figures show growth in the total number of international students, and there are now 32 percent more international students studying at U.S. colleges and universities than there were a decade ago. The 2010/11 rate of growth is stronger than the three percent increase in total international enrollment reported the previous year, and the six percent increase in new international student enrollment this past year shows more robust new growth than the one percent increase the prior year. Increased numbers of students from China, particularly at the undergraduate level, largely

account for the growth this past year. Chinese students increased by 23 percent in total and by 43 percent at the undergraduate level. These increases have been felt across the United States . . . Together, the top three sending countries—China, India and South Korea—comprise nearly half (46 percent) of the total international enrollments in U.S. higher education. (http://www.iie.org/Who-We-Are/News-and -Events/Press-Center/Press-Releases/2011/2011-311-14-Open -Doors-International-Students)

In other words, more American students than ever before are entering higher education in U.S. universities, accompanied by more foreign students than ever before. That enrollment pressure has caused many institutions to become increasingly competitive in terms of admissions. Honors programs are proliferating, and existing honors programs are expanding (Long, 2007). Because American university students today are quite capable of advanced work, an increasing number of professors expect that undergraduates will engage in original research—not simply learning what others have discovered but making significant new discoveries of their own—sometimes as early as the freshman or sophomore year (Nielsen, 2011; Karukstis, 2010). There are a lot of impressive strengths still to be found in American higher education today, and for every problem we encounter, we can identify ten or twenty areas where the level of success is a model for the rest of the world.

When I first presented this information to the public, one observer noted that I was glossing over the real challenges that exist in higher education today and dismissing "with a jaunty wave" all the problems that really ought to concern us. You'll find that that's a common reaction if you decide to practice positive academic leadership yourself. Despite all the hard evidence you collect, there will always be those who ignore the evidence and insist that by being pessimistic, negative, and obstructionist, they're simply being "realistic." To be sure, the inability to see what's working is a phenomenon that's much bigger than higher education alone. In 2012, Daniel Gross, the economics editor at Yahoo! Finance, published the book *Better, Stronger, Faster: The Myth of American Decline—and the Rise of a New Economy.* Gross, who has an extensive résumé of studying and writing about financial issues, presented insights into the strength of the economy that were in some ways similar to what I just said about American higher education: Although there's a widespread perception that disaster is looming and that only massive structural changes can prevent it, the evidence clearly says otherwise. An except from Gross's book appeared in the May 7, 2012, issue of

Newsweek and outlined the data that led to the author's conclusions. At a time when it's a common belief that the United States is finished as an economic power, Gross (2012b) noted:

o The S&P 500 has risen 104 percent since 2009.

o A record 62 million foreign tourists visited the United States in 2011.

o "From the fourth quarter of 2008 to the fourth quarter of 2009, productivity rose 5.4 percent. And it rose an impressive 4.1 percent in 2010." In other words, during the very period that many observers have dubbed the Great Recession, American productivity actually increased.

o Foreign direct investment increased substantially.

o Exports rose 34 percent from 2009 to 2011. Agricultural exports increased sharply, and "the U.S. ships beef to Brazil, rice to Japan, and soybeans to China ($9.19 billion worth in 2009 alone)."

o More than 4 million jobs have been created by the private sector since February 2010.

o American companies like Apple, Google, and Facebook, which either didn't exist or were insignificant in 2002, are now world leaders in market capitalization.

And that's just a sampling of the evidence Gross cited. Nor was he blind to the truly significant economic challenges that still exist: "The U.S. has a very long way to go to make up for lost ground in housing, and especially in jobs. The resurgence of the corporate sector, which provides ample reason for optimism, hasn't translated into new positions for the legions of unemployed" (Gross, 2012b).

And yet in the very next issue of *Newsweek*, a letter to the editor challenged the entire thrust of Gross's article and returned to the theme that there was little to do but despair:

> America is winning? Really? We have high unemployment. We have a public school system that can't compete with many other nations. We have a social-services system that isn't doing enough for people, including those with special needs. We have a higher education system that American students can't afford. And we have a political system that defines deadlock. Optimism may feel good, but we need some realism to create much-needed societal change. (Bazer, 2012)

It's difficult to read that letter and not think, *Did the writer read the same article I just did?* But of course he did. If those of us who are optimists (or learned optimists) have a tendency to cherry-pick positive data, pessimists and negative academic leaders, who often regard themselves as realists, tend to cherry-pick evidence to the contrary. Cynicism is more socially and academically acceptable than confidence.

The point isn't that some people see the glass as half empty, other people see it as half full, and still others complain that the size of the glass was too small to begin with, but that *the way in which we approach the success or failure of higher education affects the way in which we make decisions.* If we think that American universities are going to hell in a handbasket, we're likely to be advocates for revolutionary change; we'll want to upend the system entirely since anything we replace it with has to be better than what we have right now. That's the perspective of the crisis industry, and it results in the attempts by many state legislatures and governing boards to utterly transform the focus and structure of higher education. It's the perspective we find in books like Clayton Christensen and Henry Eyring's *The Innovative University: Changing the DNA of Higher Education from the Inside Out* (2011). But if we think that higher education, although it faces obvious challenges, is fundamentally sound, we're likely to be advocates for more modest improvements and evolutionary development; we'll regard wholesale, structural transformation as likely to do more harm than good. It's the perspective we adopted throughout this book. This approach to higher education as a whole and our day-to-day administrative work are largely inseparable. Since positive academic leadership builds on strengths rather than fixates on weaknesses, it's clear that this entire administrative philosophy is going to be more concerned with what's working in American higher education than with the problems other people are all to eager to identify.

So the question now becomes: How can we, as positive academic leaders, improve higher education in a world where negative administrative philosophies and an overall pessimistic worldview seem to be in the ascendant? I suggest that there are four major strategies we ought to consider as we move from our own departments and colleges into the wider world of higher education as a whole:

1. We should put all claims that higher education in the United States is irreparably broken into their proper context so that we can determine how much significance we should assign to them.

2. We should be candid about the challenges that actually exist in American higher education, and rather than treating them as crises,

approach them as opportunities to apply our positive leadership strategies.

3. We should apply what we've learned about systems thinking to identify areas where our own needs and desires overlap the needs and desires of others. In this case, "we" means those of us who are committed to positive academic leadership, and "others" means those who are currently advocating policies reflective of a more pessimistic outlook.

4. We should play to our strengths, using the skills we've developed in assessing outcomes and reviewing programs to demonstrate that positive approaches are more effective than negative ones.

We'll examine the first two strategies in this chapter, reserving the last two for the final chapter, where we can combine them with an action plan based on the principles set out in this book.

Putting Crisis Claims into Context

The first thing we need to realize about all those claims that American higher education is in crisis because standards are declining, students aren't learning, and the wrong skills are being taught is that these claims aren't new. In fact, they've been made for as long as American higher education has existed. Here's just a sampling of the various perceived problems and weaknesses that have led to changes in how colleges and universities are organized, drawn primarily from the wonderful history of higher education that appears in Gaff and Ratcliff (1997) with supplemental information provided by http://www.college.columbia.edu/core/timeline and http://www.columbiaspectator.com/2011/02/02/core-critic-bell-remembered-wide-intellect:

- o In 1756, the College of Pennsylvania adopted a more utilitarian curriculum because the public felt that classical education didn't prepare students sufficiently for working in the "real world."

- o Because student effort and performance were said to have declined, formal grades were first established in the United States at Yale in 1785 as a means of spurring students toward greater achievement.

- o In 1819, Harvard professor George Ticknor criticized his university "for the poor quality of its libraries, the exclusion of modern languages from the curriculum, and the lack of specialized departments" (Gaff and Ratcliff, 1997, p. 68).

o At the University of Nashville in 1825, President Philip Lindsley modified the curriculum to make it more relevant to student needs by "accenting utilitarian, vocational, and research concerns" (Gaff and Ratcliff, 1997, 69).

o Also in 1825, Harvard's first self-study sought to improve educational quality through a restructuring of the entire curriculum, creating academic departments and allowing students a small number of electives.

o Widespread public criticism led Yale University to defend its commitment to the value of a classical education in 1828.

o In 1850, Brown University's president, Francis Wayland, instituted changes to the curriculum that were abandoned four years later because of public opposition and declining enrollments.

o In 1869, Charles Eliot tried again to improve the quality of education at Harvard by allowing students to take a much larger number of electives.

o Regional accreditation started in 1885 out of a sense that uniformly high standards were needed throughout American higher education.

o Because students arriving in college had such diverse levels of competence in different subjects, College Entrance Examination Board tests were introduced in 1901 as a way of providing a more consistent and uniform measure.

o In 1909, President A. Lawrence Lowell of Harvard created general education requirements out of his conviction that since the adoption of the elective system, students had not been receiving a broad enough education.

o In 1910, comprehensive examinations were introduced at both Harvard and Reed College as a means of demonstrating that students had mastered an appropriate level of the material taught in their programs.

o By 1928, the University of Chicago began a lengthy reform of its undergraduate curriculum out of a desire to improve the quality of its educational program.

o At the end of World War II, Harvard issued a report, *General Education in a Free Society* (popularly known as the Redbook), that led to yet another phase of general education reform throughout the country.

○ The launch of the Soviet artificial satellite *Sputnik* in 1957 caused many critics to challenge the quality of math and science education in America, prompting reform of pedagogical methods and a rise in standards across what have come to be known as the STEM disciplines (science, technology, engineering, mathematics).

○ In 1963 a public outcry occurred as College Board scores were seen to decline.

○ Three years later, Daniel Bell issued a report at Columbia University recommending that the core curriculum be expanded and restructured as a "necessary condition for the survival of Columbia College as a first-rank school" (http://www.columbiaspectator.com/2011/02/02/core-critic-bell-remembered-wide-intellect).

○ A decade later, assessment began at Alverno College in Milwaukee as a way of demonstrating the effectiveness of the college's programs in meeting its educational goals.

○ The next year, the commonwealth of Virginia adopted minimum proficiency levels for students graduating from high school, seeking to verify whether high school graduates had achieved standards high enough to enter college. These minimum levels came to be known as Virginia's Standards of Learning (thus giving them the unfortunate acronym SOL).

○ In 1978, Harvard revised its general education program yet again in order to ensure that students had exposure to eleven key areas of the liberal arts. The new program was largely a reaction against the great books approach adopted at Columbia and elsewhere. It was instantly denounced by those outside academia.

○ Secretary of Education William Bennett issued a 1984 report, *To Reclaim a Legacy: A Report on the Humanities in Higher Education,* that decried the decline in quality found in university-level humanities and general education programs.

○ Three years later, Allan Bloom's *The Closing of the American Mind* prompted yet another call for universities to reform their curricula.

○ In 1989, Lynne Cheney, chair of the National Endowment for the Humanities, issued *50 Hours,* which recommended that general education programs be reformed at colleges and universities in order to make them more rigorous.

○ At Columbia University, the Committee on Undergraduate Education issued a report in 1994 concluding that major programs at the school have "insufficient attention and insufficient resources." In order to redirect funds toward academic majors, it was recommended that the general education program be scaled back.

o Congress approved the No Child Left Behind Act in 2001, placing greater emphasis on standardized tests out of a belief that students were being insufficiently prepared by schools at the precollege level for the workforce or higher education.

o In 2006, Secretary of Education Margaret Spellings proposed extending many provisions of the No Child Left Behind Act to higher education, including mandatory standardized testing, out of a belief that American higher education was weak due to decentralization, low standards, and a failure to adopt a unified strategy (http://www.huffingtonpost.com/john-seery/margaret -spellings-higher_b_30497.html).

In other words, the perception that American higher education is deeply flawed because standards have plummeted, we're teaching the wrong subjects, and universities have become too remote from the real world isn't new. It's simply normal. There have always been those who have claimed that colleges and universities in the United States used to be good (usually at some point in the past roughly equivalent to when the speaker went to college) but are now on the brink of catastrophe. But the fact is that we could radically restructure everything about higher education, implementing every single reform championed by every single one of these critics, and the same charges would still be made. Public disapproval of the content, quality, and focus of American higher education is perennial. It's like living in North Dakota and being surprised when it snows in the winter. It's not an aberration; it just comes with the territory.

Putting claims of crisis and failure into context therefore means that we realize how much of this debate has occurred before. *Often* before. In fact, if you look at the full sweep of how American higher education has been criticized throughout its history, certain patterns begin to emerge. For example, after the launch of *Sputnik* in the late 1950s, the public perception was that American education had become too soft and there was a need for increased standards in the hard sciences; as a result, higher education underwent a reform. But then, partly as a result of these changes, William Bennett's 1984 *To Reclaim a Legacy* and Allan Bloom's 1987 *The Closing of the American Mind* claimed that American students had lost touch with their own heritage because they weren't studying the humanities in sufficient depth or according to the proper methods.

So once again, higher education underwent a reform. Now a number of studies indicate that American students pursue majors in the STEM fields at a lower rate than in other countries and receive lower scores on standardized tests in these areas. A new crisis has been declared, and "new" reforms are being proposed.

Yet what we're really seeing is a historical cycle. There's a pendulum of opinion about the relative merits of science and the humanities that swings back and forth in American higher education. In fact, it's only one of ten cyclical shifts in opinion that are easily traced. According to editorials, surveys, and reform efforts, colleges are either emphasizing general education too much or aren't emphasizing it enough. Colleges are either adopting too much of a vocational focus or too little of one. Table 11.1 identifies these ten pendulum topics about where American higher education has "gone wrong."

TABLE 11.1   Ten Pendulum Topics About American Higher Education

American Education Should Be More:	
Oriented toward science and math.	Oriented toward the humanities and liberal arts.
Concerned with specialization, depth of knowledge, and job preparation. College fails if it doesn't help graduates secure well-paying jobs.	Concerned with general education, breadth of knowledge, and cultural heritage. College fails if it doesn't educate the whole person.
Devoted to exposing students to a canon of great books, works of art, and musical compositions.	Devoted to the diversity of human achievement, which is so broad that it can never be contained within a single canon.
Dedicated to the mastery of skills.	Dedicated to the mastery of knowledge.
Uniform, so that all students receive a consistent and equitable experience.	Diverse, so that each student, with different interests and goals, can best achieve his or her own individuality and independence.
Supportive of established values.	Supportive of challenging the status quo and established ideas.
Focused on the good of society.	Focused on the good of the individual.
Perceived as a universal right, an entitlement.	Perceived as a great privilege, a much cherished opportunity.
Classical in emphasis.	Modern in emphasis.
Inclusive since everyone is capable of higher-level learning.	Rigorous since standards must be maintained.

What we recognize when we view crisis claims in their proper context is that the two columns represented in table 11.1 are highly permeable. We can think of them as rather like columns of choices on a menu. Or to return to our earlier image, the ten pendulums swing at different rates. At one time, public opinion may swing closer to a view that college education should be largely vocational in nature while also devoted to the needs of society, grounded in a canon of great books, and rigorous even if the result will be that graduation rates decline. At other times, those who support the vocational nature of higher education may believe that college should place greater emphasis on the rights of the individual, modern discoveries instead of classic texts, and broader access for the public even if the result will be that academic standards must decline. As positive academic leaders, we owe it to our profession—and ourselves—to recognize the difference between a temporary sway in public opinion and a path that has brought us to the abyss. Negative academic leaders tend to be those who confuse the former with the latter.

It comes as no surprise to positive academic leaders when a pundit or government study announces that American higher education is now at a crossroads. We know that American education will always be at a crossroads because there's a constant tug-of-war between different visions of what colleges and universities should be. As one of the ten pendulums swings a bit closer to a particular side of an issue, those on the other side will interpret that change as a decline in quality. But what's actually occurring is that as we change as a nation, so do our institutions change. It can be unsettling to find yourself on the minority side of an issue where you were in the clear majority not that long ago. Unsettling, but not abnormal. The point is that if we see each of these regular shifts as a crisis, we end up wasting a great deal of our own resources by dismantling structures we'll end up rebuilding a decade or so in the future. (If you've ever been at any one school long enough to go through several general education reviews, you know exactly what I'm talking about.)

While the future of higher education is notoriously difficult to predict, here's one prophecy you can rely on: periodically a public voice—perhaps a politician, author, late-night comedian, blue ribbon commission, or self-proclaimed intellectual—will announce that a group of college graduates was asked if they knew X, and they demonstrated that they didn't know X at all. This same voice will then claim that X is the single most important thing colleges should be teaching. And then, throughout all the layers of American higher education, governing boards will become concerned, curriculum committees will meet, and a greater emphasis on X will be included in the graduation requirements of one school or another. But a decade or so later, a different public voice will say the same thing about Y, and the cycle will begin all over again. What positive academic leadership does is help us recognize the difference between a genuine crisis and one of those natural processes that helps keep higher education relevant and fluid. Our colleges and universities reflect us. We know that we change. Why are we constantly surprised when they change as well?

When we lose our sense of context, long-standing debates sometimes strike us as new and important conflicts. In a fascinating article in the *New Republic*, Philip Kitcher argued that the walls that we often erect between science and the humanities reflect a false dichotomy. Moreover, those walls aren't not particularly new:

> The conflict between the *Naturwissenschaften* [natural sciences] and the *Geisteswissenschaften* [humanities] goes back at least two centuries, and became intensified as ambitious, sometimes impatient researchers proposed to introduce natural scientific concepts and methods into the study of human psychology and human social behavior . . . The enthusiasm for natural scientific imperialism rests on five observations. First, there is the sense that the humanities and social sciences are doomed to deliver a seemingly directionless sequence of theories and explanations, with no promise of additive progress. Second, there is the contrasting record of extraordinary success in some areas of natural science. Third, there is the explicit articulation of technique and method in the natural sciences, which fosters the conviction that natural scientists are able to acquire and combine evidence in particularly rigorous ways. Fourth, there is the perception that humanists and social scientists are only able to reason cogently when they confine themselves to conclusions of limited generality: insofar as they aim at significant—general—conclusions, their methods and their evidence are unrigorous. Finally, there is the commonplace perception that the humanities and social sciences have been dominated, for long periods of their histories, by spectacularly false theories, grand doctrines that enjoy enormous popularity until fashion changes, as their glaring shortcomings are disclosed. (http://www.tnr.com/article/books-and-arts/magazine/103086/scientism-humanities-knowledge-theory-everything-arts-science)

Kircher proceeds to debunk each of these five observations, demonstrating that both the humanities and the sciences build on past discoveries in precisely the same way, have comparable records of extraordinary success, use identical rigor in their techniques, and so on. If we start to do the same and refuse to accept every claim that a crisis is new—or even that it's really a crisis—we can avoid wasting our resources by panicking over an issue that's little more than a passing fad.

Candor About Challenges

Nevertheless, placing criticism into its proper historical context doesn't mean that everything's perfect in American higher education or that we should turn a deaf ear to those who try to identify areas of weakness. Serious challenges do exist. The goal is to decide which of the following are problems and which are merely unthreatening trends:

- Students who entered American universities in 2004 as full-time degree-seeking students had a four-year graduation rate of only 37.9 percent, and that rate was higher than in any of the previous five years (http://nces.ed.gov/programs/digest/d11/tables/dt11_345 .asp).

- In 2008, only 13 percent of U.S. graduate degrees were granted in the areas of math and science versus 23.3 percent internationally and nearly 50 percent in economically struggling nations like Japan and Portugal (http://nces.ed.gov/programs/digest/d11/tables /dt11_427.asp).

- In November 2011, the *New York Times* reported that "roughly 40 percent of students planning engineering and science majors end up switching to other subjects or failing to get any degree. That increases to as much as 60 percent when pre-medical students, who typically have the strongest SAT scores and high school science preparation, are included, according to new data from the University of California at Los Angeles" (http://www.nytimes .com/2011/11/06/education/edlife/why-science-majors-change-their -mind-its-just-so-darn-hard.html?pagewanted=all).

- A 2011 Harris Poll found that among the general public, 42 percent of those surveyed believed that American universities cared more about tuition revenue than graduation rates (http://www .harrisinteractive.com/NewsRoom/HarrisPolls/tabid/447/mid/1508 /articleId/848/ctl/ReadCustom percent20Default/Default.aspx).

- In March 2011, an Associated Press/Viacom/Roper Poll found that 48 percent of students surveyed described themselves as "totally uncomfortable" with having student loans and that a full 22 percent had considered leaving or dropping out of college within

the previous three months (http://surveys.ap.org/data/GfK/AP
-Viacom percent20Youth percent20Study percent20Topline_college
percent20students percent20paying percent20the percent20bills
.pdf).

o A survey conducted by the Associated Press and Stanford University
in September 2010 found that two-thirds of Americans believed
their educational system was falling behind the rest of the world
(http://surveys.ap.org/data/SRBI/AP-National percent20Education
percent20Poll percent20Topline percent20100110.pdf).

o In a study conducted in Wisconsin, Katherine Cramer Walsh
found that the three words people most commonly associated with
university faculty in her state were *lazy, liberal,* and *elitist* (http://
wiscape.wisc.edu/uploads/media/e1d40727-38fc-433a-a8a7
-9df8b77b1a29.pdf).

o At the very time when the public seems most interested in the role
that universities play in preparing students for successful careers
and in producing practical, externally funded research, Dahlia Remler and Elda Penna found that reward systems throughout higher
education were tied to the production of any kind of research, even
if it is unfunded and without any relationship to economic development (http://www.nber.org/papers/w14974.pdf?new_window=1).

Having learned to view these issues in their larger context, we can
more easily distinguish what we need to fix from what we may safely
dismiss as bombast and overreaction. In other words, certain issues in
higher education are best addressed not through systemic changes but by
communicating more effectively what college professors actually do, why
the work of faculty members benefits society, why four-year graduation
rates really aren't valid indicators of student success, how basic research
improves our lives and adds to the economy, and what the difference is
between a belief that America is falling behind the rest of the world and
actual, verifiable evidence.

An emphasis on four-year graduation rates, for example, reflects an outdated view of college life stemming from when the vast majority of students
lived on campus, did not have jobs while they went to school, and took a
full load of classes each semester. More recently, the emphasis on providing
more students with access to higher education means that many of them
must balance their studies with full-time jobs, families, and a wide range
of personal challenges. Opening the doors of higher education to students
who wouldn't have had this option in the past means providing them with

greater educational, psychological, and social resources, encouraging certain students to take reduced loads so that they increase their likelihood of success, and abandoning the artificial constraints of the four-year degree. In addition, as positive academic leaders, we should preserve our core values and apply our methods of scholarly criticism when we're confronted with hostile political rhetoric. For instance, consider several recent proposals made about how we can improve higher education in the United States:

- o [The ExxonMobile Foundation launched a program supporting a number of educational reforms, featuring the slogan "Let's Solve This."] In 2009, the Program for International Students Assessment ranked U.S. students 17th in the world in science and 25th in math. Let's change those numbers. Let's invest in our teachers. Let's inspire our students. Let's solve this. (http://www.exxonmobil.com /Corporate/community_math.aspx?WT.srch=1)

- o [Governor of Florida Rick] Scott said Monday [October 11, 2011] that he hopes to shift more funding to science, technology, engineering and math departments, the so-called "STEM" disciplines. The big losers: Programs like psychology and anthropology and potentially schools like New College in Sarasota that emphasize a liberal arts curriculum. "If I'm going to take money from a citizen to put into education then I'm going to take that money to create jobs," Scott said. "So I want that money to go to degrees where people can get jobs in this state." (http://htpolitics .com/2011/10/10/rick-scott-wants-to-shift-university-funding-away -from-some-majors/)

- o Calling it an issue of national competitiveness, Congresswoman Eddie Bernice Johnson (D-Texas) announced a new bill on Tuesday [April 24, 2012] that seeks to increase the proportion of minority students who graduate with STEM degrees, as well as the number of minority faculty members who teach them. "When we look at researchers, engineers, we don't see America, the diversity," Johnson said Tuesday at a Capitol Hill news conference and round-table hosted by the National Action Council for Minorities in Engineering Inc., or NACME. (http://diverseeducation.com /article/17027/)

The idea many people have is that by refocusing American education on math and science, the nation's economic competitiveness will improve, its regions that are suffering heavy unemployment will recover, and our basic challenges of racial and socioeconomic equity will be addressed.

But remember what we just saw about public support for math and science over the humanities in American higher education: it's cyclic. In keeping with our principles of positive academic leadership, we need to probe a bit further before embracing major (possibly destructive) reforms designed to "solve this problem."

For instance, we should take into account the findings of authors like David Brooks (2004a, 2004b) and Richard Florida (2002) who have suggested that we're unlikely to create the next Silicon Valley or North Carolina Research Triangle by supporting initiatives that starve the arts and humanities in order to feed the STEM disciplines. As Brooks and Florida demonstrate, scientists and engineers usually aren't attracted to an area because they want to spend all their time with other scientists and engineers. The research centers that are thriving tend to be located in areas where there's deep support for culture and the arts, tolerance of diverse lifestyles, and a flourishing intellectual community across disciplines. In short, highly educated people value environments in which the full range of cultural achievement is encouraged, not simply a focus on their own particular specialty.

Moreover, many regions of the world that politicians cite as examples of how America has failed in teaching students math and science are pursuing strategies that are polar opposites of the desire to focus higher education on the STEM disciplines alone. In an article that appeared in the February 5, 2012, issue of the *Chronicle of Higher Education,* Karin Fischer reports that many high schools and universities in China are now shifting their priorities toward the liberal arts because an over-emphasis on science and mathematics has resulted in graduates who are unable to compete globally due to their deficiencies in creativity, adaptability, and critical thinking. And contrary to all the concern expressed in the United States about the poor academic preparation of workers, Fischer reports that many Chinese employers regard American graduates as much more capable than those attending universities in Asia. And so as John Tures concluded in the Columbus, Georgia, *Ledger-Enquirer,* while American politicians have jumped on the bandwagon of a "teach-to-the-test mentality," the very countries often cited as proof this approach works are moving in the opposite direction: They're reducing the amount of standardized testing and deemphasizing STEM education in favor of our own "hopelessly broken" system. Tures characterizes the crisis industry's panicked response to a perceived but non-existent problem as "following China off the educational cliff" (http://www.ledger-enquirer.com/2012/03/30/1994102/following-china-off-education.html).

Responding to the Crisis Industry

Seeing everything as a crisis ultimately means that nothing is really a crisis, even when a genuine problem emerges. The title of a 2009 article by Ronald Heifetz, Alexander Grashow, and Marty Linsky says it all: "Leadership in a (Permanent) Crisis." The authors' thesis is that leaders today frequently view themselves like doctors in an emergency room. They believe they have to respond quickly and dramatically; once the immediate danger has passed, the road to recovery will still be long and fraught with continuing danger.

In today's new economic and political world, issues are presented to us as a roller-coaster ride of one emergency after another. Organizations are urged to respond instantly to challenges that are believed to arise in an ever-changing landscape. While Heifetz, Grasho, and Linsky primarily address corporate leadership in their article, their descriptions fit many colleges and universities as well. We too work in an environment where we're constantly told that a new crisis is at hand, and this one will be even worse than the last one. Moreover, our own experience as administrators seems to confirm this perception. Every day people bring us problems to be solved and troubles to dispel. They point out to us an endless series of fires that are burning, and those fires can exhaust all our energy if we try to put them out one after another. Eventually we'll come to believe that higher education is a structure perpetually in flames. But that response is merely negative academic leadership. It's a preoccupation with what's not working (or, more accurately, with what some people claim is not working) rather than with our positive mission of educating students, producing significant research, and serving our communities. The crisis mind-set can cause us to channel resources away from our primary goals of teaching, scholarship, and service into strategic planning, institutional research, and multiple accreditations in a desperate hope that these devices will prevent our institutions from falling off a cliff—even when the cliff isn't really there.

Positive academic leadership offers an alternative to this destructive practice. As we've seen repeatedly, it's not that positive academic leaders never believe that crises occur: institutions do at times come to the brink of fiscal collapse, unsafe conditions do threaten the well-being of faculty and students, and natural disasters do occur. It's just that they recognize that not everything is a crisis. When tempers flare, problems arise, and mistakes occur, positive academic leaders don't feel that these are signs they need to reinvent their entire programs and realign every goal. Rather (and we should regard this as the essence of positive leadership) they approach each problem thinking, "This is not a crisis; it's just my job."

That perspective isn't mindless optimism; it's a commitment to using our time, funding, and other resources effectively. We can continually change our curricula and later undo those changes—expanding general education, then reducing it; becoming more vocational, then becoming less vocational; emphasizing science, then the humanities, then science again—or we can just learn to tell our story better and make it clear to others why what we're doing is important. We already have all the data we need to demonstrate that despite all those claims to the contrary, students' lives are significantly improved by attending our universities, important research is being done every day, and the broader community is better for our being here. In fact, some of this evidence appears in the very studies people cite as proving that higher education is in crisis.

In the same 2011 Harris poll indicating that 42 percent of Americans believed universities cared more about receiving tuition dollars than boosting graduation rates, 68 percent of respondents described American universities as doing an "excellent or pretty good" job of educating students. Only 21 percent rated the quality of higher education in the United States as fair or poor. In fact, those with a positive view of American universities outnumbered those with a negative view by more than four to one (http://www.harrisinteractive.com/NewsRoom/Harris Polls/tabid/447/mid/1508/articleId/848/ctl/ReadCustom percent20Default /Default.aspx).

The same Associated Press and Stanford University survey that found two-thirds of Americans describing our educational system as falling behind the rest of the world also found a larger group (74 percent) describing public four-year colleges in their own state as offering a quality of education that was good or excellent. Only 23 percent rated higher education in their state as fair, poor, or very poor (http://surveys.ap.org/data /srbi/ap-national percent20education percent20poll percent20topline percent20100110.pdf).

The same Associated Press/Viacom/Roper poll that found high rates of students worrying about student loans or considering dropping out of college because of the cost also found that despite the size of the investment, 79 percent of those who attended college thought it was well worth the time and money. Only 21 percent were neutral or less positive. A larger percentage of respondents thought that college was important for broadening their knowledge and expanding their minds (87 percent answered "extremely important" or "very important") than for career preparation (80 percent). When asked to choose between an education that focused on securing them a job and an education focused on general knowledge and critical thinking, the results were closer than many political leaders may have thought: 55 percent preferred a career-based education, 40 percent preferred a general knowledge–based education, and 4 percent found them both equally desirable (http://surveys.ap.org/data /gfk/ap-viacom percent20youth percent20study percent20topline_college percent20students percent20paying percent20the percent20bills.pdf).

Conclusion

The approaches that make positive academic leaders effective in a department, college, or university are the same ones we need to adopt when addressing higher education as a matter of national policy. It's one thing for entertainers and political commentators to engage in shock journalism; it's another thing altogether for administrators to buy into those same assumptions. While proclamations of impending crisis attract viewers, subscribers, and voters, they can also lead to wasteful and destructive administrative policies if we don't see through the rhetoric to the reality of the situation. Academic leaders have a responsibility to weigh truth claims about why higher education is flawed very carefully, distinguishing genuine concerns from cyclic patterns, tendentious sound bites, and inadequately examined assumptions. The sky isn't falling, but at the same time it's not universally sunny. The truth in American higher education, as it so often does, lies somewhere in the middle, as boring as that may seem. In order to tell our story better, we have to find ways in which we can relate our own priorities in higher education to those of the people who are responsible for determining our future. In the spirit of positive academic leadership, we also need to stop fixating on our weaknesses and begin playing to our strengths. It is to those two strategies that we turn in our final chapter.

References

Arum, R., & Roksa, J. (2011). *Academically adrift: Limited learning on college campuses*. Chicago, IL: University of Chicago Press.

Bazer, G. (2012, May 14). Letter to the editor. *Newsweek*, 2.

Bennett, W. J. (1984). *To reclaim a legacy: A report on the humanities in higher education*. Washington, DC: National Endowment for the Humanities.

Bloom, A. D. (1987). *The closing of the American mind: How higher education has failed democracy and impoverished the souls of today's students.* New York, NY: Simon & Schuster.

Brooks, D. (2004a). *Bobos in paradise: The new upper class and how they got there.* New York, NY: Simon & Schuster.

Brooks, D. (2004b). *On Paradise Drive: How we live now (and always have) in the future tense.* New York, NY: Simon & Schuster.

Cheney, L. V. (1989). *Fifty hours: A core curriculum for college students.* Washington, DC: National Endowment for the Humanities.

Christensen, C. M., & Eyring, H. J. (2011). *The innovative university: Changing the DNA of higher education from the inside out.* San Francisco, CA: Jossey-Bass.

Fischer, K. (2012, February 5). Bucking cultural norms, Asia tries liberal arts. *Chronicle of Higher Education,* A1, A3-A4, A6.

Florida, R. L. (2002). *The rise of the creative class: And how it's transforming work, leisure, community and everyday life.* New York, NY: Basic Books.

Francis, P. H. (2006). *Reconstructing alma mater: The coming crisis in higher education, a blueprint for reform.* New York, NY: Algora.

Gaff, J. G., & Ratcliff, J. L. (1997). *Handbook of the undergraduate curriculum: A comprehensive guide to purposes, structures, practices, and change.* San Francisco, CA: Jossey-Bass.

Giroux, H. A., & Giroux, S. S. (2004). *Take back higher education: Race, youth, and the crisis of democracy in the post–civil rights era.* New York, NY: Palgrave Macmillan.

Goodwin, C.D.W., & Nacht, M. (1991). *Missing the boat: The failure to internationalize American higher education.* Cambridge: Cambridge University Press.

Gross, D. (2012a). *Better, stronger, faster: The myth of American decline— and the rise of a new economy.* New York, NY: Free Press.

Gross, D. (2012b, May 7). Listen, the U.S. is better, stronger, and faster than anywhere else in the world. *Newsweek,* 22–27.

Harvard University. (1945). *General education in a free society: Report of the Harvard committee.* Cambridge, MA: Harvard University Press.

Heifetz, R., Grashow, A., & Linsky, M. (2009, July). Leadership in a (permanent) crisis. *Harvard Business Review,* 87, 62–67.

Hersh, R. H., & Merrow, J. (2005). *Declining by degrees: Higher education at risk.* New York, NY: Palgrave Macmillan.

Johnson, V. E. (2003). *Grade inflation: A crisis in college education.* New York, NY: Springer.

Karukstis, K. K. (2010). Expanding opportunities for undergraduate research through recent NSF awards to CUR. *Journal of Chemical Education, 87,* 245–246.

Kitcher, P. (2012, May 24). The trouble with scientism: Why history and the humanities are also a form of knowledge. *New Republic,* 20–23. http://www.tnr.com/article/books-and-arts/magazine/103086/scientism -humanities-knowledge-theory-everything-arts-science.

Long, A. (2007). Editor's introduction. *Journal of the National Collegiate Honors Council, 8*(2), 9–13.

Lucas, C. J. (1996). *Crisis in the academy: Rethinking higher education in America.* New York, NY: St. Martin's Press.

Natale, S. M., Libertella, A. F., & Hayward, G. (2001). *Higher education in crisis: The corporate eclipse of the university.* Binghamton, NY: Global Publications, Binghamton University.

Nielsen, N. (2011). *Promising practices in undergraduate science, technology, engineering, and mathematics education: Summary of two workshops.* Washington, DC: National Academies Press.

Smith, P. (2004). *The quiet crisis: How higher education is failing America.* Bolton, MA: Anker.

Soloway, A. H. (2006). *Failed grade: The corporatization and decline of higher education in America.* Salt Lake City, UT: American University and Colleges Press.

Sommer, J. W. (1995). *The academy in crisis: The political economy of higher education.* New Brunswick, NJ: Transaction Publishers.

Taylor, M. C. (2010). *Crisis on campus: A bold plan for reforming our colleges and universities.* New York, NY: Knopf.

Teixeira, R. M. (2011). *Higher education in a state of crisis.* Hauppauge, NY: Nova Science Publishers.

CHAPTER 12

PLAYING TO OUR STRENGTHS

In chapter 11, we explored two strategies for responding to what I've called "the crisis industry" in American higher education. In this chapter, I close the discussion of positive academic leadership by considering two additional strategies—adopting a systems approach and playing to our strengths—and putting some of the principles I've discussed into practice.

Applying the Systems Approach to a Larger System

One of the concepts we've returned to repeatedly has been Don Chu's open system model and the way it applies to our own leadership philosophies. In this chapter, I explore how we might also use this powerful idea to help spread positive leadership approaches throughout higher education as a whole. Let's begin by recalling the four questions that help us operate more effectively within any system:

1. What does the other person or group need from me?
2. What does the other person or group want from me?
3. What do I need from the other person or group?
4. What do I want from the other person or group?

The key to effective systems thinking is to find some way in which the answers to these four questions overlap or, to put it another way, to present the answers to the third and fourth questions in a way that they'll also answer the first two. The idea seems simple enough, and yet it's precisely here that we frequently go wrong in speaking about higher education to the public. We lapse into "closed system" thinking and present our needs and desires in terms that are meaningful to us and our faculties, forgetting that those same terms may not be at all meaningful to members of our open system.

Let me provide one example. In March 2012, the academic senate of the University of California began debating whether to send a memorial (essentially a petition requesting endorsement of a ballot measure or a certain piece of legislation) to the university's regents. The hope was that this memorial would encourage those with legislative influence to make funding of higher education a high priority:

> Increasingly damaging budgets have produced a downward spiral that threatens the survival of the University as the leading public university in the world as it experiences higher student-faculty ratios, larger class sizes, reduced depth and breadth in course offerings, staff layoffs, and lack of investment in infrastructure; . . . [moreover] the faculty are prepared to advocate publicly, consistently, and forcefully for the future of the University. (http://academic-senate.berkeley.edu /vote/mail_ballots/memorial_to_regents_20120305)

That's a compelling case, right? If budgets continue to be cut, class sizes will increase, course selection for students will decrease, people will lose their jobs, and the faculty will have to work even harder because of soaring student-faculty ratios. In addition, the professors pledged to voice these concerns "publicly, consistently, and forcefully." Pretty persuasive stuff. But what we may be overlooking is that these are the arguments that mostly concern only us within higher education.

To a regent, many of whom have corporate or legislative backgrounds, these arguments sound very different than they do to an academic audience. "Great," a member of the governing board may say:

> If that happens, we'll have greater efficiency. Once student-faculty ratios increase, productivity will be going up. Once there are fewer courses for students to choose from, higher education will finally be following the old *In Search of Excellence* principle of "stick to the knitting" (Peters and Waterman, 2004). We'll have fewer courses in queer studies and Marxism, forcing more students to take Shakespeare, American history, and business. And if all this means that the faculty's going to be working harder, that's terrific because a lot of them were only teaching three, six, or nine hours a week before. When you work fewer than ten hours a week, you've got too much time on your hands to address matters "publicly, consistently, and forcefully" that are really our business, not yours.

You may have heard trustees, regents, or legislators say things almost identical to this hypothetical response. And we continue to hear them because we don't keep our entire system in mind. We present arguments as though the people we're addressing are all members of the faculty, but our real audience is far broader. In the case we've just considered, for instance, the question we should be asking isn't, "Why do *we* want increased funding?" but rather, "What do the regents need, what do the regents want, and how can we provide those things better if our funding is increased?"

Consider this: in the same year that the academic senate of the University of California sought support for its memorial, the governor of that state, Jerry Brown, gave a major address in which he mentioned job creation half a dozen times and tied the state's employment needs to such fields as renewable energy, green technology, and the computer industry. In addition, Brown mentioned education five times, mostly in connection with issues of accountability, expanded local control, and reversing the trend toward expanding numbers of standardized tests. (See Brown's January 18, 2012, state of the state address at http://gov.ca.gov/news.php?id=17386.) Similar themes appeared in the state of the state addresses of other governors. In a wonderful summary prepared for the American Association of State Colleges and Universities by Thomas Harnisch and Emily Parker, nearly four of five U.S. governors mentioned education in their 2012 state of the state addresses (http://www.aascu.org/uploadedFiles/AASCU/Content/Root/PolicyAndAdvocacy/PolicyPublications/Special_Reports/State%20of%20the%20States%202012(2).pdf). But what's even more striking are the eight dominant themes that tended to occur whenever higher education was mentioned:

1. Higher education plays a major role in economic development.
2. Higher education's role in job creation and workforce training should be expanded.
3. Economic development and job creation require an emphasis on applied research and professional training in the science, technology, engineering, and mathematics (STEM) disciplines.
4. By the time students reach college, they should be fully prepared to perform the level of work expected there and should not require remedial courses.
5. Access to college should not be limited due to a person's level of income. For this reason, tuition must be kept low while financial aid packages must remain robust.

6. Students should be able to graduate from college on time and without a great deal of financial aid debt.

7. Dual-enrollment and accelerated programs are important because they help move students more rapidly from the world of education to the world of work.

8. Community colleges, technical colleges, and universities that offer baccalaureate and advanced degrees must all be part of a comprehensive system of postsecondary education.

Keep in mind that these eight themes didn't arise as a series of unrelated observations. Governor after governor described them as inextricably linked, almost as though they were eight facets of a single idea. For example, here's how Governor John Kasich of Ohio described the issue on February 7, 2012:

> We need our community colleges to begin to educate people for these jobs [in scientific and technical fields]. Now some of them are doing a pretty good job. Some of them aren't doing a very good job. You know, we only have a 10 percent graduation rate nationwide for community colleges. Community colleges should be like the emergency vehicle when there is a job. Put kids and students in there, including adults, and get them trained quickly so they can get the jobs that are available. So we have to match the community colleges with the business community and the forecasting. Sounds easy? Try it. We've been working on this for six months. This is a huge cultural change. And our universities, they've got to do a much better job of focusing kids on realistic job propositions. Do you know that we—well, I don't want to get into necessarily the negative, but some of our four-year graduation rates, they're just wrong. (http://governor.ohio.gov/Portals/0/2012%20State %20of%20the%20State%20Address%20Transcript.pdf)

Governor Bob McDonnell of Virginia carried these ideas even further in his address on January 11, 2012, combining job creation, practical training in the STEM disciplines, the need to increase graduation rates, and rapidly rising college tuition all into a single idea.

> I am proposing a dynamic new funding model for higher education that ties new general funds to achieving our statutory goals. Institutions will be rewarded for increasing the number of degrees, especially in STEM-H (science, technology, engineering, and mathematics, plus health care) fields; improving graduation rates; and expanding practical research. It will also require colleges to be more accountable

and efficient by reprioritizing 5 percent of their current general fund dollars by 2014 to meet the key policy goals we enacted last year, including year-round use of facilities and greater use of technology to leverage more programs and courses. Taken together, these actions cement the nexus between higher education and job creation and begin to reverse the unacceptable trend over the past ten years during which the average college tuition for our constituents has doubled. Parents and students can't afford it. Those days are over (http://www .governor.virginia.gov/MediaLibrary/Speeches/2012/SOC.cfm).

In other words, in 2012—the same year that the University of California's academic senate was seeking to preserve funding for higher education on the basis of how destructive budget cuts were because of higher student-faculty ratios, larger class sizes, and more limited course offerings—those issues didn't seem to matter at all to the people who were actually making decisions about higher education funding. We can argue all we want that those concerns should have mattered to the legislators. But when the governors spoke and the legislators listened, they didn't. To someone like Governor Kasich who sees postsecondary education as similar to an "emergency vehicle when there is a job," arguments that the international reputation of our scholars is in jeopardy are likely to fall on deaf ears. "Those days are over!" we'd probably be told, and that'd be the end of it. It may be gratifying to complain among ourselves that regents and legislators "just don't get it" when it comes to what a university education is all about, but our sense of gratification won't get us very far. We need a more positive approach.

Many of the ideas covered throughout this book, from appreciative inquiry to leading upward, emphasize the importance of seeing an issue from the stakeholder's perspective. If we were to adopt that approach, we could have made more effective arguments to legislators for making higher education a priority in their funding decisions:

o Investments in higher education repay the states that make them many times over. Data collected by the College Board revealed that in 2008, college graduates not only had median annual incomes that were significantly higher than those with only high school diplomas ($55,700 versus $33,800) but they also paid more in taxes ($13,000 versus $7,100). Moreover, those who continued their education at the graduate level had (and thus conveyed to their states) a far greater economic impact than those who held only baccalaureate degrees or attended community colleges: graduates with a master's degree had a median income of $67,300 and paid taxes of

$16,200, those with a doctorate earned $91,900 and paid taxes of $23,100, and those with professional degrees had incomes of $100,000 and paid taxes of $25,600 (http://trends.collegeboard.org /education_pays/report_findings/indicator/Education_Earnings _and_Tax_Payments). What all of this means is that over a thirty-year career, people earning doctorates pay nearly half a million dollars more in taxes than did those with high school diplomas. In addition, their higher incomes add to economic growth at a rate many times that of the state's investment in their degrees because their salaries allow them to afford additional goods and services.

o The same study found that those with a bachelor's degree were far less likely to be a drain on state and federal social services (such as Medicaid, food stamps, and school lunch programs) than those with no diploma, only a high school diploma, or an associate degree (http://trends.collegeboard.org/education_pays/report _findings/indicator/Public_Assistance_Programs).

o Similarly, those who received their education at a college or university had lower rates of smoking, obesity, and low birth weight in their children than did other groups (http://trends.collegeboard .org/education_pays/report_findings/health).

o Moreover, the anecdotal evidence that boards and legislatures often cite about the low skill levels of American college graduates or employer dissatisfaction with the curricula and standards found throughout American higher education is not supported by data. In a joint study conducted by the Conference Board, Corporate Voices for Working Families, the Partnership for 21st Century Skills, and the Society for Human Resource Management, employers indicated that the majority of graduates from American four-year colleges or universities were rated as proficient or excellent in every skill listed in the survey and had far more areas of excellence than they had deficiencies. Those results did not occur when employers were asked about those who had earned only a high school diploma or a two-year degree (Casner-Lotto, 2006).

o Finally, it makes little political sense for those in positions of authority to treat higher education and the holders of advanced degrees as though they were the cause, not the solution, of economic and social problems. University-educated citizens are more likely to vote than any other segment of the population, including those with associate degrees (http://trends.collegeboard.org/education_pays /report_findings/indicator/Voting).

In making these arguments, positive academic leaders understand that trustees, regents, and legislators aren't "the enemy"; they're merely one important group of constituents in the open system of a modern college or university. Every member of such a complex system has his or her own needs and desires, but every member is also affected by the choices made by others elsewhere in the system. For this reason, rather than taking the negative approach of seeing trustees and legislators as problems needing to be solved, positive academic leaders view them as stakeholders who, while they may have perspectives different from their own, are ultimately interested in what's best for the system as a whole. For many of these stakeholders, economic arguments will always trump all other concerns. For others, however, the issues that were significant throughout so many of the state of the state addresses in 2012 won't necessarily be the same in the years to come. Positive academic leaders thus understand that they can't dismiss any group of stakeholders as "bean counters" or "nothing more than accountants," but recognize that each constituent is a distinct individual whose concerns will evolve over time.

Assessment and Positive Leadership

At several points in our discussion, I've spoken about assessment, strategic planning, and quality assurance in ways that must seem disparaging, calling them "invasive species" that migrated into the system of higher education from the world of business. As someone who routinely provides training in these very areas, I'm fully aware of the irony. (In my own defense, I believe that those of us in academia who feel far too much money is devoted to these accountability exercises have an obligation to demonstrate to others how they can be done more effectively, at a lower cost, and with a greater appreciation for what makes higher education unique as a working environment.) I certainly wouldn't deny the claim that assessment, strategic planning, and accreditation have helped improve colleges and universities. Nevertheless, I also believe that people may be forgiven for wondering whether higher education could fulfill its mission better and at a far lower cost if the staggering expense devoted to funding strategic plans, offices of institutional effectiveness, and accreditation reviews were directed instead to teaching and research. Be that as it may, if higher education has become expert in anything over the past half-century, it has been in establishing strategic goals, setting measurable outcomes related to those goals, assessing the degree to which those outcomes have been achieved, using those data to improve internal processes ("closing the loop"), and documenting how that improvement has occurred. All of us in higher education have become masters of using assessment, accreditation, and strategic planning to demonstrate to external constituents that we really are doing what we say we're doing. But suppose for a moment that we decided to apply this expertise not to a constant tweaking of our programs in a game of (we may as well admit it) rapidly diminishing returns, but to the way in which positive academic leadership is more effective than traditional administrative strategies. What might be the result?

In *Positive Leadership* (2008), Kim Cameron suggested several possible ways to measure the degree to which someone had adopted more constructive management approaches. For instance, Cameron noted that during a self-evaluation, supervisors could rate the frequency with which they

- Forgave mistakes rather than punished errors
- Expressed gratitude to those who reported to them
- Encouraged employees to support one another
- Provided feedback that emphasized strengths rather than weaknesses
- Gave criticism in the most constructive possible way
- Spent time with their most capable employees rather than their most problematic ones
- Identified and respected the core values of those who report to them
- Related goals to the overall mission and vision of the organization

The result is a positive leadership assessment form on which Cameron identifies twenty-four desirable behaviors to which managers should aspire. Yet since our focus is higher education rather than the corporate world, we might augment Cameron's form with a number of positive leadership strategies that relate specifically to what we do as administrators. For instance, we might rate ourselves on how often we

- End weeks, semesters, and academic years by summarizing the good things that happened during that time
- Make a conscious effort to see our systems not as closed (i.e., consisting of only faculty, students, and staff) but open (i.e.,

including a broad range of constituents, such as the local
community and general public)

o Reflect on our core values and consider whether they're informing
the decisions we're making

o View our administrative role as coaching and mentoring others
rather than manipulating and controlling them

o Take full advantage of the knowledge and experience of our
faculties by empowering them rather than just assigning
responsibilities to them

o Receive genuine delight from the accomplishments of the people we
supervise rather than just from our own successes

o Act in a way that underscores for others what they've gained when
they make a compromise, not what they've lost

o Promote the highest possible standards of excellence in teaching,
research, and service

o Evaluate the members of the faculty and staff both as individuals
and as members of a team that contributes to the mission of the
program

o Convey a positive image of the program and institution to all constituents

By themselves, these behaviors in conjunction with Cameron's positive leadership assessment provide a useful way of determining how
well we're adhering to the principles we've been advocating. But these
instruments can become even more valuable if we cross-tabulate the
items on them with our progress in reaching our long-term goals. For
instance, consider the issues that came up repeatedly in the state of
the state addresses we considered earlier: the placement of graduates
into jobs, helping students achieve on-time graduation without a great
deal of financial aid debt, the economic impact of higher education,
and so on. Then combine those metrics with other factors we're likely
to track anyway:

o Student retention rates

o Number of declared majors

o Faculty research productivity

o Student research productivity

o Placement of baccalaureate graduates into graduate and
professional programs

o Rates of faculty morale

o Rates of student satisfaction

o Annual giving rates

o Amount of external funding a program has received over a rolling three-year period

o Number of refereed publications produced by a program each year

o Number of regional and national awards received by students and faculty members

And so on. If we were to use a 360-degree process to rate administrators on how well they've adopted positive leadership strategies and then correlate those results with the factors that we (or our stakeholders) regard as integral to the success of our programs, we would begin to assemble a singularly useful body of data. Over time we could trace which positive leadership approaches had the strongest correlation with specific measures of success. We could then use this information to document the efficacy of positive academic leadership as a whole, improve the metrics that we've identified as most significant, and demonstrate that progress on soft goals (such as improving morale) doesn't have to be sacrificed in order to achieve hard goals (such as increasing enrollment).

By collecting and analyzing data in this way, we'd be playing to our strengths in two important ways. First, we'd be applying everything we learned about assessment, program review, and strategic planning in a manner that more effectively relates to the unique structure of the academy. Second, we'd be acquiring insight into how we can build on our successes even more by discovering which positive leadership techniques correlate best with the outcomes we want our programs to achieve. In the spirit of positive academic leadership, we'd be using our current assets and resources to provide the greatest number of benefits to the greatest number of people.

Mini-Case Studies on Positive Academic Leadership

We've had an opportunity throughout these chapters to explore the theoretical aspects of positive academic leadership and the research suggesting that it would be effective in different academic environments. But the real test of an administrative approach is whether it affects the way we respond to actual situations. I end our discussion therefore by examining four short case studies and seeing how we might apply positive academic leadership if challenges such as the following were to occur.

Positive Leadership in a Negative Environment

Case Study

You've already been practicing positive academic leadership for quite some time when you find yourself reporting to a new supervisor who's been hired from outside the institution. One of the first opportunities your new boss has to gain an impression of you comes at a meeting of your faculty where, as usual, you strive to find win-win solutions in some extremely difficult situations and demonstrate your ability to view matters from the faculty's perspective.

After the meeting, you feel pretty good about what happened and regard the meeting as an overall success. But as you're walking out of the building, you find yourself alone with your new supervisor who says:

> What did you think you were doing back there? You let people walk all over you. You're supposed to be in charge, but I didn't observe a trace of leadership on your part. In fact, what I witnessed just isn't working. You're never going to start getting things done unless you make it clear to everyone who reports to you that you're their boss, not their friend. Stop trying to put a happy face on what's really a disaster in your program. If people aren't afraid of you, they'll just do whatever they want, work as little as possible, and milk the system for everything they can get. From now on, I want you to clear each faculty meeting agenda with me in advance and demonstrate some effective governance. Due to the budget situation we're in, it's going to be a bloodbath this year, and we won't be able to make any progress until everyone understands how serious the problem is.

Your immediate impulse is to think that it may be time to move on since you're not sure how successful you can be in your institution's new administrative climate. But you worry about the future of your programs and feel that if your new supervisor plays an active role in choosing your successor, the people and curriculum you value will be done a great deal of harm. Remembering that positive academic leadership involves doing the right thing even if it isn't the easiest thing, what do you do? Stop here to consider your most likely response; then continue with the case discussion.

Case Discussion

In this case study, we learn that you've done a good job seeing matters from the perspective of your faculty members. In your new administrative environment, however, your commitment to positive academic leadership requires you to lead upward and see matters from your supervisor's perspective. Obviously he is convinced that the institution's budgetary challenge constitutes a crisis (even though you may disagree) and fits several of the criteria that Daniel Goleman used to describe the "bad boss" in chapter 1: he is suspicious, assumes that leadership requires intimidation, blames problems on others, and takes a cynical view of each employee's motives. But your supervisor also wants results, and that may be the most productive way to approach this challenge. Try working with your boss to set up specific goals and a time line for achieving them. Then, using your own words and style, say something like the following:

> I know the people I work with, and I've got a pretty good record at getting things done with them. [You may need to cite some of your successes since your supervisor is new.] Let's accept the goals we've set, but let me work to reach them my way. I'm convinced there's more than one effective style of leadership, and I've discovered an approach that I believe works best in my area. If you like, I'll give you constant updates on our progress toward meeting these goals, but I also want the liberty to use my best professional judgment in how they can best be met.

This strategy comes with a risk: you're probably putting your job on the line if you can't reach the goals you've set. But positive academic leaders don't shy away from calculated risks when the potential advantages outweigh those risks. Besides, you've already been tempted to explore your options by looking for another position, returning to the classroom, or retiring, so you may well decide that "the worst possible thing that can happen" isn't really that bad after all.

A Double Bind of Your Own Creation

Case Study
You're responsible for conducting the evaluation of someone whose performance has been declining for several years and has reached a particularly low point during the past six months. It's time for you to schedule an evaluation session, and you're starting to gather your thoughts about what you'll say to the person about how to increase the likelihood of improved performance and what the consequences will be if these targets aren't reached. Before you complete your preparation, however, this faculty member appears in your doorway and asks if the annual evaluation can be done immediately. You mention that you're not quite ready and

suggest that sometime later, perhaps even tomorrow, would be better. "But don't you remember?" she asks you. "After today I'm on leave for the next month to take that language immersion course overseas. You approved it ages ago. If you can't meet with me right now, we can't do it for another five or six weeks." You quickly calculate that a delay of more than two weeks would cause you to miss the deadline your institution has imposed for this person's annual review. At best, such a delay would make it almost inevitable that any criticism or sanction would be overturned during an appeal, grievance, or lawsuit. At worst, your own job could be in jeopardy because your supervisor is particularly adamant that all evaluations be done correctly and on time. As a positive academic leader, what do you do?

1. Do you go ahead and conduct the review anyway?
   - If so, how do you strike the proper balance between being constructive, supportive, and forward looking while still underscoring the serious message that significant changes will need to be made?
   - How do you discuss the possibility that there will be consequences for not achieving the goals you set without utterly discouraging the person and without being too specific (since you haven't had time yet to decide what you would do)?
   - What steps should you take in order to protect yourself since you're going into this evaluation less prepared than you'd like to be?
2. Do you postpone the review until the person returns from leave?
   - If so, how do you address your supervisor's impression that you didn't follow his or her instructions about conducting all evaluations properly and on time? Imagine that you try contacting your supervisor to explain the situation in advance and learn that he or she is off-campus without access to telephone or e-mail for more than a week.
   - How do you reduce the likelihood that any criticism or suggestions of possible consequences will be invalidated by an appeal, grievance, or lawsuit?
3. Are there any alternatives that you can think of besides the two already mentioned (doing the review today versus waiting for the employee to return in a month)?

Once you have in mind how you'd probably proceed if you were to find yourself in this predicament, continue to the case discussion.

Case Discussion

The toughest decisions aren't those that require you to identify the right choice from a number of wrong choices. They're the ones where there are no right options at all or where you have plenty of satisfactory choices but not one that's clearly the best. The current situation places you in one of these awkward situations: you're wrong no matter which way you go, so positive leadership becomes a matter of finding the outcome that provides the greatest amount of good while resulting in the least amount of harm. If you were actually to find yourself facing a situation like the one in this case study, your first temptation would probably be to indulge in a certain amount of self-reproach: "Why didn't I remember that I had agreed to that leave of absence? What was I thinking of when I let this deadline creep up on me?" We all have a tendency to beat ourselves up when we don't meet our own expectations. And the scenario described here is particularly vexing because we're in the awkward position of having to fault someone for poor performance when we ourselves are guilty of something similar. But that type of self-recrimination is a waste of time. If a little bit of guilt helps you become better at planning your time so that you're not caught unaware again in the future, then that's a healthy thing. In keeping with the principles of positive academic leadership, you'll have developed a good result in the midst of a bad situation. But if you find yourself becoming distracted because you can't get this mistake out of your mind, then that's not a productive use of your time. You'd be better off spending your energy on figuring out what to do now than on becoming preoccupied with what you should have done before.

The third question asks whether you still have any alternatives to conducting the review now or doing it after the deadline. That's a good place to begin your approach to this challenge. We already know that your supervisor can't be reached for more than a week, but is there anyone else who is authorized to extend the deadline for you? With all the technology available today, is there a way in which you can perform the review before the deadline even if the person you're evaluating is in another country? In other words, can you conduct the review by videoconference, telephone, or some other means? Even though your own preference (and perhaps the institution's policy) has led you to think of this evaluation as an oral review, is it possible on this one occasion for the process to occur in writing only? The positive leadership strategy that you should use is to avoid settling for one of two unsatisfactory alternatives simply because those are the only options initially presented. Don't ever consent to something unsuitable without first exploring whether that's all that's available.

Nevertheless, suppose that the two alternatives presented in the case study are all that's available. Then what? You'll need to weigh the two choices carefully to determine which of them conveys the greater benefits and the lesser harm. If, in the end, you decide to proceed with the review immediately, keep in mind the techniques of appreciative inquiry from chapter 2: don't assume that the person you're reviewing hasn't been successful because she doesn't want to be or is intentionally trying to harm your program. The vast majority of people truly want to do a good job and will respond favorably to helpful advice about how to do so. No one enjoys hearing criticism that comes across as judgmental, trifling, or directed at their personality rather than their performance. So you can make the best of a bad situation if you don't lose sight of your positive leadership ideals simply because you're feeling unprepared. If you decide that it's best to conduct the review after the deadline, then be candid with your supervisor about the choice you made and explain your rationale clearly and concisely. Be sure that you can articulate why you believe that you've chosen the best option available and what you learned from the situation. As we saw in chapter 7, there's a huge difference between explaining your reasons and rationalizing your behavior; if your supervisor senses that you're indulging more in the latter than in the former, you'll be making a bad situation even worse.

One final way of applying positive academic leadership to the current situation is to take advantage of this problem to improve your entire system of evaluation. Ian Macdonald, Catherine Burke, and Karl Stewart (2006) suggest that supervisors create a "review the reviewer" form that employees can use to evaluate their supervisor's evaluation skills. The sample form they provide includes the following topics:

o My leader prepared adequately for the review.
o My leader devoted an appropriate amount of time for the meeting.
o My leader honored commitments made to me in my last review.
o I was able to provide honest advice to my leader on his or her leadership.

If you substitute the words *dean, chair,* and so on for *leader* in these questions, you'll have a valuable source of advice about how you can conduct better reviews in the future (particularly if you're coming across as rushed or unprepared). In addition, by demonstrating your own willingness to accept constructive criticism, you'll be making it more palatable for others to do the same.

Seizing the (Wrong) Teachable Moment

Case Study

Part of your positive leadership philosophy is that you encourage the people in your area to grow in their own leadership roles through the work you perform together. One of your direct reports has a tendency to be careless in the materials he sends you. For instance, there have been a number of occasions on which this person failed to proofread documents or missed something by not reading e-mails in their entirety. For a while, you've simply been correcting the resulting errors yourself, but now you realize that you've been enabling poor performance, not improving it. Due to yet another round of budget cuts, your institution has imposed a requirement that no course can be offered during the summer unless it enrolls at least thirty-five people. That minimum was established to guarantee that each summer course would generate a profit, helping the budget for the coming academic year. You're a bit uneasy about that requirement, since a number of courses in your own area are better taught as small seminars, labs, or studios than in a larger, mostly lecture format. Nevertheless, you're not in a position to change this policy, and your arguments in favor of flexibility have gone unheeded. In an e-mail to the administrators in your program, you explain that while you'll be enforcing the institution-wide minimum enrollment of thirty-five students per section, you won't approve any minimums higher than thirty-five since you don't want to depart too far from the close student-faculty relationship that you believe is vital to your program.

As usual, the same person who's been careless in the past once again appears not to have read your entire message. Or perhaps he just made yet another typographical error when submitting that summer's course list. Almost every course on this person's summer schedule does have its minimum enrollment set at thirty-five, but one highly paid full professor's course is listed as requiring at least thirty-six students. Ordinarily you would've just corrected the listing and the problem would be solved. But rather than encouraging this administrator's inattentive behavior, you decide to seize the teachable moment. The result is a series of e-mails and text messages that continues for the next five days.

> You: Please review the summer course list you've submitted and make sure everything is correct.
> Reply: Sure will. I just checked it over again, and everything is right.

You:	Please examine it very carefully. I think you're missing something.
Reply:	I guess I'm just not spotting it. What do you mean?
You:	Take a look at the guidelines I sent out earlier.
Reply:	Which set of guidelines: The ones about summer courses in particular or the ones about how we should format reports for your office?
You:	Summer courses.
Reply:	I just went over the list again and then had two colleagues review it as well. We all think the list complies fully with all your guidelines.
You:	Examine again the minimum enrollment policy.
Reply:	I did. The courses all meet or exceed those minimums.
You:	That's the problem.
Reply:	Now I'm really confused. The problem is that I met the minimums???
You:	Or exceeded.
Reply:	For which course?
You:	XOL 4191.
Reply:	The minimum's thirty-five, as you said.
You:	No, thirty-six.
Reply:	Wait. You want it raised to thirty-six?
You:	No, it IS thirty-six. It's supposed to be thirty-five.
Reply:	Oh. Sorry. We didn't catch that before. It's fixed now.

He then goes to those two colleagues who reviewed the list earlier and says, "Can you believe it took five days for the boss to have me correct a mistyped 36 to 35? What a waste of our time!" How do you evaluate your own positive academic leadership strategies in this situation?

Case Discussion

This case study is an exercise in empowerment gone awry. While you began with the honorable intention of creating an environment in which people would deal with their own challenges rather than expecting you to fix everything for them, that goal became lost somewhere along the way. It's apparent from the e-mail exchange that both you and the other person were miscommunicating from the start and eventually becoming exasperated. A great deal of effort could've been saved if you'd stopped e-mailing and had a conversation (in person if possible, or by phone if that proved to be the only option) to clear the air a bit. The message you thought you were conveying was, "I'm trusting you to figure out on your own how best to handle this situation." But the message that the other person received was, "I'm expecting you to read my mind." In short, the whole problem should have been avoided through good lateral leadership strategies, including awareness of how stakeholders are likely to interpret our communications because of the frames and perspectives they bring to the conversation. (See chapter 10.)

Nevertheless, the incident has already occurred and, as we saw in the previous case study, remorse and second-guessing yourself are usually a waste of time. The real positive leadership question here is: How do I transform what has happened into something beneficial, and how do I avoid making similar mistakes in the future? Let's begin with the first part of that question.

Although it would've been preferable to have a face-to-face conversation about this matter earlier in the process, it's not too late to take that step now. Sit down with the other person in a neutral area. Don't use one of your offices. Somewhere off campus, such as a quiet restaurant or coffee shop, is best. It provides a more relaxed environment than can be found in any official setting. Clear the air, saying that you know that the e-mail exchange didn't go well and indicating your hope that the two of you can still straighten things out. Explain your philosophy of trust, empowerment, and responsibility and, in that context, take responsibility for your own contribution to the miscommunication. Note why it's important to you that details be correct and that by the time memos and reports reach you, you expect that careless errors will be caught so that you can focus on the bigger issues. Listen to what the other person has to say, letting him or her vent if that seems necessary. Avoid becoming defensive about the shortcomings the other person finds in your own handling of the situation. Instead, view the conversation as an opportunity for you to see your administrative style as others see it.

As for the second part of the question that concerns how you can avoid similar situations in the future, regard this experience as a lesson in how to pick your battles. In retrospect, a single-digit difference in an enrollment minimum is probably not the best issue to draw a line in the sand over. In the future, a challenge like this one may best be handled with a quick call that goes something like the following: "I was just going over the summer course list you sent me, and I noticed that you had the minimum for XOL 4191 set at thirty-six when we were going to set it at thirty-five for all courses. Was there a reason you need an extra student in the course?" If the answer is that because the professor's salary is so high, it'll take the tuition of thirty-six students to cover the cost, you'll have an opportunity to clarify your view on why it benefits the students to hold the line on class size. If the answer is that the number was just a typo, you'll have an opportunity to talk about why paying attention to details is important and your concerns about carelessness in the past. Remember that in accordance with positive leadership strategies, you're not trying to attack the person or make him or her feel bad, simply indicating your confidence that an improved performance is possible in the future.

Full Frontal Assault

Case Study

You go to a faculty meeting one day expecting a rather dull session since there isn't much on the agenda and the items that are listed as scheduled topics are all quite routine. As a result, you're stunned when during the announcement section at the end of the meeting, a faculty member proceeds to attack you by name, blaming you for almost everything that's recently gone wrong at the institution and describing you as ineffective, incompetent, and weak. You instantly recognize that what you regard as many of the strengths of your positive leadership style— your nonauthoritarian manner, willingness to consider different points of view, desire to empower members of the faculty and staff, and frequent use of humor—is regarded by this particular faculty member as an absence of leadership. You expect that the verbal attack will be over soon, that the chair of the meeting will eventually intervene, and that others will then rise in your defense, but none of these things occur. The tirade continues for ten unbearable minutes, concluding with a motion that the faculty take a vote of no confidence in you. When the faculty member finally sits back down, you can feel that all eyes are on you. What do you do?

Case Discussion

After reading about so many instances in which I encourage you to see matters from the perspective of others and recognize that most people are just trying to do what they think is best for the institution, you probably think I'm going to say something like, "Before you reply, try to relate to this person's situation. Understand the matter from his or her point of view. Consider the degree to which he or she may be right." But I'm not. What I *am* going to say is that being a positive academic leader is one thing; being a doormat is another. The faculty member hasn't been guilty of merely a slight lapse in judgment; he or she has engaged in profoundly unprofessional, noncollegial behavior. There's no reason that you should simply sit there and take it. (I probably wouldn't have allowed the full ten minutes to go by.) Although not a crisis in the sense that this verbal assault constituted an imminent threat to the survival of your program or the personal safety of a student, this situation is one in which a little bit of crisis management seems in order. Take back control of this turn of events and don't deceive yourself that the best response to this attack is a smile and optimism.

For one thing, notice that although the faculty member has made a motion, no one immediately seconded it. That itself may be the vote of confidence that you were expecting from others; they may just be feeling too intimated by this bully to speak up in your defense. Start by exerting your right to respond to the allegations that have just been made. Note that although your positive style of leadership may look a bit different from more hierarchical approaches to management, it's no less effective; in fact, it is ultimately much more beneficial to the program you all care about. (The References and Resources sections in this book can provide you with plenty of studies to cite.) Go through some of the achievements that have resulted from your administrative methods. Share the limelight freely; point out when your leadership style made it easier for someone to win a teaching award, receive a prestigious grant, complete an important publication, or achieve any other success you regard as significant. If that person is present, look him or her in the eye and cite that faculty member as an example of what you're trying to do. Emphasize why a command-based model of governance simply isn't appropriate in higher education and why your type of leadership may be more understated than an "in your face, down in the weeds" approach. Note that you trust the faculty enough to know that it's better for them (and the entire institution) if your area isn't controlled from the top down.

Ironically, this demonstration of resilience may be just what's necessary to undermine the faculty member's claim that you're not a genuine leader. Your speech may even win that person over. (But don't get your hopes up.) Conclude by expressing a willingness to continue this discussion further with the faculty member in a more appropriate setting. And once the situation has been resolved, bear no grudges. Negative academic leaders never forget a slight; positive academic leaders never forget that it's the program, not their own feelings, that is ultimately most important.

Conclusion

British journalist Russell H. Ewing (1885–1976) wrote:

> A boss creates fear; a leader confidence. A boss fixes blame; a leader corrects mistakes. A boss knows all; a leader asks questions. A boss makes work drudgery; a leader makes it interesting. A boss is interested in himself; a leader is interested in the group. (cited by Harris, 2000, p. 97)

While most of this book has explored positive academic leadership as a strategy that individuals can use to improve their own effectiveness as administrators, the full impact of these strategies will become apparent only when they spread throughout higher education as a whole. When that occurs, we can expect those annoying motivational posters to be removed from our conference rooms and posters of new statements of principles to take their place:

○ Negative academic leaders effect change by commanding and intimidating others.

○ Neutral academic leaders effect change by managing and organizing others.

○ Positive academic leaders effect change by empowering and inspiring others.

And when that occurs, we'll know we've won.

The essence of positive academic leadership is respect—respect for our colleagues, respect for those who report to us, and respect for the ability of higher education to change people's lives for the better. When we resort to firefighting and fault finding, we trivialize the profession that, as we saw in chapter 5, quite literally makes dreams come true for millions of people every year. To build on what's best in our colleges or universities, we don't have to commission new studies or create new governmental programs. All we have to do is to remember what it was about higher education that attracted us to this field in the first place. We can tell that story to those inside the academy and to the critics outside its walls. We can shift our language, perspective, and thinking just slightly so we tell this story through our choices and actions, as well as through our words. It is, after all, a good story to tell.

References

Cameron, K. S. (2008). *Positive leadership: Strategies for extraordinary performance.* San Francisco, CA: Berrett-Koehler

Casner-Lotto, J. (2006). *Are they really ready to work? Employers' perspectives on the basic knowledge and applied skills of new entrants to the 21st century U.S. workforce.* New York, NY: Conference Board Partnership for 21st Century Skills, Corporate Voices for Working Families, and Society for Human Resource Management. http://p21.org/documents /FINAL_REPORT_PDF09-29-06.pdf.

Harris, D. (2000). *Warriors@work: What the smartest business leaders are saying.* Salt Lake City, UT: Franklin Covey.

Macdonald, I., Burke, C. G., & Stewart, K. (2006). *Systems leadership: Creating positive organizations.* Aldershot, England: Gower

Peters, T. J., & Waterman, R. H. (2004). *In search of excellence: Lessons from America's best-run companies.* New York, NY: HarperBusiness Essentials.

INDEX

Page references followed by *fig* indicate an illustrated figure; followed by *t* indicate a table.

A

Aarts, H., 87
Academic administration: centrifugal leadership strategy of, 38, 186–188, 199–201
   environmental or essential leadership strategy of, 192–199
   lateral leadership strategy of, 188–192
   leading upward strategy of, 183–186
   transforming other strategies into positive, 199–201
Academic administrators: "change agent" or "in-your-face" type of, 77
   "fuels" versus "catalysts" approach by, 174–175
   honeymoon period of newly hired, 76–77
   peak-end rule significance for positive leadership by, 56–60*fig*
   positive academic leadership as antidote to stress of, 52
   positive administration by, 183–1202
   questions that should be asked periodically by, 177
   six daily activities typical for, 90
   taking positive perspectives practice by, 83–98
   when not to use positive academic leadership, 60–62. *See also* Crisis management; Faculty; Positive academic leadership

Academic interaction: client/professional, 43, 44–46, 47*fig*, 48
   distinction between other models and the client/professional, 43–48
   leadership orders as sign of failed relationship, 48–50
   positive language used in, 68–69
   power politics as great bane of, 49–50
   promoting maximum collegial flow in, 50–53
Academic leader roles: as coach, 123–141
   as conductor, 161–178
   as counselor, 143–159
   historic and worldview of, 33–34
Academic leaders: client/professional interactions by, 43, 44–46, 47*fig*, 48, 68–69
   core values of, 101–111, 196–197
   historic and worldview of, 33–34
   leadership failure implication of orders given by, 48–50. *See also* Department chairs
Academic leadership: Ahearn's description of, 3–4, 20
   aligning programs and institution to your philosophy of, 112–114
   catalytic, 174–175
   client/professional type of interactions by, 43, 44–46, 47*fig*, 48
   core values used to develop philosophy of, 108–111

Academic leadership: *(continued)*
  danger of adopting military or
    corporate language in, 29
  discrete tasks used to achieve goals
    of, 116–118
  mind mapping for philosophy of,
    110*fig*
  moving from theory to practice of,
    114–116
  orders as sign of failure by, 48–50
  resilience significance in, 31
  responding to the crisis industry,
    211, 222–224
  the road to positive, 39. *See also*
    Higher education
Academic leadership models:
  administrative resilience, 29–32
  appreciative inquiry and positive
    change, 35–37
  centrifugal, 38, 186–188, 199–201
  common themes of all of the, 39
  environmental or essential, 192–201
  hope-based leadership, 25–28
  joyful leadership, 32–34
  lateral, 188–192, 199–201
  leading upward, 183–186, 199–201
  servant leadership, 37–39. *See also*
    Positive academic leadership
*Academically Adrift: Limited
  Learning on College Campuses*
  (Arum and Roksa), 206
*The Academy in Crisis: The Political
  Economy of Higher Education*
  (Sommer), 205
Active listening, 139–140
Administrative resilience model:
  description of, 29
  examining resilience in context of
    the, 30–31
  strategies for developing resilience,
    31–32. *See also* Resilience
Administrators. *See* Academic
  administrators
Ahearn, F. L., 3–4, 20, 90
Alessandra, T., 12, 151
Alverno College (Milwaukee), 213
American Association for the
  Advancement of Science, 167

American Association of State
  Colleges and Universities, 229
American Council on Education
  (ACE), 116, 117
Anderson, J. R., 26
Antioch College bankruptcy, 60
Antonides, G., 55
Appreciative inquiry: comparing
  traditional administrators with
  those using, 35–36
  4-D model and 4-I model
    foundations of, 36–37
  leading to positive change through,
    35
  powerful questioning element of,
    139, 140
Aristotle, 87
Arum, R., 206
Assessment: higher education metrics
  tracked during, 235–236
  positive academic leadership role of,
    233–236
  positive leadership desirable
    behaviors to rate during,
    234–235. *See also* Evaluation
Associated Press and Stanford
  University poll (2010), 219, 223
Associated Press/Viacom/Roper Poll
  (2011), 218–219, 223–224
Authentic leaders, 145
Authority: college and hospital
  hierarchies of, 45–46, 47*fig*
  history of pyramid structure of,
    183–184
  systems approach understanding of
    power and, 167
  triangle or pyramid shape
    of corporate and military,
    45*fig*–46*fig*
Averill, J., 85
Avolio, B., 145

B
Bad vs. good bosses, 19–20, 238
Baldwin, M. R., 72
Baumgartel, H., 57
Bay of Pigs incident, 85–86
Bays, J. C., 118

Bazer, G., 209
Beard, R., 72
Beck, A. T., 26
Becker, D., 9
Behavior: assessment to rate positive leaders' desirable, 234–235
how experience shapes our, 87–88
neuroscience approach to, 87
positive reinforcement of, 13–14, 68
rational choice view of, 87
study on teachers' expectations and student, 67
subconscious motivations shaping, 87
Behavioral control, 85
Behaviorism backlash (late 1950s to 1990s), 85
Bell, D., 213
Bennett, W., 213, 214
Bernstein, D., 13
Berry, J., 192, 193
Beswick, K., 167
Better, Stronger, Faster: The Myth of American Decline—and the Rise of a New Economy (Gross), 208–209
Bilsky, W., 102
Birnbaum, H., 52
The Black Swan (Taleb), 166
Blanchard, K., 11
Blind optimism, 18
Bloom, A., 213, 214
Boin, A., 30
Bolman, L., 93
Borysenko, J., 30
Boston Philharmonic Orchestra, 161
Brems, C., 72
Brinkman, D. R., 75
Brooks, D., 221
Brooks, R. B., 30
Brophy, J., 67
Brown, J., 229
Brown University, 212
Buller, J. L., 43, 72, 76, 124, 157, 191
Bundgaard, L., 189
Burke, C. G., 14, 49, 136–137, 173, 241
Burke, W. W., 77

Burt, C.D.B., 55
Butler, E. A., 17
Butterfly effect, 167

C
Cahn, D. D., 136
Cameron, K. S., 10, 16, 19, 234, 235
Carr, A., 8
Carson-Newman College, 32
Casner-Lotto, J., 232
Catalytic leadership, 174–175
Catherine the Great, 14
Catholic University of America, 3
Center for Applied Ethics (renamed Greenleaf Center for Servant-Leadership), 37
Center for Leadership and Change Management (Wharton School of Business), 184
Centrifugal leadership: questions to ask for implementing, 187
similarities between servant leadership and, 187
transforming into positive academic leadership, 199–201
visualizing, 38, 186–187fig, 188
Chain-of-command organizations: corporate customer/business interactions, 43, 45fig–46fig
hospital and academic client/professional interactions, 43, 44–46, 47fig, 48
military soldier/command interactions, 43–44, 45fig–46fig
Change: administrative resilience on acceptance of inevitable, 31
appreciative inquiry and positive, 35–37
defining positive, 35
4-D model and 4-I model for effective implementation of, 37
importance of positive language in effecting, 76–79
nurturing the system to promote constructive, 176–178
O'Toole's thirty-three hypotheses on resistance to, 77
overcoming resistance to, 78–79

Chaos theory, 167
Cheney, L., 213
Choices. *See* Making choices
Chomsky, N., 85
Christensen, C., 210
Christopher, J., 9
Chronicle of Higher Education, 51,
    221
Chu, D., 57–58, 186
Chung, H.-Y., 14
Churchill, W., 73–74
Clance, P. R., 72
Cleveland's annual sustainability
    summits, 33
Client/professional model of
    interaction: college hierarchy of,
    45–46, 47*fig,* 48
  description and example of, 44–45
  distinction between other models
    and the, 43–48
  hospital hierarchy example of,
    44–46, 47*fig*
  positive language used in, 68–69
  as typical in academic world, 43
Cline, F., 124
Closed academic system, 58
Closed system thinking, 227–228
The Closing of the American Mind
    (Bloom), 213, 214
Coach Carter (film), 125
Coaches: characteristics of good,
    140–141
  department chairs as, 138–140
  differences between teachers and,
    124–126, 133
  powerful questioning and active
    listening by, 139–140
Coaching strategies: inspiring
    confidence even in trouble times
    quality of, 127, 128–131
  motivating others to achieve highest
    possible standards quality of,
    127, 131
  moving from delegation to
    empowerment quality of, 128,
    137–138
  positive qualities of the academic
    leader as, 126–128

providing constructive criticism
    quality of, 128, 134–137
  recognizing when an excuse is
    merely a barrier quality of, 127,
    132–133
  taking responsibility for the group
    as a whole quality of, 128,
    133–134
Cognitive control, 85
Cojuharenco, L., 55
Colleagues: collegial and professional
    interactions with, 17
  relationship building between, 27
College Board declining scores (1963),
    213
College Entrance Examination Board
    tests (1901), 212
College of Allied Health and Nursing
    (Minnesota State University), 25
College of Pennsylvania (1756), 211
Colleges. *See* Institutions
Collins, J., 6
Columbia University, 213
Comfort, L. K., 30
Command authority: indicating a
    failure in academic leadership,
    48–50
  triangle or pyramid shape of
    corporate and military, 45*fig*–
    46*fig*
Committee on Undergraduate
    Education report (1994),
    213–214
Communication: active listening for
    effective, 139–140
  crisis management leadership
    strategy for, 61–62
  inspiring confidence through
    frequent and open, 130–131
  nurturing the system through
    constructive, 176–178
  powerful questioning for effective,
    139, 140
Complex Sale, 29
Compromise: love-hate relationship
    with, 195
  without being compromised,
    195–197

Concierge medicine health care,
4–5, 6
Conductors: being "fuels" versus
"catalysts" in the system,
174–175
exploring the components of your
system, 168–174
how they inspire others, 161–163,
178
nurturing the system, 176–178
systems approach to positive
leadership by, 163–167
Confidence building. *See* Inspiring
confidence
Conflict: developing ground rules
governing, 155
nine policies to help create positive
conflict out of, 155–158
nurturing the system to reduce,
176–177
positive conflict out of,
154–155
"Congratulations!" cards, 150
Conley, D., 27–28
Constructive criticism: coaching
strategies for giving, 134–137
description of, 128, 134
Constructive criticism strategies: be
discreet, 134
be future oriented, 135
focus on the behavior instead of the
person, 135
never criticize in anger, 134
pick your battles, 134
praise what you can, 136
prepare your remarks in advance,
134
suggest instead of tell people what
to do, 135–136
Conveying realistic confidence,
129–130
Cooperrider, D., 35, 140
Core values: compromising without
compromising your, 196–197
description of, 101–102
developing philosophy of leadership
based on your, 108–111
identify your, 102–108

Core values identification: mind
mapping for, 103–106
paired comparisons method for,
103
responding to uncompromising
statements for, 106–108
structured brainstorming for,
102–103
Corporate interactions: comparing
client/professional and soldier/
command models to, 43–48
customer/business model of,
43
triangle or pyramid shape of
authority in, 45*fig*–46*fig*
Côté, S., 144
Counseling: dealing with grief and
suffering, 158–159
on developing attitude of gratitude,
145–154
on making conflict positive,
154–158
Counselors: accepting inevitability of
having to act as, 144–145
fears related to taking on role of,
143–144
Coussons-Read, M. E., 137
*Crisis in the Academy: Rethinking
Higher Education in America*
(Lucas), 205
Crisis industry: applying the systems
approach to the, 227–233
arguments for increasing state
funding of higher education,
231–233
positive academic leadership
response to the, 211,
222–224
putting crisis claims into context,
210, 211–218
state of the state addresses that
mention the, 229–231
Crisis management: examples of
situations requiring, 60
four categories of, 61
leadership tools required during,
61–62. *See also* Academic
administrators

Crisis management leadership
strategies: action before analysis,
61
decisiveness precedence over
consensus building, 61
use different communication styles
and methods as needed,
61–62
leadership roles will be blurred, 61
*Crisis on Campus: A Bold Plan for
Reforming Our Colleges and
Universities* (Taylor), 206
Csíkszentmihályi, M., 7, 8, 50
Cuban missile crisis, 86
Curriculum: caution against ignoring
arts and humanities, 221
false dichotomy of conflict between
science and humanities,
217–218
reform history of U.S., 211–215
STEM discipline, 213, 215, 218,
220, 221, 229, 230
"teach-to-the-test mentality," 221
ten pendulum topics about U.S.
higher education, 215t–216. *See
also* Higher education
Currie, W., 167
Custers, R., 87
Customer/business model of
interaction: description and
example of, 43
distinction between other models
and the, 43–48
triangle or pyramid shape of
authority in, 45fig–46fig

D

Daniels, D., 128
"Dave's Rules of Order," 157
Davis, L., 72
"A Day in the Life of a Dean"
(Ahearn), 3–4, 90
De Geest, E., 167
de Hoog, H.A.N., 55
De Luca, B., 51
Dead Poets Society (film), 125
Deal, T., 93
"Deanlets," 137

Decision making: how experience
shapes our, 87–88
by positive academic leadership in
response to crisis, 222–224
rational choice view of, 87
subconscious motivations shaping
our, 87
systems approach to, 163–166. *See
also* Making choices
Decisional control, 85
*Declining by Degrees: Higher
Education at Risk* (Hersh and
Merrow), 205
Deiser, R., 189
Delegation: managerial approach
using, 137
moving to empowerment from,
137–138
Demchak, C. C., 30
Deming, W. E., 15
Denning, S., 80
DePalma, J., 138–139, 140
Department Chair (Mallard and
Sargent), 32
The Department Chair Primer (Chu),
58
Department chairs: as coaches,
138–140
four primary behaviors of the
"best," 33
who appreciate uniqueness, 33. *See
also* Academic leaders
*Designing Resilience: Preparing for
Extreme Events* (Comfort, Boin,
and Demchak), 30
Diener, E., 8, 55
Directive leadership, 57
Do, A. M., 55
Drapeau, A. S., 102
Dream frame, 93
Dudley, D., 38
Dutton, J., 10

E

Edwards, E., 29
Egloff, B., 17
80/20 rule (Pareto principle), 11
Electronic praise, 147

Eliot, C., 212
Ellsworth, P., 55, 56
Elsewhere, U.S.A. (Conley), 27–28
Emergent leadership: becoming
an authentic leader through,
144–145
definition of, 144
Emmons, R., 147
Empowerment: "Deanlets" who have
responsibility without, 137
leadership approach to, 137
moving from delegation to,
137–138
seizing the (wrong) teachable
moment mini-case study on
negative, 242–245
"Energy vampires," 97
England, G., 102
English, S., 138–139, 140
Environment: catalytic approach to
leadership inspiring creative, 175
closed academic, 58
created to encourage maximum
collegial flow, 56
"feedback gap" common to work,
146
for maximizing peak experiences,
56–60*fig*
positive climate of, 10
positive leadership in a negative,
237–238
Environmental (or essential)
leadership: complex system work
facilitated through, 192–193
compromising without being
compromised strength of, 193,
195–197
description of, 192
goal of transforming stress into
eustress, 199
leading in the midst of uncertainty
strength of, 193, 197–199
transforming into positive academic
leadership, 199–201
understanding the system strength
of, 193–195
Epley, N., 55, 56
Erickson, E. A., 17

Erickson, R. J., 102
Etcoff, N., 8
European feudalism, 184
Eustress, 199
Evaluation: a double bind of your
own creation mini-case study on,
238–241
suggestions for self-evaluation
questions to ask during, 234. *See
also* Assessment
Evans, L., 128
Ewing, R. H., 247
Excuses: coaching strategies to
overcome barrier of, 132–133
recognized as lack of effort, 127, 132
Experience: how our behavior is
shaped by our, 87–88
how to maximize peak, 60*fig*
imposter syndrome, 72
peak-end rule on, 53–55, 56–60
studies on three things that occur
when recalling, 55–56
ExxonMobile Foundation, 220
Eyring, H., 210

F
Faculty: administrative leading
upward leadership of, 184–186
creating environment that
maximizes peak experiences for,
56–60*fig*
dealing with grief and suffering by,
158–159
establishing boundaries for
unproductive attitude by, 96
full frontal assault mini-case study
on handling angry, 245–246
general public beliefs about, 219
joyful leadership approach to tenure
of, 34
overcoming resistance to change by,
78–79
positive academic leadership as
antidote to low morale of, 52
positive language used to facilitate
behavior change in, 69–70
promoting maximum collegial flow
for, 50–53, 56

Faculty: *(continued)*
    systems approach to thought
        experience on salary increase
        request by, 163–166
    taking positive perspective of
        leave taken by, 83–85. *See also*
        Academic administrators
    Teachers
Faculty Incivility (Twale and De
    Luca), 51
*Failed Grade: The Corporations and
    Decline of Higher Education in
    America* (Soloway), 206
Failure: recognizing when an excuse is
    lack of effort, 127, 132–133
    taking responsibility for, 128,
        133–134. *See also* Mistakes
Faris, S. K., 201
Fay, J., 124
"Feedback gap," 146
Fellows Program (American Council
    on Education), 116, 117
Ferriss, T., 6
50 Hours (Cheney), 213
Fischer, K., 221
Fisher, R., 189
Fisk, G. M., 17
Fleishman, E., 102
Flora, S. R., 13
Florida, R., 221
Flow: Csíkszentmihályi's concept of,
    50
    group achievement of, 50–51
    maximum collegial, 50–53
Foresight, servant leader quality of, 38
4-D model of change, 36–37
4-I model of change, 36–37
Francis, P., 205
Fredrickson, B. L., 55, 140–141
Free Will (Harris), 87
Freud, S., 87
Frick, W., 128
Frohnmayer, D., 157
Furneaux, L., 55

G
Gaff, J. G., 211, 212
Galbraith, J. R., 189

Galford, R. M., 102
Galliers, R., 167
Gandhi, M., 67
General Education in a Free Society
    (Redbook) [Harvard University],
    212
Gentry, W. A., 102
Georgia Southern University, 38, 74
Gilbert, D., 8
Girnius-Brown, O., 136
Giroux, H., 205
Giroux, S., 205
Gleason, C. A., 87
Goal setting: motivating other to
    achieve high standards through,
    127, 131
    why positive language is important
        in, 74–75
Goals: administrative resilience
    approach to achieving, 31
    discrete tasks used to achieve
        leadership, 116–118
    hope-based leadership approach to
        setting, 28
The golden rule (Do unto others), 12
"Goldilocks" moment, 50
Goldman, B. M., 102
Goldstein, S., 30
Goleman, D., 19, 20, 238
Good, T., 67
Good vs. bad bosses, 19–20, 238
Goodbye, Mr. Chips (film), 125
Goodwin, C., 206
Google Alerts, 149
Gordon College, 32
Gordon, J., 192, 193
*Grade Inflation: A Crisis in College
    Education* (Johnson), 205
Graduation rates, 218
Grandey, A. A., 17
Grashow, A., 222
Gratitude: appropriate ways to
    express thanks and, 150–154
    developing the attitude of, 145–150
    as factor driving job satisfaction,
        145
    five simple rules for writing thank-
        you notes, 141

four mechanisms for offering, 147

measures taken to access good news worthy of, 149

roundtable recognition technique for expressing, 147–149. *See also* Rewards/recognition

Gratitude principles: make the gratitude clear, 152–153

make the gratitude personal, 151–152

make the gratitude sincere, 153–154

make the gratitude specific, 152

make the gratitude timely, 154

Great Recession (2008), 209

Greenleaf, R. K., 37

Grief counseling, 158–159

Gross, D., 208–209

Gross, J. J., 17

Group needs: department chairs who match strengths with, 33

questions that should be asked by administrators on, 177

Grube, B., 74

Guignon, C., 9

H

Hackman, J. D., 167

Harland, L., 14

Harnisch, T., 229

Harris Poll (2011), 218, 223

Harris, S., 87

Harter, S., 102

Harvard University, 212, 213

Hayward, G., 205

Healing, servant leader quality of, 37

Health care models: common factors found in different, 6–7

concierge medicine, 4–5, 6

P4 Medicine Institute's holistic, 5–6

personal trainer approach to, 6

positive psychology similarities to other, 8–9

surgeon, 6

Heifetz, R., 222

Helicopter parents, 124

Helland, M., 25, 26

Heraclitus, 158

Herbst, P. G., 184

Hersh, R., 205

Herth, K., 25, 26, 27, 28, 38–39, 123

Hickinbottom, S., 9

Hierarchies: college and hospital, 45–46, 47*fig*

history of pyramid structure of authority and, 183–184

how they impede maximum collegial flow, 51

triangle or pyramid shape of corporate and military, 45*fig*–46*fig*

Hierarchy of needs, 194*fig*, 195

Higher education: arguments for increasing state funding for, 231–233

Associated Press and Stanford University poll (2010) on American beliefs about, 219, 223

challenges facing U.S., 218–221

differing perceptions of the current state of, 209–210

dire realities of today's, 29

history of development and reform of, 211–215

increasing enrollment, growth, and competitive admissions to, 206–208

international enrollment in U.S., 207–208

sample list of titles written about crisis in, 205–206

state of the state addresses that mention, 229–231

ten pendulum topics about U.S., 215*t*–216

types of metrics tracked for, 235–236. *See also* Academic leadership; Curriculum; Institutions

Higher education crisis: false dichotomy of conflict between science and humanities in, 217–218

inevitable continued cycle of the, 216–217

myth of U.S. economic decline due to, 208–209

Higher education crisis: *(continued)*
  positive academic leadership
    response to, 222–224
  putting crisis claims into context,
    210, 211–218
  sample list of titles written about,
    205–206
  ten pendulum topics about
    American, 215t–216
Higher Education in a State of Crisis
  (Teixeira), 206
Higher Education in Crisis: The
  Corporate Eclipse of the
  University (Natale, Libertella,
  and Hayward), 205
Higher education strategies: academic
  leadership responses to the crisis
  industry, 211, 222–224
  candor about the challenges we
    face, 210–211, 218–221
  playing to our strengths, 211,
    227–247
  putting crisis claims into context,
    210, 211–218
Hope: Lazarus' work on how
  perspective impacts, 85
  learned optimism as form, 28
  rejected as strategy, 29
  as servant leader's greatest
    contribution, 39
Hope-based leadership: basic
  assumptions of, 25–26
  main objection raised about, 29
  strategies for, 27–28
  three major components of,
    26
Hope-based leadership strategies:
  building relationships among
  colleagues, 27
  reflect on achievements before
    moving on to next project,
    27–28
  set meaningful goals for institution
    and individuals, 28
  underscore meaning and
    importance of tasks, 27
Hospital chain-of-command hierarchy,
  44–46, 47fig, 48

Hu, D.-C., 14
Human resource frame, 93
Hunt, T. L., 26

I

Idealism frame, 93
Imes, S. A., 72
Imposter syndrome, 72
In Search of Excellence (Peters and
  Waterman), 228
Inner dialogue/imposter syndrome, 72
The Innovative University: Changing
  the DNA of Higher Education
  from the Inside Out (Christensen
  and Eyring), 210
Inspiring confidence: as coaching
  quality, 127, 128
  communicate frequently and openly
    strategy for, 130–131
  convey realistic confidence strategy
    for, 129–130
  explore alternative rewards strategy
    for, 129
  invest in people strategy for, 128–129
Institutions: aligning philosophy of
  leadership to your, 112–114
  client/professional hierarchy and
    interaction in, 43, 45–46, 47fig,
    48
  Harris Poll (2011) on general public
    beliefs about, 218, 223
  moving from theory to practice of
    leadership at, 114–116
  positive administration throughout
    the, 183–202. *See also* Higher
    education
Interaction models: client/professional,
  43–48, 68–69
  customer/business, 43–48
  distinguishing between different,
    43–48
  soldier/command, 43–48
Investing in people, 128–129
Irving, L. M., 26
Ishikawa, K., 15
It's Not the End of the World:
  Developing Resilience in Times of
  Change (Borysenko), 30

J

Jacobson, L., 67
Japanese feudal system, 184
Johnson, E. B., 220
Johnson, S., 11
Johnson, V., 205
Jones, L., 13
Joyful leadership model: origins and description of, 32–33
strategies of the, 33–34
Joyful leadership strategies: enforcing policies as collegially as possible, 34
four primary behaviors of "the best chairs," 33
vertically looking through time approach of the, 33–34

K

Kahneman, D., 54, 55
The Karate Kid (film), 126
Karl, K., 14
Karukstis, K. K., 208
Kasich, J., 230, 231
Kelly, K., 132
Kemp, S., 55
Kennedy, D., 27
Kennedy, E., 85
Kennedy, J. F., 85–86, 177
Kennedy, R., 86
Kernis, M. H., 102
Kida, T. E., 80
The King's Speech (film), 127
Kirschner, D. R., 75
Kitcher, P., 217
Knope, S. D., 5
Kochanska, G., 135, 136
Kopf, J., 68
Kotter, J., 76, 77
Krovetz, M. L., 29
Krugman, P., 29
Kuczynski, L., 135

L

Laissez-faire leadership, 57
Language: how reality can be shaped by rhetoric and, 70–74
our inner dialogue, 72

three Ps of constructive phrasing, 74–75. *See also* Positive language
Lao Tzu, 162
Lateral leadership: building bridges through, 189
cross-functional teams application of, 191–192
description of, 188–189
thought experiment for judging your comfort with, 189, 190–191
transforming into positive academic leadership, 199–201
Lawler, E. E., 189
Lazarus, R., 85
Le Guin, U., 162
Leadership: authentic, 145
catalytic, 174–175
centrifugal, 38, 186–188, 199–201
emergent, 144–145
environmental or essential, 192–201
by good vs. bad bosses, 19–20, 238
lateral, 188–192, 199–201
leading upward, 183–186, 199–201
negative, 19–20
Seven C's of developing leadership, 201–202
"Leadership in a (Permanent) Crisis" (Heifetz, Grashow, and Linsky), 222
Leading Change (Kotter), 76
Leading Change (O'Toole), 77
Leading in uncertainty, 197–199
Leading upward strategy: applied to higher education, 184–186
questions to ask for using the, 185–186
traditional pyramid structure of authority expanded by, 183–184
transforming into positive academic leadership, 199–201
Learned optimism: dire realities of higher education ignored by, 29
hope-based leadership based on, 28
Ledger-Enquirer (Tures), 221
Lee, R., 102
Leeds, D., 32
Lester, D., 26

"Let's Solve This" slogan
(ExxonMobile Foundation), 220
Levin, D., 68, 175
Levoy, B., 146
Li, Y., 55, 56
Liao, S.-H., 14
Libertella, A., 205
Libet, B., 87
Liebenberg, L., 29
Life coaching, 17
Lindsley, P., 212
Linsky, M., 222
Lombardi, V., 127, 140
Long, A., 208
Longenecker, C. O., 20
Lopes, P. N., 144
Lopez, S., 25
Lorenz butterfly effect, 167
Lorenz, E., 167
Lowell, A. L., 212
Lucas, C., 205
Luthans, F., 145
Luthar, S. S., 29

M
Macdonald, I., 14, 49, 136–137, 173, 241
Mad Libs approach, 109–110
Making choices: how experience shapes, 87–88
positive perspective for reframing, 92–94
rational choice view of, 87
subconscious motivations shaping, 87. See also Decision making
Mallard, K., 32–33, 34, 39
Marecek, J., 9
Marsh, J., 124
Martin, G., 13
Martin, S. B., 192
Maslow, A., 8, 19, 194
Maslow's hierarchy of needs, 194fig, 195
Master Class (play), 127
Maximum collegial flow: achieved by members of a team, 52–53
creating environment for, 56
description of concept of, 50

how hierarchies impede, 51
making a conscious decision to pursue, 51–53
Mayfield, J., 68
Mayfield, M., 68
McCullough, M., 147
McDonnell, B., 230
McMahon, K. N., 201
Media coverage, 85
Merrow, J., 205
Military interaction: comparing corporate and academic models of interaction to, 43–48
soldier/command model of, 43–44
triangle or pyramid shape of authority in, 45fig–46fig
Mind mapping: of core values, 103–106
for philosophy of leadership statement, 110fig
Miners, C. T., 144
Miracle (film), 125
Miron-Shatz, T., 55
Missing the Boat: The Failure to Internationalize American Higher Education (Goodwin and Nacht), 206
Mission frame, 93
Mistakes: definition of, 70
showing empathy when others make, 70
understanding the inevitable nature of making, 32. See also Failure
Motivation: five factors driving job satisfaction, 145–146
inspiring confidence by helping to inspire, 127, 131
Motivational speaking, 17
Mowle, T. S., 29
Mr. Holland's Opus (film), 125

N
Nacht, M., 206
Namyniuk, L., 72
Nasiry, J., 55
Natale, S., 205
National Action Council for Minorities in Engineering Inc. (NACME), 220

Negative attitude boundaries, 96
Negative bias, 19
Negative leaders, 20
Negative leadership, 19–20
Negativity: considering resources for
    handling a person's, 97–98
  establishing boundaries for, 96
  examining effect of, 95–96
  positive leadership in an
    environment of, 237–238
  positive perspective challenged by, 95
  as springboard for finding positive
    solutions, 96–97
  tracing the source of, 97
Negativity effects, 95–96
Nelson, B., 12, 146, 147
New Republic, 217
New York Times, 218
Newspapers notices, 149
Newsweek magazine, 209
Nielsen, N., 208
No Child Left Behind Act (2001), 214

O
O'Brien, E., 55, 56
Occupy Wall Street movement, 11
O'Connor, M., 12, 151
The 1 percent, 11
1001 Ways to Energize Employees
    (Nelson), 12
1001 Ways to Reward Employees
    (Nelson), 12, 146
Open Doors report (2011), 207
Optimism: blind, 18
  learned, 28, 29
  positive psychology approach to,
    18–19
  resilience context of, 30
Orchestras: Benjamin Zander's
    perspective on conductors of,
    161, 162, 178
  "fuels" vs. "catalyst" conductors
    of, 175
  perceived as a system, 163
Organizations, four frames of
    operations by, 93
Orloff, J., 97
Outcalt, C. L., 201

P
P4 Medicine Institute, 5–6
Page, D., 13
Page, R., 29
Paired comparisons method, 103
Parachin, V., 14
Pareto principle (80/20 rule), 11
Pareto, V., 11
Parker, E., 229
Parkman, A., 72
Parseghian, A., 127
Parsons, J., 128
Participatory leadership, 57
Peak-end rule: applications to
    different disciplines, 54–55
  description of the, 54
  trip to Capri story on the, 53–54
Peak experiences: Baumgartel's study
    on group satisfaction related to,
    57
  creating environment that
    maximizes, 56–60*fig*
  thought experiment on creating,
    58–59
Pear, J., 13
Pearl, D. K., 87
Peluchette, J., 14
Penn State sex abuse scandal, 60
Penna, E., 219
Personal control: behavioral,
    cognitive, and decisional, 85
  over our day-to-day perspective,
    85–86
Personal leadership style, Baumgartel's
    study on group satisfaction under,
    57
Personal praise, 147
Personal trainer wellness approach, 6
Peters, D., 102
Peters, T. J., 228
Philosophy of leadership: aligning
    programs and institution to your,
    112–114
  core values used to develop,
    108–111
  example of statement of, 111
  moving from theory to practice of,
    114–116

Piaget, J., 85
The platinum rule ("do unto others as they'd like done unto them"), 12, 151
Plato, 166
Platonicity thinking, 166
Political beliefs, 17–18
Political frame, 93
Pollyanna's "glad game," 85
Pop! Tech, 30
Popescu, I., 55
Positive academic leader roles: as coach, 123–141
  as conductor, 161–178
  as counselor, 143–159
Positive academic leadership: assessment role in, 233–236
  common themes of all models on, 39
  foundations of, 40
  inadvisable during crisis situations, 60–62
  maximum collegial flow during interactions under, 50–53, 56
  peak-end rule significance for, 56–60fig
  positive perspectives practice of, 83–98
  respect as the essence of, 155, 247
  responding to the crisis industry, 222–224
  role of positive language in, 67–81
  transforming administrative leadership strategies into, 199–201. See also Academic administrators
  Academic leadership models
Positive academic leadership mini-case studies: a double bind of your own creation, 238–241
  full frontal assault, 245–246
  positive leadership in a negative environment, 237–238
  seizing the (wrong) teachable moment, 242–245
Positive academic leadership strategies: step 1: identify your

core values as an academic leader, 101–108
step 2: develop philosophy of leadership based on core values, 108–111
step 3: align philosophy of leadership with your programs and institution, 112–114
step 4: move from theory to practice, 114–116
step 5: break goals and projects into discrete tasks, 116–118
Positive bias, 19
Positive change: appreciative inquiry for creating, 35–36
  defining, 35
Positive climate, 10
Positive communication: active listening for effective and, 139–140
  constructive criticism for, 128, 134–137
  description of, 10
  inspiring confidence through frequent and open, 130–131
  nurturing the system through constructive and, 176–178
  using positive language for, 67–80
Positive conflict: developing ground rules to facilitate, 155
  goal of turning conflict into, 154–155
  nine policies to help conflict become, 155–158
Positive conflict policies: always focus on the issue and not the person, 155
  end disagreement by reaffirming support for all parties, 157
  move forward following disagreement, 157–158
  offer a better alternative when objecting to an idea, 156
  periodically paraphrase to facilitate clear communication, 156
  reducing personal criticism by deflecting statements toward yourself, 155–156

reiterating mutual support even during conflict, 157

speak in your own voice, 156–157

state your reasons when objecting to an idea, 156

Positive language: client/professional interactions using, 68–69

encouraging faculty behavior change through, 69–70

examining leadership role of, 68–70

how reality can be shaped by, 70–72

importance in effecting change, 76–79

importance in goal setting, 74–75

storytelling versus use of, 79–80

study on student performance and teachers,' 67. *See also* Language

Positive leadership: affirmative bias of, 16

four key strategies of, 10

introduction to, 9–10

systems approach to, 12, 163–166

ten principles of, 10–16

what it is not, 16–19. *See also* Academic leadership

Positive Leadership: Strategies for Effective Performance (Cameron), 10

Positive Leadership and Positive Organizational Scholarship: Foundations of a New Discipline (Cameron, Dutton, and Quinn), 10

Positive Leadership (Cameron), 234

Positive leadership principles: 1: greater emphasis on developing what works rather than correcting flaws, 10–11

2: supervisory time spent on best performers instead of problem people, 11

3: personalizing guidance given to each employee, 11–12

4: adoption of a systems approach, 12, 163–166

5: being future oriented and proactive, 13

6: emphasizing rewards and recognitions over punishment, 13–14

7: being people oriented as well as goal oriented, 14–15

8: team-based and collaboration over rigid hierarchies, 15

9: valuing each member of the group, 15–16

10: guidance versus authoritarian management style, 16

Positive leadership strategies: positive climate, 10

positive communication, 10

positive meaning, 10

positive relationships, 10

Positive meaning, 10

Positive perspective: dealing with negativity to maintain a, 95–98

on faculty member taking leave due to prestigious award, 83–85

increasing options by changing to, 89–92

reframing choices through, 92–94

slowing down responses as key to, 88–89, 90

strategies for shifting into a more, 94–95

Positive psychology: commonalities with other health care models, 8

compared to traditional psychology, 7–8, 9

resilience research in the field of, 29–30

Positive relationships, description of, 10

The Power of Resilience: Achieving Balance, Confidence, and Personal Strength in Your Life (Brooks and Goldstein), 30

Powerful questioning, 139, 140

Practicality frame, 93

Praise, 147

Predator drone parents, 124

"Predictability: Does the Flap of a Butterfly's Wings in Brazil Set Off a Tornado in Texas?" (Lorenz), 167

Price, R., 109
Problem frame, 93
Ps of constructive phrasing, 74–75
Psychology: comparing traditional
    and positive models of, 7–9
    scientific advances made in, 7
    self-actualizing focus of, 8
Public praise, 147
Punishment: criticism perceived as
    form of, 136
    emphasizing rewards over, 13–14
    negative impact on behavior
    change by, 68. See also Rewards/
    recognition
Pygmalion in the Classroom
    (Rosenthal and Jacobson), 67
Pyramid-shaped hierarchies: corporate
    and military, 45fig–46fig
    history of, 183–184

Q
Questions: administrative resilience on
    importance of asking the right,
    31–32
    for applying the leading upward
    strategy, 185–186
    asked by traditional vs. appreciative
    inquiry administrators, 35–36
    communication through asking
    powerful, 139
    helping us to operate effectively
    within any system, 227
    for implementing centrifugal
    leadership, 187
    that should be asked periodically by
    administrators, 177
The Quiet Crisis: How Higher
    Education Is Failing America
    (Smith), 205
Quinn, R., 10

R
Radke-Yarrow, M., 136
Ratcliff, J. L., 211, 212
Rational choices, 87
Recognition. See Rewards/recognition
Reconstructing Alma Mater: The
    Coming Crisis in Higher

Education, a Blueprint for
    Reform (Francis), 205
Redbook (General Education in a Free
    Society) [Harvard University],
    212
Reed College, 212
Reframing Organizations (Bolman
    and Deal), 93
Reisser, U., 85
Reivich, K., 30
Relationship building, 27
Religious beliefs, 17–18
Remember the Titans (film), 125
Remler, D., 219
Resilience: academic leadership
    significance of, 31
    academic research in positive
    psychology on, 29–30
    defined as maintaining core
    functions under stress, 30
    full frontal assault mini-case study
    on, 245–246
    as modern buzzword, 29
    optimism in context of, 30. See
    also Administrative resilience
    model
Resilience development strategies:
    accept the face that change is
    inevitable, 31
    asking the right questions,
    31–32
    be experimental, 32
The Resilience Factor: Seven Keys
    to Finding Your Inner Strength
    and Overcoming Life's Hurdles
    (Reivich and Shatté), 30
The Resiliency Advantage: Master
    Change, Thrive Under Pressure,
    and Bounce Back from Setbacks
    (Siebert), 30
Respect: department chairs who show,
    33
    positive conflict facilitated through
    mutual, 155, 247
Responding to uncompromising
    statements: description of, 106
    identifying core values using,
    106–108

Rewards/recognition: Appreciation
    Calendar used for, 147*fig*
  avoiding punishment and
    emphasizing, 13–14
  behavior change through positive
    reinforcement of, 68
  "Congratulations!" cards used for,
    150
  as driving people to make best
    efforts at work, 145–146
  four mechanisms for offering
    gratitude or praise, 147
  inspiring confidence by exploring
    alternative, 129
  measures taken to access good news
    worthy of, 149
  roundtable recognition technique
    for, 147–149
  study findings on research
    production tied to, 219. *See also*
    Gratitude; Punishment
Rhetoric: how other people's reality is
    shaped by our, 72–74
  how our reality is shaped by our,
    70–72
  of our inner dialogue, 72
Richardson, F., 9
Richardson, J., 189
Rockne, K., 127
Rodie, A., 14
Roksa, J., 206
Rosenthal, R., 67
Roundtable recognition, 147–149
Royal Pains (USA Network series), 4
Rupert, A. V., 55
Ryvkin, D., 55

S
Sabatine, J., 138–139, 140
Sadri, G., 102
Salovey, P., 144
Sargent, M., 32–33, 34, 39
Sarin, R., 55
Schwartz, S. H., 102
Schwarz, N., 55
Scott, R., 220
SEAL Team Six, 51
SEAL Team Six parents, 124

Seel, R., 36
Self: neuroscience research on the, 87
  rational choice view of, 87
  subconscious motivations shaping,
    87
Seligman, M., 7, 8, 18, 28,
    85, 123
Selye, H., 199
Sense of community, 10
Servant leaders: contribution of hope
    by, 39
  ten qualities characterizing,
    37–38
Servant leadership model: Dudley's
    open letter on the, 38
  origins and development of, 37
  similarities between centrifugal and,
    187
  on ten qualities characterizing
    servant leaders, 37–38
Seven C's of developing leadership,
    201–202
Sharp, A., 189
Shatté, A., 30
Siebert, A., 30
Sinatra, N., 132
Sit, H. W., 189
Smart Questions (Leeds), 32
Smith, B., 200
Smith, N. C., 17
Smith, P., 205
Snee, T., 17
Snyder, C. R., 25, 26
Soldier/command model of
    interaction: description and
    example of, 43–44
  distinction between other models
    and the, 43–48
  triangle or pyramid shape of
    authority in, 45*fig*–46*fig*
Soloway, A., 206
Sommer, J., 205
Southern Association of Colleges and
    Schools Commission on Colleges,
    30
Southwest Airplanes, 51
Sparks, T., 102
Spears, L., 37, 38

Spellings, M., 214
Sputnik (1957), 213, 214
Staff: creating environment that
maximizes peak experiences for,
56–60*fig*
dealing with grief and suffering by,
158–159
overcoming resistance to change by,
78–79
promoting maximum collegial flow
for, 50–53, 56
Stakeholder frame, 93
Stakeholders: arguments for
increasing state funding by
legislature, 231–233
becoming accustomed to catalytic
approach to leadership, 175
questions that help us operate in
any system with, 227
thought experience on maximizing
peak experiences of, 58–60*fig*
Stand and Deliver (film), 126
Stealth bomber parents, 124
Steiner, D. D., 17
STEM disciplines: caution against
ignoring arts and humanities for,
221
efforts to increase minority students
in, 220
Florida governor efforts to increase
funding to, 220
graduation rates in, 218
higher education reform of, 213,
215
state of the state addresses that
mention, 229, 230
STEM-H fields, 230
Stern, L., 109
Stewart, K., 14, 49, 136–137, 173,
241
Stone, T., 137
Stories/Storytelling, 79–80
Strauss, E., 128
Strengths: department chairs who
match group needs with, 33
responding to higher education
crisis by playing to our, 211,
227–247

Stress: academic context of, 198
centrifugal leadership focus on
reducing stakeholders,' 187
eustress as "upside" of, 199
nurturing the system to reduce
stakeholders,' 177–178
Structural frame, 93
Structured brainstorming: description
of, 102–103
identifying your core values
through, 103
Student enrollment: increased access
to higher education evidenced by,
208
of international students in the U.S.,
207–208
Students: Associated Press/Viacom/
Roper Poll (2011) on, 218–219,
223–224
concerns over declining graduation
rates of, 218
impact of teacher expectations on
performance of, 67
Seven C's of developing leadership
of, 201–202
STEM disciplines, 213, 215, 218,
220, 229, 230
Thank a professor (online form)
provided to, 149
Subconscious motivations, 87
Success Dynamics, Inc., 146
Surgeon model of medicine, 6
Swindoll, C., 31
Symbolic frame, 93
Systems: applying the systems
approach the crisis industry,
227–233
closed system thinking on, 227–228
conclusions to draw about the,
172–174
contributions made by each person
to the group, 168–169
"fuels" versus "catalysts" of,
174–175
Lorenz butterfly effect on, 167
network connections between
people in the system, 168,
170–172

nurturing the, 176–178
orchestra, 161, 162, 173, 175, 178
questions that help us operate in
    any, 227
roles played by people in the
    system, 168, 169–170
Systems approach: applied to the crisis
    industry, 227–233
exploring the system components,
    168–174
Platonicity thinking and, 166
positive leadership adoption of, 12,
    163–166
power flow in the, 167
questions that help us operate using
    the, 227
thought experiment on faculty's
    salary increase request, 163–166
Systems Leadership: Creating Positive
    Organizations (Macdonald,
    Burke, and Stewart), 49

T
Take Back Higher Education:
    Race, Youth, and the Crisis of
    Democracy in the Post–Civil Rights
    Era (Giroux and Giroux), 205
Taking responsibility: coaching
    strategies for, 133–134
"Dave's Rules of Order" on, 157
how teachers versus coaches
    approach failure by, 128, 133
Taleb, N., 166
Tao Te Ching (Lao Tzu and Le Guin),
    162, 174, 177
Taylor, J. B., 92
Taylor, M., 124, 206
Taylor, W., 14
"Teach-to-the-test mentality," 221
Teachers: differences between coaches
    and, 124–126, 133
link between student achievement
    and expectations of, 67. See also
    Faculty
TED conference (2008), 161, 178
Teixeira, R., 206
Tenure, 34
Texas Tech University, 200

Thank a professor (online form), 149
Thank-you note rules, 151
A Theory of Human Motivation
    (Maslow), 194
Think Big and Kick Ass in Business
    and Life (Zanker), 19
Thorndike, E., 13, 68
Three Ps of constructive phrasing,
    74–75
Ticknor, G., 211
Time to Get Tough: Making America
    #1 Again (Trump), 19
Tinto, V., 167
To Reclaim a Legacy: A Report on the
    Humanities in Higher Education
    (Bennett), 213, 214
To Sir, with Love (film), 126
Toastmasters International, 40
Trexler, L., 26
True Compass (Kennedy), 85
Trump, D., 19
Tsang, J.-A., 147
Tures, J., 221
Turner, J. F., 132
Tuskegee Airmen, 51
Twale, D., 51
Tyree, T. M., 201

U
Uncertainty: discomfort with,
    197–198
environmental (or essential)
    leadership in the midst of,
    198–199
Ungar, M., 29
Union University tornado damage
    (Tennessee), 60
United States: history of higher
    education development and
    reform of the, 211–214
international enrollment of students
    in the, 207–208
myth of economic decline of the,
    208–209
ten pendulum topics about higher
    education in the, 215t–216
University of California at Los
    Angeles (UCLA), 97, 218

University of California memorial
   debate (2012), 228–229, 231
University of California-San Marcos,
   57
University of Chicago, 212
University of Kansas, 57
University of Michigan, 55
University of Nashville (1825), 212
University of Nebraska-Lincoln, 38
University of North Carolina at
   Chapel Hill, 140
University of Oregon, 157
University of Pennsylvania's Wharton
   School of Business, 184
U.S. Army's Comprehensive Soldier
   Fitness program, 29
Useem, M., 184

V

Verhoef, P. C., 55
Virginia's Standards of Learning
   (SOL), 213
Viriginia Tech shootings, 60
Vision: department chairs with, 33
   framing with the, 93
Vision statements: constructing your,
   115
   rephrasing into list of tasks,
   115–116
Vygotsky, L., 50, 131

W

Wakker, P. P., 55
Walsh, K. C., 219
Waterman, R. H., 228

Watson, A., 167
Wayland, F., 212
Weber, T. J., 102
Webster, H., 193
Wegner, D. M., 87
Wei wu wei (action without action)
   principle, 175
Weissman, A., 26
Wheeler, D., 37, 38, 39
Whitney, D., 35, 140
"Why Professors Hate Their Jobs"
   (Daniels, Strauss, and Evans),
   128
Wiley, C., 145
Wilhelm, F. H., 17
Windle, G., 29
Winston, B., 25, 26
Wolford, G., 55
Wright, E. W., 87
Written praise, 147
Wrzesniewski, A., 86

Y

Yahoo! Alerts, 149
Yale School of Management, 86
Yale University, 211, 212

Z

Zander, B., 161, 162, 178
Zanker, B., 19
Zen flow, 50
Zen Life (Levin), 68, 175
Zolli, A., 30
Zone of proximal development, 50,
   131

Atlas

ATLAS: Academic Training, Leadership, & Assessment Services offers workshops, retreats, books, and materials dealing with collegiality and positive academic leadership. Its programs include

- Positive Academic Leadership
- Creative Academic Leadership
- Mindfulness-Based Academic Leadership
- Promoting Collegiality
- Conflict Management
- A Community of Scholars: Developing Teamwork
- Best Practices in Faculty Evaluation
- Best Practices in Academic Benchmarking
- Best Practices in Strategic Planning
- Best Practices in Academic Delegation
- Communication Skills for Academic Leaders
- The Art and Science of Grant Writing

ATLAS programs can be offered on your own campus or through regional leadership institutes that provide administrators with intensive training over two to four days. ATLAS also offers reduced prices on leadership books and distributes the Collegiality Assessment Matrix (CAM) and Self-Assessment Matrix (S-AM), which allow academic programs to evaluate the collegiality and civility of their faculty members in a consistent, objective, and reliable manner. The ATLAS e-Newsletter addresses a variety of issues related to academic leadership and is sent free to subscribers.

For more information, contact:

ATLAS: Academic Training, Leadership, & Assessment Services
4521 PGA Boulevard, PMB 186
Palm Beach Gardens FL 33418
800–355–6742; www.atlasleadership.com
E-mail: questions@atlasleadership.com